Trust

Trust

How Citizens View Political Institutions

Ben Seyd

Great Clarendon Street, Oxford, OX2 6DP,
United Kingdom

Oxford University Press is a department of the University of Oxford.
It furthers the University's objective of excellence in research, scholarship,
and education by publishing worldwide. Oxford is a registered trade mark of
Oxford University Press in the UK and in certain other countries

© Ben Seyd 2024

The moral rights of the author have been asserted

All rights reserved. No part of this publication may be reproduced, stored in
a retrieval system, or transmitted, in any form or by any means, without the
prior permission in writing of Oxford University Press, or as expressly permitted
by law, by licence or under terms agreed with the appropriate reprographics
rights organization. Enquiries concerning reproduction outside the scope of the
above should be sent to the Rights Department, Oxford University Press, at the
address above

You must not circulate this work in any other form
and you must impose this same condition on any acquirer

Published in the United States of America by Oxford University Press
198 Madison Avenue, New York, NY 10016, United States of America

British Library Cataloguing in Publication Data

Data available

Library of Congress Control Number: 2023944403

ISBN 9780198896449

DOI: 10.1093/oso/9780198896449.001.0001

Printed and bound in the UK by
Clays Ltd, Elcograf S.p.A.

Links to third party websites are provided by Oxford in good faith and
for information only. Oxford disclaims any responsibility for the materials
contained in any third party website referenced in this work.

For Pat: with gratitude, affection, love.

Acknowledgements

Various papers that form the basis of this book's chapters were discussed at conferences organized by the International Political Science Association, the Elections, Public Opinion and Parties group, the Political Studies Association, and the University of Tampere, and at a workshop at the University of Kent. I would like to thank the participants at each of these events for their very helpful comments and suggestions.

I would also like to thank colleagues who read and commented on draft chapters of the book: Laurence Durham, Joseph A Hamm, Will Jennings, Aaron Martin, James Weinberg, Andrew Wroe, and Sonja Zmerli. Their comments immeasurably strengthened the analysis, although they will not always agree with my arguments or interpretations. I absolve them of any responsibility for these while extending to them my gratitude for their effort and wisdom.

I would also like to thank colleagues who provided useful guidance and who identified profitable avenues to probe and relevant data sources to consult, notably Christopher Anderson, Tereza Capelos, Nicolas Dimertzis, Theofanis Exadaktylos, and David Farrell. I would also like to thank my Oxford University Press editor, Dominic Byatt, for his receptiveness to my proposal and general counsel. Also thanks to the Press's reviewers for their supportive and helpful comments.

My final acknowledgement is the most important. I was a late covert to political science, only entering the field after an early career in industrial research and lobbying. My father, an established and respected member of the political science profession, might have been a bit put out at my late decision to enter his field. Not a bit of it. He welcomed me with open arms, a constant source of advice and encouragement. I could not have asked for more. This book is a small payback for his generosity.

Contents

List of figures — x
List of tables — xii

Introduction: Why study trust? — 1

SECTION 1. WHAT ARE WE TALKING ABOUT? THE NATURE AND MEASUREMENT OF TRUST

1. What is trust? — 21
  1.1 Defining trust — 22
  1.2 States of trust — 24
  1.3 What do we trust? — 27
  1.4 How do we trust? — 35
  1.5 Conclusion — 45

2. Why focus on trust? — 48
  2.1 The nature of political support — 49
  2.2 The status of trust — 51
  2.3 Forms of political support — 53
  2.4 Is trust distinctive? — 56
  2.5 The relevance of trust — 61
  2.6 Does it make sense to 'trust' government? — 67
  2.7 Conclusion — 69

3. Measuring trust — 71
  3.1 Practices and problems in the measurement of trust — 71
  3.2 Is trust an attitude or a behaviour? — 81
  3.3 Conclusion: Moving on with measurement — 83

SECTION 2. WHAT IS GOING ON? LEVELS AND CAUSES OF TRUST

4. Is there a problem of trust? — 87
  4.1 Levels of trust — 87
  4.2 Trust within the population — 88
  4.3 Trends in trust — 90
  4.4 Trust in Britain compared — 94
  4.5 Conclusion — 97

5. Why has trust declined? — 98
5.1 Changes of trust within the population — 99
5.2 The role of political beliefs and engagement — 104
5.3 Modelling the impact of demographic and political factors — 113
5.4 Conclusion — 116

6. Why do citizens trust (or not)? — 118
6.1 What shapes trust? — 119
6.2 What do we know about the sources of trust? — 120
6.3 How do we know about the causes of trust? — 126
6.4 Identifying the sources of trust in Britain — 128
6.5 Variations in the sources of trust: People, institutions, and contexts — 135
6.6 Conclusion — 143

SECTION 3. SO WHAT? THE CONSEQUENCES OF TRUST

7. The effects of trust — 147
7.1 Identifying the effects of trust — 148
7.2 The 'voice' consequences of trust — 150
7.3 The 'exit' consequences of trust — 167
7.4 Conclusion: What does a low trust society look like? — 179
7.5 Coda: What does a very low trust society look like? — 182

Conclusion: The problem of trust — 186

Appendix — 203

Appendix 2.1 Measures used to assess dimensionality of political support — 204
Appendix 2.2 Measures used to assess different forms of political discontent — 205
Appendix 4.1 Survey questions used to measure trust (in Figure 4.7) — 206
Appendix 5.1 Media effects on trust — 207
Appendix 5.2 Pooled models of trust, 1986–2016 — 208
Appendix 6.1 Details of model summarized in Figure 6.5 — 210
Appendix 6.2 Details of model summarized in Figure 6.6 — 211
Appendix 6.3 Impact of evaluations on trust in different institutions — 212
Appendix 7.1 The relationship between trust and protest participation — 215
Appendix 7.2 Impact of change in trust on vote choice, 2015 — 216
Appendix 7.3 Trust and support for government activism — 217
Appendix 7.4 Trust and electoral abstention, 2015–2019 elections — 220
Appendix 7.5 Items used to measure acceptance/verification of official information — 221

Appendix 7.6A	Acceptance of collective obligations—items from the European Social Survey.	222
Appendix 7.6B	Acceptance of collective obligations—items from the Citizen Audit	224
Notes		225
Bibliography		243
Index		271

List of figures

1.1	Trends in trust and political crises, 2005–2015	30
1.2	Trust in government on different functions	32
1.3	Trends in trust at the aggregate and individual levels	34
1.4	Trust in institutions among Germans, 2014–2022	35
1.5	Negative and positive evaluations and trust	44
1.6	The impact of negative and positive information on trust in food outlets	45
2.1	The spectrum of political support	50
2.2	Trust among government and opposition supporters	51
2.3	Structural model of different forms of political support	61
4.1	Trust in public office-holders	88
4.2	Trust in government in Britain, 1973–2020	92
4.3	Trust in public actors, 1983–2022	93
4.4	Trends in political discontent, 1966–2016	93
4.5	Trust in core political institutions in nine Western European countries	94
4.6	Trust in two core institutions in eleven advanced democracies	95
4.7	Trends in trust in advanced democracies	96
5.1	Trends in trust by education—Britain	100
5.2	Trends in trust by education—selected countries	101
5.3	Trends in trust by economic status	102
5.4	Public expectations of government, 1985–2016	106
5.5	Trends in trust, by expectations of government	107
5.6	Trends in trust, by policy positions	109
5.7	Levels of trust, by representation gap	110
5.8	Differences in trust, by newspaper readership	112
5.9	Trends in trust, by interest in politics	113
5.10	Impact of economic feelings and education on trust over time	115
5.11	Impact of newspaper readership on trust over time	116
6.1	Typology of factors shaping trust judgements	119
6.2	Relationship of different dimensions of trustworthiness with trust: cross section	130
6.3	Association with trust of different judgements	132

6.4	Relationship of different dimensions of trustworthiness with trust: over time	134
6.5	Association with trust of judgements about parties	135
6.6	Association with trust of evaluations, by knowledge	138
6.7	Association with trust of economic evaluations, 2005 and 2010	142
6.8	Association with trust of fairness evaluations, 2005 and 2010	143
7.1	Association of trust and protest participation	152
7.2	Association of trust and efficacy with protest	153
7.3	Association of change in trust with party vote	155
7.4	Association of trust with vote choice in US presidential elections	156
7.5	Democratic norms, by trust	158
7.6	Trends in trust and support for active government	163
7.7	Support for active government, by trust	164
7.8	Trends in electoral turnout and trust, 1973–2019	168
7.9	Compliance with the law, by trust	179
7.10	Levels of trust in countries hit by financial crash	183
7.11	Levels of trust and tax evasion in Greece, 2001–2018	184

List of tables

1.1	Association of personality traits with trust	37
2.1	The behavioural correlates of different types of political support	64
2.2	The behavioural correlates of different types of political discontent	65
4.1	Levels of trust among population sub-groups	89
5.1	Levels of trust, by year and age cohort	103
6.1	Associations between competence, benevolence, and fairness appraisals and trust	131
7.1	Key outcomes of trust	149
7.2	Support for government activism in various fields, by level of trust	166
7.3	Association of trust with collective obligations (European Social Survey)	176
7.4	Association of trust with collective obligations (Citizen Audit)	177
7.5	Key outcomes of trust	181

Introduction
Why study trust?

Politics has long been defined by conflict between social groups over access to power and wealth (Lasswell, 1936). For much of the twentieth century, in industrialized countries at least, that conflict primarily involved political parties of the left and the right. Political conflict took a largely horizontal form, based on ideological competition between parties and their followers. Today, despite the predictions of some analysts (Fukuyama, 1989), horizontal forms of political conflict have not withered. Indeed, parties on the political left and right still disagree about the basic goals of social and economic life, and elections are still fought over distinctive ideological positions. Yet alongside horizontal political conflict, many advanced democracies are now witnessing an additional, acute, and vertical form of conflict. This pits citizens against their rulers, with the former often viewing the latter, at best, as ignorant of their needs or, at worst, as harmful to them.

Conflictual relations between citizens and their rulers are nothing new and can be traced back to the development of representative political relations in the eighteenth century (Manin, 1997: chapter 4). Well-organized movements pitting citizens against state actors and institutions have operated in western countries for well over a century; examples stretch from populism in the late nineteenth-century United States to Poujadism in mid-twentieth-century France. Yet across many advanced democracies, citizens appear more critical of their elected representatives today than in the past and more prone to negative judgements about their actions, and even their status and role. Modern democratic societies seem to be witnessing a widening of the arena of political conflict, extending from the horizontal level—where parties compete over different visions of the good society—to the vertical level—where that good society has fragmented into distinctive conceptions of mass and elite interests. Horizontal-level frictions between parties of the left and right have been supplemented—if not supplanted—by frictions in citizens' relations with their political rulers (Mair, 2013: 71–73).[1]

These frictions appear to be evident in recent political events such as the Brexit referendum in Britain in 2016, the rise in electoral support for anti-system or populist parties in various western democracies, and the increase in

Trust. Ben Seyd, Oxford University Press. © Ben Seyd (2024). DOI: 10.1093/oso/9780198896449.003.0001

citizen-initiated forms of political protest. What these events apparently share is public discontent with political elites and the institutions they inhabit. In an op-ed article in the *New York Times*, Cohen (2016) noted how, across western democracies, 'Ordinary folk reckon the [political] system is rigged, that elites are not in it for the people but, rather, the money'. The vertical relations between citizens and their political rulers seem to have soured, with more and more people apparently seeing politicians as out for themselves rather than as acting for the good of society. As a result, citizens appear to have grown increasingly discontent with those exercising political authority. We live, concluded Cohen, in an 'Age of Distrust'.

There is plenty of evidence to support Cohen's claim. In 1986, four in ten people in Britain said they trusted their government 'almost always' or 'most of the time'. Just one in eight people said they 'almost never' trusted government. Yet just over three decades on, the proportion of high trusters had more than halved (to 16 per cent), while the proportion of low trusters had almost trebled (to 35 per cent).[2] A similar picture can be found in the United States. In the late 1950s, three quarters of people believed the government in Washington could be trusted 'almost always' or 'most of the time', while just one quarter trusted government 'none of the time' or only 'some of the time'. Six decades on, these distributions have reversed; in 2020, almost eight in ten of the population expressed only occasional trust in the government, while just two in ten mostly or always trusted government.[3] Levels of public trust in institutions like government and parliament have also declined in some Western European countries (Martini and Quaranta, 2020: 90). By 2022, in ten of the seventeen Western European countries surveyed by Eurobarometer, majorities of citizens said they did not trust their national government.

Hardly surprisingly, these bleak figures have triggered a response among policymakers, who have highlighted the issue and identified the need for urgent corrective action. *The Economist* magazine warned in 2014 that in western countries, 'flaws in the system have become worryingly visible and disillusion with politics is rife'. The Chief Executive of Edelman, a market research company that runs an annual global survey of trust, suggested in response to the low rates of trust recorded in 2016 that 'We have moved beyond the point of trust being simply a key factor in product purchase or selection of employment opportunity; it is now the deciding factor in whether a society can function' (Edelman, 2017a). In 2021, leaders of the World Economic Forum noted that 'The lack of trust is apparent all around us – among voters and politicians, consumers and multinationals, and between countries and heads of states …. This is extremely worrying. We know that trust is a must, if we are to solve the challenges we are facing as a collective.'

Global leaders and media commentators have been quick to highlight the perils of low and declining public regard for government and to urge action to tackle the problem because low trust is seen to impair the quality of government and democracy (and also, it must be said, to call into question politicians' own standing). The lower the citizens' trust in politicians responsible for official rules and laws, the less willing individuals are seen to be to abide by them. This problem became particularly acute during the coronavirus pandemic that gripped countries across the world from 2020. This forced citizens to confront the question of whether rules, guidelines, and information sponsored by national governments should be accepted and followed. For the vast majority of citizens around the world, the decision about whether to comply with personally inconvenient and costly official guidelines and rules will have been the most acute and serious they will have faced in their lifetimes. Commentators and policymakers alike concluded from their experience of the pandemic that trust—which refers here, and in the rest of this book, to the vertical ties between citizens and rule-makers[4]—played a central role in encouraging individuals to bear those costs and to comply with intrusive official constraints on their freedoms.

Trust is seen as a vital resource, not only in encouraging citizens to behave in ways that enhance social benefits but also in avoiding behaviours that cause political disruption. Many countries have recently witnessed what might euphemistically be termed 'political turbulence', in particular the rise of candidates and parties opposed to established and mainstream representative bodies, widespread demands for reform of the political system, and the spread of grassroots or citizen-initiated protest activities and movements. Some of these outcomes have generated serious problems for countries' stability and policymaking capacity. In the United Kingdom, Brexit has raised numerous knotty problems for the country's international relations and internal cohesion. The election of Donald Trump in the United States in 2016 brought with it significant challenges to the operation of that country's political system, culminating in a mass invasion of Congress in January 2021. Citizen-led protests like the *gilets jaunes* movement in France have introduced significant new pressures on official policy agendas and processes. In various ways, and in different forms, governments across the world are now faced with new groups or movements that challenge established political conventions and processes, often seemingly on the back of popular distrust of mainstream political institutions and actors. These currents of distrust are sometimes even seen as inducing a widespread questioning of democratic norms and practices themselves (Mounk, 2018: 99–112).

We appear to find ourselves today in an invidious position in relation to trust. On the one hand, trust appears to be a vital democratic commodity if, as is often suggested, it shapes important outcomes ranging from compliance with collective rules to support for democracy itself. On the other hand, trust in many countries appears to have declined and to be at a low ebb. If trust does have such important consequences, shortages of this commodity seem to portend dark days ahead.

Before accepting this bleak picture, however, we might want to pause, to take stock of what we know about trust and to assess whether the picture is as serious as sometimes made out. In particular, we might want to reflect on what we mean by trust and what trust signifies, to identify whether trust really is in decline, and to explore what the effects of low and declining levels of trust might be.

To start with, we need to understand more clearly what trust consists of. As we will shortly see, many academic studies approach trust in broad conceptual terms. While such theoretically inclined studies are important, another angle on the nature of trust also requires attention, notably the meanings that individuals themselves attach to the concept. When individuals express 'trust' or 'distrust' in a particular actor or institution, what do such judgements consist of? We can glean a lot of valuable information about the meaning of this seemingly important political commodity by understanding more precisely what individual expressions of the concept mean.

Armed with a clearer understanding of trust, we can then explore how far citizens trust their political rulers, and how far levels of trust have declined over time. Has there been a decline in people's trust across all state actors and institutions? Are levels of trust declining across all western democracies? Has trust declined more among certain groups within the population than among others? Few analysts seriously question the concern among policymakers and media commentators with the state of trust in contemporary societies; after all, not all the doomsday claims can be wrong. Yet is the picture of trust presented in policy pronouncements and media headlines quite as bleak as made out? We need to go beyond generalized claims and examine current levels and historical trends in trust if we are to establish whether we currently face a general 'crisis of trust' and, if not, where the particular problems of trust might reside.

Finally, we need to establish more clearly what the consequences of low and declining trust might be. On the face of it, it is not obvious that low levels of trust are as damaging for political and civic governance as is sometimes made out. For a start, levels of trust among citizens have, in some countries, been in long decline without many serious wider consequences. We must also remember that low trust might have beneficial consequences as well as adverse ones. In *The Winter's Tale*, Autolycus asserts 'What a fool honesty is! And trust, his sworn brother, a very simple gentleman' (Act IV, scene 4). Trust that breeds credulity enables governments to mislead and hoodwink citizens, much as Autolycus gulls the unwary in Shakespeare's play. By contrast, an absence of trust might stimulate greater vigilance, better equipping citizens to exercise important democratic functions such as monitoring their governments' performance and behaviour.

Yet it would be dangerous to dismiss low trust as inconsequential or to complacently assume it is likely to breed a vigilant citizenry. Instead, this is surely the time to examine more closely what the effects of low trust are likely to be. What kind of outcomes follow from low levels of trust among a country's citizens? How far are these effects amenable to being dealt with, and accommodated by, the political system? Or are the effects unlikely to be resolved within the constraints of existing political institutions and norms? Do low and declining rates of trust pose a readily surmountable *challenge* to western political systems, or do they represent a more fundamental *crisis* for those systems?

Today, more than in the immediate past, political debate centres on the relationship between those who draw up political rules and those who must abide by them. Trust stands at the centre of this debate. Yet policy and media discourse about trust and its problems has run ahead of the research base on trust. As a result, discussions of trust often rest on rather shaky foundations. It is not always clear what the 'trust' at the heart of the discourse consists of, how far that trust has genuinely declined in recent years, and whether the consequences of low trust are as damaging as is often supposed. This book attempts to provide answers to these issues, and thus to underpin the foundations of our knowledge about this important political commodity.

Studying trust

Empirical studies of the way citizens relate to politicians and political institutions date back over six decades. The earliest attempt to systematically measure and analyse what people make of their political rulers was Sidney Verba and Gabriel Almond's *Civic Culture* study, published in 1963. Since then, there have been numerous studies on the relations between citizens and politicians, including several recent books on political trust. Some of these studies have adopted a cross-national or comparative approach (Klingemann and Fuchs, 1995; Pharr and Putnam, 2000; Dalton, 2004; Hooghe and Zmerli, 2011; Norris, 1999, 2011, 2022; Shockley et al., 2016; Zmerli and van der Meer, 2017; Uslaner, 2018; van Ham et al., 2017; Sasaki, 2019; Schnaudt, 2019; Martini and Quaranta, 2020; Mauk, 2020), while others have focused on a particular country (Craig, 1993; Hibbing and Theiss-Morse, 1995, 2002; Hetherington, 2005; Cleary and Stokes, 2006). In addition, numerous journal articles have been devoted to the topic, both wide-ranging reviews of the academic literature (e.g. Levi and Stoker, 2000; Citrin and Stoker, 2018) and more specific studies which, according to the Web of Science, number almost 5,000 in the last five years.

This book therefore joins a long line of studies into how citizens relate to political actors and institutions, a set of analyses that has burgeoned in recent years as the depth and scope of citizen discontent with political elites has become clearer. These studies have greatly expanded our knowledge and understanding of trust. In particular, conceptual inquiries have identified more clearly the broad contours of trust and helped specify the concept's core meaning. Descriptive accounts have mapped the distribution of trust over time, between different actors and institutions, and across countries. In so doing, they have provided a clearer picture of how much trust exists among national populations, how levels of trust vary across different actors and institutions, and how those levels have changed over time. Empirical analyses have delved into the determinants of trust, extending our knowledge of the conditions—both macro-level contextual factors and micro-level individual characteristics—associated with trust. Empirical studies have also explored how trust shapes individuals' attitudes and patterns of behaviour, thereby providing important insights into the broad effects of trust and the potential implications of any decline in trust for the health of democratic systems.

Existing studies on trust have therefore provided scholars and analysts with important tools with which to understand the conceptual contours of trust, along with its distribution, causes, and consequences. Yet certain features of trust have been less explored in academic analyses, and as a result, our understanding of these issues is more impaired.

One such feature is the *nature* of trust. As just noted, a great deal of effort has been invested in identifying the conceptual nature of trust, both within political science (e.g. Hardin, 2002) and within other academic disciplines such as sociology (e.g. Luhmann, 1979), management (e.g. Mayer, Davis and Schoorman, 1995), and psychology (e.g. Shockley et al., 2016). Yet the thrust of these discussions has proceeded in a largely 'top-down' or deductive manner, in which conceptual meaning is determined from first principles and abstract reasoning. This approach is useful for identifying trust's broad conceptual nature. However, it is less useful for identifying how individuals might understand trust and how they might form trust judgements. If the study of trust is to produce more than conceptual or definitional knowledge and shine some light on the nature of citizens' attitudes in a social setting, it needs to pay greater attention to the way trust is expressed by individuals. A central purpose of this book is thus to explore how individuals form trust judgements, and what their expressions of trust comprise. The analysis presented here rebalances the existing investigatory lens on trust: from a top-down perspective to a more bottom-up one. In doing so, the book provides a clearer picture of what trust means and signifies to citizens.

A second feature of trust only partially explored in existing studies concerns its *status* as a barometer of the relations between citizens and political rulers. In representative democracies, trust is central to the vertical relations between rulers and ruled (Bianco, 1994). The very act of delegating authority from citizens to governments requires the former to trust that the latter will not abuse their authority and act against citizens' interests.[5] Trust therefore captures an important aspect of the relationship between citizens and political rulers. But it is not the only concept that does so. Existing studies have paid considerable attention to the notion of 'political support' (Easton, 1965), a portmanteau term covering different forms of the relations between citizens and political actors. However, few studies have systematically explored where trust stands in relation to other forms of political support. The bulk of existing studies (at least within the discipline of political science) have focused their attention on whether and how various forms of political support map onto different tiers or levels of the political system, such as political authorities, political institutions, and the political community as a whole (e.g. Klingemann, 1999; Dalton, 2004: chapter 2). While it is useful to distinguish between these levels, the exercise tells us little about the relations between trust and other forms of political support such as alienation, legitimacy, cynicism, and dissatisfaction. These concepts are often deployed—alongside trust—in academic studies and media commentary with little sense of how they relate to one another and of which aspects of the vertical relations between citizens and political rulers each captures.

To gain a clearer understanding of how citizens orientate themselves to political actors, we need more clarity about where trust sits alongside these other forms of political support. Hence one of the goals pursued in this book is to respond to Levi and Stoker's plea (2000: 497) for 'scholars […] to develop a clear sense of how trust differs from other kinds of judgments about political actors or institutions'. Put simply, we need to answer the question 'why trust?'

What is gained by focusing on trust rather than on one of the other forms of political support?

A third feature of trust to have attracted less scholarly attention than it deserves is the *measurement* of the concept. Unlike many political attitudes (perceptions of economic conditions, for example, or evaluations of the incumbent prime minister), trust is not straightforward to measure. Yet few empirical studies devote much attention to how trust should be measured and to the validity of existing—primarily survey-based—indicators. The empirical analysis of political trust has arguably regressed from the situation in the 1970s, when academic studies of political trust (along with associated concepts such as alienation and disaffection) paid significant attention to concept measurement. Since then—and simplifying somewhat—studies of trust have taken one of two routes, either exploring the definition and meaning of trust at a broad conceptual level or engaging in data-driven analysis based on existing survey indicators. Rarely have scholars combined attention to the meaning of trust with careful consideration of its measurement. This neglect may be partially explained by empirical scholars' reliance on existing data that are usually confined to narrow survey-based indicators of trust.

This book is not immune to these constraints and also has to rely for much of its empirical analysis on a narrow set of indicators (although it also introduces various broader—and arguably better—measures of trust into the analysis). However, it would be helpful if analysts were more reflective of the relationship between the concept of trust and its measurement, and of the potential gap between the two. This book explores this relationship and considers how closely typical measures of trust approximate its conceptual nature. In doing so, it highlights potential problems in the way trust tends to be gauged and points to ways our measurement of this important concept might be improved.

A fourth feature of trust that has only received partial coverage in the existing literature concerns its *effects* or *outcomes*. This is not to say that the effects of trust have been ignored. Far from it; there is now a lively set of studies considering the potential implications of trust for a variety of civic and political outcomes. Yet attempts to identify these implications have lagged behind attempts to identify the levels and determinants of trust. Attempts to answer 'what' and 'why' questions about trust have run ahead of attempts to answer 'so what' questions. This stands in contrast to studies of interpersonal or social forms of trust, where a long line of enquiry has sought to understand the effects or consequences of individuals' trust in other people. Early explorations of institutional or political forms of trust suggested that low rates of trust among citizens might damage the quality of countries' civic and political infrastructure. These analyses date back to the *Civic Culture* study of the 1960s (Almond and Verba, 1963) and studies of governing crises from the 1970s (Crozier Huntington and Watanuki, 1975). In many cases, however, the negative effects of low trust have been assumed rather than empirically demonstrated.

This shortcoming has partially been addressed in recent years by studies that have explored the link between trust and voters' support for populist parties (e.g. Hooghe, Marien, and Pauwels, 2011). The outbreak and spread of SARS-CoV-2 (or coronavirus) in 2020 also encouraged a slew of studies on the role of trust in shaping outcomes such as popular compliance with government rules (see Seyd and Bu, 2022, and references therein). In general, however, consequences or effects remain—alongside issues of measurement—the Cinderella topics of trust, lagging as they do scholarly attention on its distribution and causes. This book seeks to redress the imbalance by systematically examining the relationship between trust and a variety of civic and political outcomes. In doing so, it provides a clearer picture of the potential consequences of trust for democratic governance, helping to place in a broader context policymakers' concerns about declining levels of trust among citizens.

Approach

This book studies political trust from the perspective of citizens located predominantly in a particular country: Britain. This geographical focus reflects the high level of detail needed to extend our understanding of key aspects of trust. Such detail would be difficult to achieve in a comparative study, which examined trust across multiple countries. Some of these details are touched on in existing cross-national studies, notably those by Dalton (2004), Norris (2011, 2022), Schnaudt (2019), and Martini and Quaranta (2020). Yet comparative studies cannot provide the level of detail that is possible where the context is limited to a single country. The virtues of the case study approach adopted in this book therefore complement the virtues of existing comparative studies, supplementing their broad panorama with a more detailed focus on particular aspects of trust.

Britain was selected as the primary case study for two reasons. First, because Britain has, relative to many other comparable countries at least, fairly good data resources that enable analysis of the key issues on trust identified above. In particular, thanks to reputable and long-established population surveys such as the British Election Study and British Social Attitudes, there are both contemporary and longitudinal data that help us explore levels of trust and changes in these distributions over time. In addition, there are stand-alone sources of data in Britain—some of which were conducted by others and some of which I was involved in collecting and which are presented here for the first time—that help to fill in some of the gaps among more established data sources.

The second reason for selecting Britain as a case study is because it is something of an extreme case. Levels of trust among British citizens have declined more sharply than in most other advanced democracies (as we will see in Chapter 4). Although potentially worrying for policymakers, these conditions are valuable for analysts. They enable us to explore why trust might have fallen, and what the effects of low and declining levels of trust might be. These issues are less easily explored in countries where levels of trust have remained high or at least fairly constant. While this latter situation currently applies to many western countries, in others there is evidence of declining trust among citizens. Thus, although some countries may not currently face quite the trust challenge of countries like Britain, it is as well for all to be aware of why trust has fallen and of what the consequences of this might be. By virtue of its low and declining rates of trust among citizens, Britain provides a useful case study through which to study, and to raise wider awareness of, these issues.

Granted, findings on trust drawn from one country may not always 'carry' to other countries. While there are important similarities in the nature, causes, and potential effects of trust across national contexts, there are also differences. For example, comparative studies have pointed to variations between countries in the association with trust of particular individual evaluations, such as economic appraisals (Torcal, 2017). It is thus sensible to explore how far key findings on trust derived from the case of Britain might also apply in other countries. For this reason, the focus on trust in the British context is supplemented at various points by analyses of trust among populations in other countries. These excursions are used to test whether conclusions on trust reached in the British context also apply in other contexts and also to fill in gaps where relevant data on trust are absent in Britain. To give some examples, data are drawn in the following chapters from:

- *Norway*, to explore how far levels of trust vary by particular tasks or 'domains'.
- *Germany*, to examine the over-time variability of trust among individuals.

- *Canada and the United States*, to analyse where trust sits as a measure of general political support.
- *Western Europe, the United States, and Australia*, to explore trends in levels of trust.
- *Various Western European countries*, to analyse the effects of education on changes in trust.
- *Greece and Spain*, to examine the effect of low trust on various civic behaviours.

These examples do not make this book a comparative study. It is a study of a single country, yet one that retains an eye to trust in other countries where these cases help us to understand the wider application of key findings or supply useful additional data to plug gaps in our understanding of trust.

When it comes to approach, the book blends conceptual reasoning and empirical investigation. The emphasis is on the latter over the former. For example, there is no attempt to replicate the secondary literature's extensive conceptual discussions about the nature of trust. Instead, and for reasons already explained, the analysis focuses on what people's expressions of trust tell us about its nature. The book's empirical analysis of different aspects of trust draws primarily on data collected from population surveys. Surveys provide the bulk of our data on political trust and present some clear advantages for trust scholars, notably in facilitating cross-national and longitudinal analyses. Yet a reliance on survey data also presents potential problems, notably in the form of concerns over the validity of survey indicators as accurate measures of the underlying concept. These questions and concerns are real, as we will find out in Chapter 3. If it is appropriate to begin a book with a health warning, it would be that many of its conclusions—and indeed many of the things analysts tell us about political trust—rest on the particular ways (warts and all) in which we usually measure the concept. The potential implications of this are considered in more detail in the Conclusion.

Finally, a word on the type of academic studies drawn on in this book. Trust arises in numerous settings and across numerous relationships: for example, between patients and doctors, workers and managers, defendants and judges, victims and the police, and local communities and risk managers. Studies of trust in these settings have mushroomed across academic disciplines. This book focuses on the relations between citizens and institutions in the political realm. Most of the studies shedding light on those relations unsurprisingly derive from the field of political science. Yet studies in other fields—notably sociology, psychology, criminology, management studies, health service research, and risk management—have contributed important perspectives that aid our understanding of trust in the political realm. Political scientists could learn much from the perspectives and findings of trust scholars in these and other academic disciplines (whose focus on trust, I suggest, has sometimes been rather deeper and broader than that among political scientists). Where appropriate, therefore, the analysis in the following chapter draws on those perspectives, blending the findings from political scientists with those of scholars in other academic disciplines.

Outline of the book

The book is organized into three sections, each of which poses a broad question about trust. Section 1 asks 'What are we talking about?' It explores how we define trust and what trust signifies. It also explores where trust sits as an indicator of citizens' relations with political rulers. Finally, it considers how trust is measured, and how its measurement might be improved. Section 2 asks 'What is going on?' It explores people's trust in different institutions, how levels of trust have changed over time, and how far these changes apply across countries. It also considers which factors shape trust, both over time and at single points in time. Section 3 asks 'So what?' and focuses on the consequences of trust. In particular, it explores how far low trust undermines civic and political norms and practices in ways that threaten effective democratic governance.

Section 1: What are we talking about? The nature and measurement of trust

We begin in Chapter 1 with the meaning of trust. The chapter opens with a brief definition of the concept, although it argues that abstract reasoning about trust only gets us so far. Instead, we gain additional insights into the nature of trust by exploring different states of trust, and the relationship between trust and distrust. The analysis suggests that rather than categorizing people as either trusting or distrusting, we would do well to recognize the mixture of feelings—or ambivalence—people have towards political actors. Moreover, people who are identified as having low levels of trust may not necessarily be distrustful. There is an important difference between low trust and distrust that is often elided in scholarly analyses and media commentaries. In turn, such elisions may help explain why the consequences of trust—which are explored in Chapter 7—are sometimes less significant than often supposed.

Another route to a clearer understanding of trust is via exploring individuals' expressions of trust. Chapter 1 thus pursues an individual-focused, or 'bottom-up', perspective on trust, via two principal questions: *what* do individual expressions of trust consist of, and *how* are these trust expressions formed?

In terms of *what* trust consists of, Chapter 1 explores the extent to which trust reflects specific or generalized evaluations. Are individual expressions of trust specific in being attached to particular institutions and particular tasks or functions? The evidence presented in the chapter points to some specificities in people's trust judgements. For example, individuals manifest very different levels of trust in different institutions, while events that affect their trust in one institution do not necessarily affect their trust in others. Yet if trust judgements are sometimes specific, they more often show signs of generalization. Notably, the chapter identifies commonalities in people's trust in different political and civic institutions and in different tasks or functions undertaken by these institutions. Individual trust judgements are also shown to be fairly stable over time. The implication is that individual expressions of trust often represent generalized judgements, ranging across objects, functions, and periods of time.

Chapter 1 also probes *how* individuals form trust judgements. It explores the features—ranging from individual personality traits to different levels of information—that trust judgements typically rest on. Particular attention is paid to the role in trust formation of cognitive considerations alongside simpler cues involving feelings and impressions about an actor. Additional evidence presented suggests that individuals may not readily update evaluations of trust when presented with new information about an actor's performance or behaviour. Trust may be too engrained or 'sticky' for this. The chapter also considers how far individuals' trust is shaped by different types of information, in particular by positive and negative forms of information. To the extent that trust is particularly affected by negative information—the 'negativity bias' in trust—this might help explain why in recent years countries such as Britain have witnessed declining rates of trust.

Having examined the *nature* of trust, Chapter 2 turns to the *status* and position of trust. A question that has hovered over research in the field for almost fifty years is what types of judgements are captured by (survey) measures of trust? In particular, do people's expressions of trust primarily reflect evaluations of the government of the day or appraisals of the wider political system? In the parlance of political scientists, is trust a 'specific' or a 'diffuse' form of political support? This distinction is important, since if trust is found to operate simply as a form of specific support, its effects and implications are likely to be limited. The evidence presented in Chapter 2 suggests that trust incorporates both specific and diffuse elements; it reflects people's evaluations of incumbent actors while also reflecting broader appraisals of the political system. Trust therefore appears to constitute a 'middle-level' judgement; neither a specific appraisal of particular politicians nor a generalized appraisal of how well democracy is working but, rather, an assessment that straddles both specific and diffuse evaluations.

Even with this conclusion, one might wonder about the volume of attention paid to trust by academics, policymakers, and media commentators, when trust is by no means the only concept capturing the vertical relations between citizens and political rulers. The second part of Chapter 2 considers where trust sits in relation to these other forms of political support. Conceptual and empirical analysis shows that while there are some overlaps between different forms of political support, some important distinctions also exist. There are also some observable distinctions when it comes to the effects of different forms of political support. Thus, while trust is not a wholly stand-alone or distinctive form of political support, it shows particular features which distinguish it from other evaluations. This, in turn, reinforces the value of studying trust.

Chapter 3 turns to the issue of how we measure trust. While there are various ways in which an individual's trust might be identified and quantified, most empirical analyses draw on survey indicators fielded on samples of national populations. This assumes that trust can be measured as an attitude (i.e. what an individual believes) rather than as a behaviour (i.e. what an individual does). Yet treating trust as an attitude involves some tricky measurement issues. Traditional survey indicators of trust should (but rarely do) come with important health warnings. There are important questions to ask about the validity of the trust indicators routinely deployed to underpin empirical analysis. The chapter explores these questions and potential shortcomings in the way trust is conventionally measured. It also identifies how analysts might 'move on with measurement', to provide more robust ways of gauging individuals' trust.

Section 2: What is going on? Levels and causes of trust

Having laid the ground by analysing the nature, status, and measurement of trust, the attention in this section turns to patterns of trust within the population. Chapter 4 provides a comprehensive picture of people's trust in different state actors and institutions, of how levels of trust vary within the population, and of how far levels of trust have changed over time. The chapter points to a decline in people's trust in partisan actors (such as governments, legislatures, and political parties) but not in other public actors. It also explores how far changes in trust among British citizens have been mirrored among populations in comparable countries. Overall, the chapter provides a clearer picture about whether western societies, and Britain in particular, face a 'crisis of trust'.

Chapters 5 and 6 turn to explaining trust. To start with, the analysis picks up the trends in trust identified in Chapter 4 to explore why levels of trust in Britain have declined over the past four or more decades. The longitudinal analysis in Chapter 5 identifies changing levels of trust among individuals located in different socio-economic groups within the population. In particular, the results point to a growing gap in trust between society's 'haves' and 'have nots'. Extending the analysis to other European countries provides important clues about why trust has declined in many advanced democracies. At the same time, the evidence from Britain does not suggest that declining trust reflects the particular effects of age or generation. Beyond socio-economic and demographic factors, the chapter also considers how far declining trust might be attributable to people's attitudes, in particular feelings of political representation and evaluations and expectations of government delivery.

To complement the longitudinal picture presented in Chapter 5, the following chapter examines in more detail the types of appraisal that shape citizens' trust at particular points in time. The analysis presented in Chapter 6 highlights the range of considerations involved in individuals' trust judgements, covering perceptions of what politicians do, their concern with citizens' interests, and their integrity. Trust is shown to be a complex judgement, not reducible to any particular criterion or consideration. Yet the evidence considered in this chapter suggests that individuals' trust rests more heavily on whether political actors are perceived as being motivated in the right ways than by whether these actors are seen as competent or effective.

If the sources of people's trust in their political rulers are broad, their application can often be specific. Chapter 6 examines whether the factors associated with trust are consistent or variant between different individuals, between different institutions, and at different points in time. The evidence marshalled suggests that the factors associated with trust often vary between different individuals, different objects of trust, and different time-points. Trust may have some generalized features (as suggested in Chapter 1), but the analysis here points to important specificities in how individuals form trust judgements.

Section 3: So what? The consequences of trust

Trust may shape what people think and how they behave in all sorts of ways. To give a structure to these various outcomes, the analysis in Chapter 7 identifies two potential effects or consequences of trust. If trust represents 'loyalty' in Hirschman's (1970) well-known triumvirate of behaviours, the alternatives are represented by 'voice' or 'exit'. Voice relates to the expression of grievances, manifested in the political realm by activities such as protest, voting for anti-system parties, seeking reform of the political system, and rejecting an active role for governments. Employing a variety of data, the impact of trust on each of these behaviours is reviewed. Trust is found to have some effect on each, although these effects are often conditional. Thus, trust is found to be positively associated with protest activities, particularly where protest is a substitute for electoral engagement not an addition to it. Low trust is also found to be associated with support for protest parties; but it is associated with support for some mainstream parties, too. Moreover, while a lack of trust appears to be one of the factors behind the Brexit referendum vote in Britain in 2016, the 'Leave' vote was not a straightforward consequence of declining trust. Nor does low trust appear to trigger individual preferences for non-democratic practices and norms or individual rejection of an active role for government policymaking and capacity.

Citizens who are low in trust may choose not to engage in 'voice' behaviours by expressing their grievances but instead to 'exit' the political system. Exit entails opting out of engagement with the political system and may take various forms such as abstaining from elections, ignoring official information and guidance, and failing to comply with important collective obligations. Should such exit forms of behaviour become widespread among the population, the damage to a country's civic and political life would be serious. The analysis in Chapter 7 considers how far trust is associated with each of these behaviours. It concludes that trust does not have consistent effects on citizens' engagement with the political system. Thus, the effects of trust on electoral abstention are fairly modest, although trust appears more closely associated with people's receptiveness to government information. There is some evidence that trust is associated with people's observance of collective obligations such as obeying the law, paying taxes, and—over the past few years—complying with official restrictions around viral (coronavirus) prevention. Yet trust does not appear to be consistently and strongly related to compliance; during the coronavirus pandemic, for example, many governments were able to secure public acceptance of their measures even when a large proportion of their citizens expressed a lack of political trust. Indeed, looking beyond Britain to cases where popular trust has fallen to extremely low levels—such as in Greece and Spain after the global financial crash in 2007–2008—there is evidence that important civic behaviours did not deteriorate. While low trust appears to trigger some negative behaviours among citizens, it, by no means, induces a general and widespread turn away from political and civic norms and duties. Trust is often important for effective politics and governance, and declining public regard for political actors in countries like Britain should not be ignored. Yet neither should the problems be exaggerated. For, as Chapter 7 concludes, declining trust and the problems to which this gives rise represent a challenge to the political system rather than a crisis for democratic governance.

SECTION 1
WHAT ARE WE TALKING ABOUT? THE NATURE AND MEASUREMENT OF TRUST

Chapter 1
What is trust?

What does it mean to say that a citizen either 'trusts' or 'distrusts' a political actor or institution? Numerous studies of trust dedicate extensive space to the term's conceptual nature, within the disciplines of political science (Levi and Stoker, 2000; Hardin, 2002; Uslaner, 2002; Bauer, 2014; PytlikZillig and Kimbrough, 2016; Citrin and Stoker, 2018), sociology (Luhmann, 1979; Robbins, 2016), management (Mayer, Davis, and Schoorman, 1995; McKnight and Chervany, 1996; Bigley and Pearce, 1998; Rousseau et al., 1998; Kramer, 1999; Schoorman, Mayer, and Davis, 2007; Searle, Nienaber, and Sitkin, 2017), psychology (Shockley et al., 2016), and risk studies (Earle, Siegrist, and Gutscher, 2010). These studies are helpful in identifying the broad conceptual boundaries of trust. In this chapter, I draw on these studies to establish what I understand trust to mean. But I do so fairly concisely. This is partly to avoid repeating discussions presented elsewhere. It also reflects a belief that we only learn so much about trust by attending to its conceptual basis. As we will see in Chapter 3, we generally measure the concept by asking people how much they trust a particular actor or institution. Understanding the nature of trust at least partly consists of attending to the ways it is used, and exploring how the term is interpreted and deployed by citizens in the political arena. As a concept, trust might be defined in broad terms. But as a social phenomenon, it requires reference to its comprehension and expression by individuals. Few studies consider what these understandings and usages consist of, preferring instead to explore trust through abstract conceptual discussions. This approach risks leaving us with a rarefied account of trust: long on conceptual detail but short on its practical meanings and social significance. And it is surely this social significance—of what trust entails for the way citizens think and behave—that has sparked the interest and concern of so many policymakers and commentators.

Accordingly, this chapter is light on conceptual definitions of trust. Instead, it seeks to extend our understanding of trust by fleshing out some overlooked details of its nature and by exploring how individuals apply and form trust judgements. In the first part of the chapter, close attention is paid to two issues often overlooked in existing studies, namely distinctions between different

Trust. Ben Seyd, Oxford University Press. © Ben Seyd (2024). DOI: 10.1093/oso/9780198896449.003.0002

states of trust and the relationship between trust and distrust. The second part of the chapter explores what trust means for people and the ways they deploy it. Particular attention is paid to two issues. The first concerns the focal points of individuals' trust judgements, or *what* people trust. The analysis here concentrates on how far individual expressions of trust comprise either specific or generalized judgements. The second issue concerns the way in which trust judgements are formed, and thus *how* people trust. This section concentrates on how far trust judgements reflect individuals' personalities, cognitive and affective appraisals of political actors, and negative and positive forms of information to which individuals are exposed. The results laid out in this chapter have important implications for our understanding of trust and for our awareness of its potential consequences.

1.1 Defining trust

While there are lively scholarly debates about the meaning of trust, a core definition of the concept has emerged from discussions across different academic disciplines. This core consists in a belief on the part of an individual that another actor or organization is likely to behave in a manner that upholds, or is consistent with, the individual's interests. In some accounts, trust is held to comprise a *belief* that another actor is likely to act on those interests. Hence Gamson's (1968: 54) definition of trust as the 'probability ... that the political system (or some part of it) will produce preferred outcomes even if left untended'. Similarly, in his many writings on trust, Hardin (notably 2002; 2006) defines trust as a belief that another person will behave in a manner consistent with the trustor's interests because they have some incentive or motivation to do so. Gambetta (1988: 217) adopts the same approach in suggesting that trust entails a judgement that 'the probability that [an agent] will perform an action that is beneficial or at least not detrimental to us is high enough for us to consider engaging in some form of cooperation with him'. This statement ends by introducing a behavioural element to trust. Indeed, some accounts treat trust as comprising an *action*, or an *intention to act*, on the part of an individual in making themselves vulnerable to, or cooperating with, another actor. Hence Levi and Stoker (2000: 476) define trust as involving 'an individual making herself vulnerable to another individual, group or institution that has the capacity to do her harm or to betray her', and Warren (1999: 311) takes trust to involve 'a judgment ... to accept vulnerability to the potential ill will of others by granting them discretionary power over some good'.[1]

The two forms of trust contained in these definitions—namely, a belief held about another person or an action or intention to act in relation to another person—are linked in Mayer, Davis, and Schoorman's (1995: 712) highly cited formulation of trust from the field of management studies. Here, trust is defined as 'the willingness of a party to be vulnerable to the actions of another party based on the expectation that the other will perform a particular action important to the trustor'. A similar conceptualization underpins another widely cited definition from the management field, in which trust represents 'a psychological state comprising the intention to accept vulnerability based upon positive expectations of the intentions or behaviour of another' (Rousseau et al., 1998: 395). Within the field of risk management, trust has similarly been defined as 'the willingness, in expectation of beneficial outcomes, to make oneself vulnerable to another based on a judgement of similarity of intentions or values' (Earle, Siegrist, and Gutscher, 2010: 30).

While trust is conceptualized both as a belief and as an action or intention to act, the degree to which these overlap among individuals might be limited (for more on this, see Chapter 3, Section 3.2). Some analysts suggest that people's actions represent a better measure of their underlying trust than their beliefs, which may comprise little more than 'cheap talk' (O'Neill, 2002). Yet it is also possible that people form trust beliefs that do not spill over into actions; we may trust another person without necessarily engaging with, or making ourselves vulnerable to, them. Hence it seems somewhat restrictive to focus the definition of trust on people's behaviour rather than on their beliefs. Moreover, while definitions of trust as a willingness to make oneself vulnerable to another person make sense in the context of interpersonal relations—involving a manager and a colleague in the workplace, for example—they are less intuitive in the realm of political relations. An individual has little or no choice about whether to make herself vulnerable to most state actors and agencies; these have authority over her by dint of her status as a citizen. It makes more sense to treat trust as willing vulnerability in cases where individuals can exercise choice over engaging with public service providers, as in the case of selecting a local doctor or school, for example. It is also useful to separate out people's attitudes and behaviour—rather than treating both as potential forms of trust—since this enables us to distinguish more clearly between the manifestations of trust and its outcomes or consequences.

When evaluating people's trust in political actors and institutions, it is helpful to follow Hardin (2002, 2006), who argues that trust rests heavily on the notion of *trustworthiness*. Here, an individual will trust (or distrust) another person or agency to the extent that they are perceived to be trustworthy (or untrustworthy). In principle, a person or agency may be assessed as trustworthy or untrustworthy against a multitude of factors, although empirical studies stress the importance of factors such as benevolence, ability, and integrity in people's appraisals of an actor (these features and qualities are explored more fully in Chapter 6).

Pulling these threads together, we can define trust as a summative judgement made by an individual about whether another person or organization will operate (i.e. behave and make decisions) in a way consistent with the individual's interests. This judgement is based on perceptions of the object's relevant qualities—notably their benevolence, ability, and integrity—the presence of which in the object suggests both motivation and competence to act in the individual's interests. While trust can consist of a willingness to engage with, or make oneself vulnerable to, another actor, it can also consist of a belief about that actor, notably about whether they are likely to act in a way consistent with one's interests. This belief or judgement formed by an individual of another actor comprises the core of trust deployed in the rest of this book.

1.2 States of trust

When an individual forms a trust judgement about another person or agency, three broad outcomes are possible. First, the individual may trust the object. Second, they may distrust the object. Third, they may hold conflicting feelings about the object, and thus be neither fully trusting nor distrusting (see Emborg, Daniels, and Walker, 2020).

This latter condition of trust—in which someone experiences both positive and negative feelings about an actor or institution—can be characterized as one of 'ambivalence'. Few of us are likely to wholly trust or wholly distrust a political actor or agency; most people's attitudes are likely to be more qualified than that. An individual may harbour negative sentiments about some features of an actor, but more positive sentiments about other features. Indeed, studies of American citizens have identified widespread ambivalence in attitudes towards core political institutions; between 50 and 70 per cent of Americans have been found to hold attitudes towards Congress, the Supreme Court, and the incumbent president that contain both positive and negative feelings (McGraw and Bartels, 2005; Gainous, Craig, and Martinez, 2008).

This ambivalence can be seen in data on attitudes to politicians I collected in 2019 from a sample of British citizens. The data derive from a survey containing various measures of trust and were gathered from a sample of participants on Prolific Academic, a UK-based online recruitment platform.[2] Some measures were positively worded (e.g. 'Most politicians are good at what they do') while others were negatively worded (e.g. 'Most politicians do not do a capable job'). We can count agreement with positively worded items as indicating trust and agreement with negatively worded items as indicating distrust. By tallying up each of the positive and negative items into scales tapping trust and distrust and then comparing their distribution, we can identify the degree of consistency in people's trust evaluations. The results show that fairly few people consistently trust politicians (by agreeing with all positive items and disagreeing with all negative items) or distrust them (by agreeing with all negative items and disagreeing with all positive items). Only 25 per cent of respondents were consistent distrusters, with 11 per cent consistent trusters. The remaining 64 per cent were ambivalent, manifesting signs of both trust and distrust.[3]

Aside from ambivalence, people's evaluations of political objects appear in the forms of either trust or distrust. Two issues arise here that need disentangling. The first is whether survey measures designed to tap trust can also tap distrust. The second is whether trust and distrust originate from similar or distinct factors and should thus be measured on the same scale or on different scales.

Let me start by considering the measurement of trust and distrust. Many empirical measures (such as those fielded on surveys like the European Social Survey (ESS) and the British Election Study (BES)) assess trust by asking respondents to evaluate a particular institution on a scale anchored by the options of 'complete trust' (ESS) or 'a great deal of trust' (BES) at one end and by 'no trust at all' (ESS) or 'no trust' (BES) at the other. Yet the lower anchor indicates only that people lack trust in the institution, not that they actively distrust it. Studies that have purposively asked people about their 'distrust' as well as their 'trust' in a political object have found that an absence of trust does not equate to active distrust. When faced with a question on trust whose response options run from 'high' to 'low', people may indicate that they do not trust. Yet when faced with a response scale that runs from 'trust' to 'distrust', they often select a point in the middle of the scale (Mishler and Rose, 1997; Cook and Gronke, 2005). For instance, Cook and Gronke (2005) fielded two questions on trust in government among a sample of United States citizens. One provided response options that ranged from 'just about always' to 'almost never', while the second provided response options that ranged from 'strong trust' to 'strong distrust'. The researchers found that among survey respondents who answered 'almost never' to the first question, the modal response to the second question was the mid-point 'neither trust nor distrust'.

We should therefore be wary about assuming that people who respond negatively to survey measures of trust are therefore distrustful (see also Hardin, 2002: 90). It may well be that people who report lacking trust in politicians and governments are thereby indicating a belief that those actors do not manifest the trustworthy qualities required for trust. Yet a lack of trust does not necessarily indicate that an individual judges an object to be untrustworthy.[4]

The second issue is whether trust and distrust spring from similar or distinct sources. For some scholars, distrust is simply the obverse of trust. For example, in their analysis of political cynicism—which they define as a contemptuous distrust of human nature—Agger, Goldstein, and Pearl (1961) identify its antonym as trust. Hence to trust is to believe that politicians act responsively, while to be cynical or distrustful rests on a belief that politicians act self-interestedly. Ullmann-Margalit (2004) takes a similar position. She suggests that individual A will trust actor B if they believe that B is motivated to act in their (A's) interests. They will not trust B if they do not believe that B is motivated to act in their interests. They will distrust B if they believe that B is motivated to act against their interests. The factors shaping trust and distrust are identical, albeit with opposite valence: trust arises from positive evaluations of B, while distrust arises from negative evaluations of B.

If trust and distrust share common origins, it makes conceptual and empirical sense to measure them using a single scale (anchored by explicit 'trust' and 'distrust' end-points). However, other analysts suggest that trust and distrust do not cohabit on a single scale, but instead spring from distinct sources. On this argument, an individual may trust an actor for one reason but distrust them for another. Yet arguments about the distinctiveness of trust and distrust have been made at the conceptual level (Sitkin and Roth, 1993; Lewicki, McAllister, and Bies, 1998; Van der Walle and Six, 2014; Bertsou, 2019a), but with rather little empirical support. Some studies that claim to identify distinctive sources for trust and distrust are underpinned by empirical results that fail to corroborate such distinctiveness (Saunders, Dietz, and Thornhill, 2014).[5] Additional studies claim to measure distrust as a separate construct (Rose et al., 2014); but the extent to which distrust is distinct from trust cannot be explored since no equivalent measures of trust are fielded.

Where studies have attempted to measure distinctive conditions of trust and distrust, they have tended to find that the indicators of each concept fall within the same attitudinal dimension, suggesting that they comprise opposite poles of a singular concept rather than distinct constructs

(Omodei and McLennan, 2000; Saunders and Thornhill, 2004; see also Schoorman, Mayer, and Davis, 2007). For example, in a study of organizations involved in managing food risk, Frewer and colleagues (1996) showed that the grounds on which people rested their trust were similar (albeit in positive form) to those on which they rested their distrust (see also Poortinga and Pidgeon, 2004). A similar picture arises in relation to people's trust in the media in the United States. When asked which factors explained their lack of trust in media outlets, the most prevalent complaint—identified by over four in ten respondents—was inaccurate reporting and bias. When asked which factors explained their trust in media outlets, the most cited virtues were truthfulness, accuracy, and a lack of bias, nominated by between three and four in ten respondents (Gallup, 2018). Thus, negative and positive orientations towards the media were found to rest on the same grounds, not on different grounds.[6] Even when studies have identified different grounds for trust and distrust, these differences are fairly minor (Kavanagh et al., 2020: 73–74).[7]

In sum, we can identify various states of trust among citizens. Some individuals might feel internally conflicted or ambivalent, holding positive feelings about some aspects of politicians' behaviour but more negative feelings about other aspects. Other citizens might hold more consistent positive or negative orientations. Yet individuals may not trust an actor without necessarily distrusting them. Moreover, there is little evidence that trust and distrust spring from specific considerations; instead, they appear to reflect different—positive and negative—reactions to the same sort of considerations. Overall, we should be careful how we interpret survey results showing low levels of trust among a population. These results often reveal a popular lack of trust in politicians, but not necessarily widespread hostility to those actors.

1.3 What do we trust?

This section moves on from defining trust and identifying its different states to considering ways in which trust is interpreted and expressed by citizens. It explores two key issues. The first is whether people's trust judgements take a specific or general form. Do people express trust in specific institutions and in relation to specific functions, or is trust a more generalized judgement? The second is whether people's trust judgements are consistent or variable over time.

The specificity of trust

In her 2002 Reith Lectures on the topic of trust, the philosopher Onora O'Neill made the case for the specificity of trust and pointed to inadequacies in the generalized, undifferentiated way in which trust is often measured:

> Most of us would want to say that we trust *some* but not *other* professionals, *some* but not *other* office-holders, in *some* matters but not in *others* .... In answering the pollsters we suppress the complexity of our real judgements, smooth out distinctions we draw between different individuals and institutions, and average our judgements about their trustworthiness in different activities.
>
> (O'Neill, 2002: 9–10; emphases in original)

If, in broad terms, trust comprises a belief that another person will act in a way that is consistent with my interests, its potential specificity is quickly apparent. For example, I may trust an academic colleague when they promise to produce a brilliant piece of research but not when they promise to deliver a decent student lecture. The specificity of trust judgements is likely to be greater in the case of relations between individuals than in the case of relations between individuals and institutions. When we enquire whether individuals trust an organization like 'government' or 'the courts', many are likely to form an evaluation based on how well these bodies serve their general interests rather than any specific interest. That said, it is possible that governments or the courts may be trusted on one function (to act efficiently, say) while not trusted on another (to be impartial and fair). If trust is a judgement in three parts (Hardin, 2002: 9)—an individual (A) trusts an actor (B) in relation to some function (X)—O'Neill's injunction to identify what X consists of is, in principle, sound.

Yet do we observe such specificities in the way people express trust judgements? In fact, many analysts suggest that trust takes a fairly general, rather than a specific, form. Comparative analyses show a high level of consistency in people's trust in different bodies like parliament, political parties, politicians, the legal system, and the police. While levels of trust in these bodies might vary—typically being higher in the case of courts and the police than in the case of more partisan institutions (see Chapter 4)—empirical analyses often find that these judgements comprise—or 'load onto' in statistical terms—a single dimension rather than multiple dimensions (Mishler and Rose, 2001; Zmerli et al., 2007; Marien, 2011; Zmerli and Newton, 2017; van der Meer and Ouattara, 2019). People's trust in different bodies thus appears to manifest considerable consistency or similarity. In some cases, the consistency of people's trust judgements appears to extend well beyond core political institutions. For example, in a study of British citizens, Rose (2014: 34–35) found high interrelationships between individuals' trust judgements across a range of public officials, from government ministers, through health service managers, to police officers and even school head teachers.

The specificity of trust judgements has also been addressed by Hooghe (2011), who examines citizens' trust in political parties and politicians. Hooghe finds a singular structure to people's trust in these two bodies. He concludes that citizens' trust in core political institutions is not distinctive but instead comprises a 'comprehensive judgement on political trust' (Hooghe, 2011: 274) extending across institutions. His explanation for this generalized judgement is that actors within different political institutions tend to behave in broadly similar ways, in turn reflecting the dominant political culture or operation of a country's political system. An alternative explanation is that in answering survey questions, respondents economize on information processing and effort and rely on shortcuts or report generalized assessments. Suggestive evidence for this comes from studies that have found people's trust in regional tiers of government is shaped by the same factors that influence their trust in national government (Uslaner, 2001; Wolak and Kelleher Pelus, 2010; however, for somewhat contrary evidence, see Chapter 6, Section 6.5) and from studies in the field of risk management that have found trust in the regulation of genetically modified food to covary strongly with a more general measure of trust in government (Poortinga and Pidgeon, 2006).

Against this generalized picture of trust judgements, other studies point to distinctiveness in the way individuals evaluate trust. Thus, people's trust in 'representative' institutions (such as parliament, parties, and government) has been found to be distinctive to their trust in 'implementation' institutions (such as the army, the police, and legal bodies) (Denters, Gabriel, and Torcal, 2007; Rothstein and Stolle, 2008; Allum et al., 2010; Schnaudt, 2019: 56–59; see also Liu et al., 2018). People express trust in core political institutions in distinctive ways to their trust in commercial bodies (such as banks and large companies) and the press (van Elsas, 2015).

We can see these kinds of trust distinctions among British citizens by drawing on the 2018 British Social Attitudes survey which asked respondents about their trust in seven institutions: government, parliament, the civil service, the courts, the police, the media, and banks. Answers were recorded against four options: 'trust a great deal', 'tend to trust', 'tend to distrust', and 'distrust greatly'. People's trust judgements about government were very similar to their trust judgements about parliament, with 77 per cent of respondents picking exactly the same response option when asked about their trust in the two bodies. Yet when it came to the civil service, only 44 per cent of respondents expressed the same level of trust as they did in government. For courts and the police, the figure—at 36 per cent—is even lower.[8]

It is also apparent that external events have varied effects on people's trust in different institutions. Figure 1.1 plots levels of trust among British citizens for various public actors over the period 2005–2015.[9] This period straddles two major crises in international and British politics: the 2008 financial crash and the 2009 MPs' expenses scandal (which involved the widespread misuse of legislative expenses and allowances among British members of parliament (MPs)). As is clear from the plotted lines for each actor in Figure 1.1, the financial crash did not serve to depress people's trust in public actors.[10] The MPs' expenses scandal, however, had a clear depressive effect on people's trust in government ministers and politicians, along with their trust in business leaders, civil servants, and the police.[11] Yet the scandal did little to affect people's trust in judges and doctors. In other words, particular events or national crises do not lead to people tarring all public actors with the same low-trust brush.[12]

Some important distinctions are thus apparent in people's expressions of trust in different public actors and institutions. These distinctions may be even more visible if trust was measured in a different way. As we will see in Chapter 3, survey questions taking a very generalized form

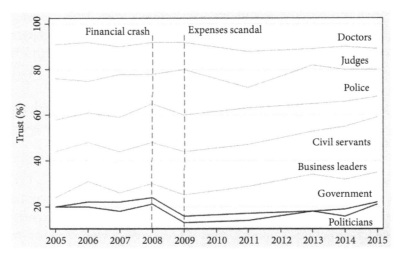

Figure 1.1 Trends in trust and political crises, 2005–2015
Source: Ipsos Mori 'Trust in Professions'

('How much do you trust ...?') tend to encourage broad or generalized responses. This tendency is exacerbated if survey respondents are asked about their trust in different institutions listed together in a survey. This practice encourages 'carryover' effects, whereby answers to a survey question are shaped by respondents' answers to preceding questions (Tourangeau, Rips, and Rasinski, 1989). There is some evidence that when surveys appraise people's trust in different institutions listed together, the similarity of respondents' answers is magnified (Loosveldt and Beullens, 2017). Given this, it is difficult to distinguish how far any consistencies in people's trust judgements across institutions reflect substantive considerations or, alternatively, methodological ones. This is an area in which further empirical research would be highly valuable. In the meantime, however, we can note some distinctions in the way people express trust, while also concurring with Hooghe that when it comes to core political institutions, trust appears to be a fairly generalized evaluation.

Having explored the specificity of trust as applied to different actors or institutions, what about the function or domain of trust (the X term in the trust equation: A trusts B in respect of X)? What evidence is there that people's expressions of trust vary depending on the function an object is being evaluated against? There is some evidence for such specificity in people's trust judgements. Thus, for example, the British government has been found to be trusted more on the issue of genetic testing than on the issues of genetically modified food and climate change (Poortinga and Pidgeon, 2003). However, these differences are fairly small (similar evidence is provided by Bickerstaff et al., 2008). There is little additional data in Britain that can be used to identify variations in trust by function. However, data from Norway suggest that trust judgements are fairly similar irrespective of which aspects of decision-making citizens are asked to evaluate. In 2013, the Norwegian Citizens Panel asked its respondents how much they trusted the national government to handle various incidents: a natural disaster, a transport accident, a contagious disease, an infrastructure failure, and a terrorist attack. As shown in Figure 1.2, levels of trust in government were highest in relation to a transport accident and lowest in relation to a terrorist attack. While these variations in trust in different tasks are all statistically significant (as shown by the non-overlapping error bars), they are not that substantive. Citizens' trust in their government to execute one particular task or function appears to be fairly similar to their trust in government to execute other tasks or functions.

Yet individuals may show other evidence of specificity in their trust judgements. In particular, as Citrin (1977: 387–388) suggested, assessments of trust in different institutions may rest on different criteria. Studies have shown

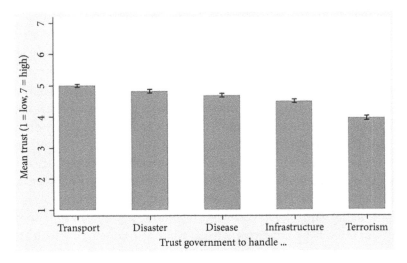

Figure 1.2 Trust in government on different functions
Source: Norwegian Citizens Panel, Wave 1 (2013)

that in the case of 'executive' bodies (such as presidents or central banks), trust may rest on perceptions of competence or performance while, in the case of 'delivery' bodies (such as family courts) or 'representative' bodies (such as legislatures), trust may rest more strongly on perceptions of responsiveness and understanding of citizens' needs (Feldman, 1983; Braithwaite, 1998; see also Kelleher and Wolak, 2007) for similar results for state-level institutions in the United States). Similarly, citizen satisfaction with a variety of federal government agencies in the United States has been found to rest on how well those agencies are seen to perform particular functions. Thus, for example, while satisfaction with some agencies (e.g. those concerned with medical care) is driven by perceived service quality, satisfaction with other agencies (e.g. those concerned with tax collection) is driven by the nature and quality of the information provided to citizens (Morgeson and Petrescu, 2011). As we will see in Chapter 5, there is also some evidence from Britain of variation in the factors shaping people's trust in different political institutions. Yet we should not overdo the distinctiveness of people's trust judgements. Research conducted in the United States by PytlikZillig and colleagues (2016) found that the dimensionality of people's judgements about objects' trustworthiness—the structure of the criteria on which trust rests—is similar across different institutions and individuals. The authors conclude from this that people tend not to form specific evaluations of trust in particular agencies and at particular points in time. Instead, they carry around general—positive or negative—evaluations of public agencies, which inform their responses when stimulated to express a trust judgement in a specific institution.

Onora O'Neill's injunction to treat trust in differentiated terms—to focus on how individuals apply trust judgements across different objects and in relation to different functions—is well made. In this section, we have seen examples of such specificity, notably when it comes to the way individuals evaluate different objects and the criteria on which those evaluations rest. Yet people do not tend to compute fresh judgements every time a trust dilemma is faced. Instead, they tend to draw on generalized evaluations, which are often applied across institutions. The implication is that any attempts to stimulate higher levels of trust will need to be generalized in form rather than specific to particular institutions.

The variability of trust

People's attitudes and evaluations of political actors and agencies have often been found to manifest little prior thought and reflection and to be changeable over time (Zaller, 1992; Tourangeau, Rips, and Rasinski, 2000). Indeed some analysts have suggested that trust—as conventionally measured in surveys—overlaps strongly with evaluations of incumbent political actors and, as a result, fluctuates as much as does party popularity (Citrin, 1974). Yet as we have just noted, trust often represents a more generalized evaluation of political actors and institutions. This would suggest that trust judgements are—or should be—fairly stable over time.

Exploring the consistency of people's trust judgements requires tracking the same individuals over time. We can do so in two cases—Britain and Germany—by drawing on appropriate panel data. In Britain, we can use the British Election Study Internet Panel (BESIP), which questioned the same individuals over an eight-year period between spring 2014 and spring 2022. These individuals were asked how much they trusted MPs in general, with responses measured on a 1 (no trust) to 7 (great deal of trust) scale. The results are shown in Figure 1.3. Mean levels of trust across individuals are reported in the left-hand panel of the figure. This shows a broad consistency in trust until spring 2019, at which point trust fell dramatically (almost certainly as a result of the protracted process of Britain leaving the European Union (EU) following the Brexit vote in 2016). Levels of trust among individuals are reported in the right-hand panel of the figure. This shows fairly limited variability in trust across successive survey waves. Between

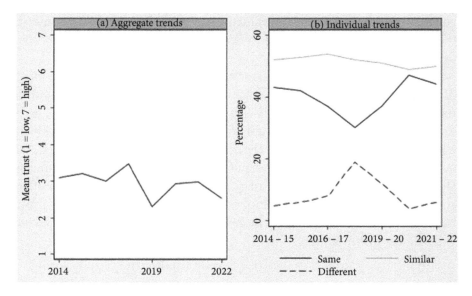

Figure 1.3 Trends in trust at the aggregate and individual levels
Source: British Election Study internet panel

three and five in ten people gave exactly the same trust rating across consecutive survey waves (indicated by the line marked 'same'), while slightly more gave trust ratings that differed by one or two points on the seven-point scale (line marked 'similar'). Only around 5 per cent of respondents changed their level of trust between consecutive survey waves by three or more points (line marked 'different'). And only between 2017 and 2019 did noticeably more people make substantial changes to their trust ratings across survey waves; even here, the proportion of people giving 'different' trust ratings only reached 19 per cent.[13]

We get a similar picture from panel data in Germany, collected by the social research organization GESIS. These data have the added advantage of measuring people's trust in different institutions, notably the government, parliament, the federal (or constitutional) court, and the police. Measures of trust were carried on the GESIS panel survey between autumn 2013 and spring 2022. Just as with the British data, I measure variations in trust across successive waves of the panel, starting in 2013–2014. Trust is measured on a 1 (don't trust at all) to 7 (entirely trust) scale. Figure 1.4 shows the trends in people according exactly the same level of trust to each institution across consecutive survey waves ('same' trust) along with people giving a level of trust that is one or two points different between waves ('similar' trust). The

What is trust? 35

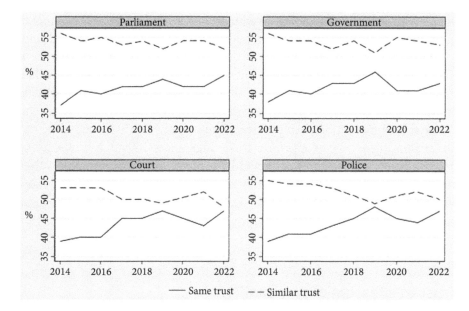

Figure 1.4 Trust in institutions among Germans, 2014–2022
Source: GESIS panel

results show high rates of consistency in trust judgements, and that this consistency maintains—and even increases slightly—over time. Moreover, this consistency is as high for people's trust in partisan actors (parliament and the government) as it is for their trust in non-partisan ones (the court and the police).

These data from Britain and Germany suggest that outside critical or crisis incidents, individuals' trust tends to be largely stable. Trust judgements formed at one point in time carry over to trust judgements formed at later points. Trust appears to have a consistent and deep-rooted quality (for similar evidence, see Siegrist, 2019).[14] But where does the rooted nature of trust judgements derive from? This requires us to consider the second major theme of this chapter: how trust is formed.

1.4 How do we trust?

The formation of individuals' trust judgements is often treated wholly or largely as a function of the qualities or features of the object being evaluated. The issue of *how* trust evaluations are formed is thus often reduced to identifying whether an object manifests trustworthy qualities, and if so, which ones. As already suggested, perceived trustworthiness is a central element of individuals' trust judgements. Yet the formation of those judgements cannot wholly be reduced to the qualities of the object. It is also important to consider other 'inputs' to trust judgements, such as the nature of the individual trustor, the role of feelings as well as of cognitive evaluations, and the effect of positive and negative forms of information about an object.

The following sections explore these issues, with a view to extending our understanding of how people form trust judgements. I begin by considering how far trust judgements are shaped by an individual's personality. I then consider how far trust is shaped by cognitive evaluations alongside more affective factors such as feelings. Finally, I explore the role of different forms of information, in particular the evidence for a 'negativity bias' in the formation of trust judgements.

Trust as a feature of personality

Some people may be predisposed to trust or to distrust particular objects. Just as an individual may express a fear of crime predominantly out of a predisposition to fear rather than from an evaluation of risk (Chadee and Ying, 2013), so a person's trust may rest less on evaluations of an actor than on that person's generalized propensity to trust or distrust those holding political office. Indeed, trust in other people—a social or interpersonal form of trust—is frequently explained by reference to individuals' dispositions (Rotter, 1967; Yamagishi and Yamagishi, 1994; Uslaner, 2002). Trust in political actors and institutions has similarly been traced back to some underlying features of individuals, notably their personality traits. Studies have shown that trust tends to be higher among people manifesting altruistic tendencies or sympathetic feelings towards other people (Mondak and Halperin, 2008). Recent analysis by Mondak, Hayes, and Canache (2017; see also Cawvey et al., 2018) suggests that three personality traits in particular—agreeableness, openness to new experiences, and extraversion—have particularly strong connections with trust. While the association between personality traits and interpersonal, or social, trust is rather stronger than the association with institutional trust (Cawvey et al., 2018), there still appears to be a sufficiently strong relationship to suggest that trust judgements might reflect some key features within our psychological make-up.

To test the application of such effects in Britain, I constructed a model of trust drawing on data from a survey conducted by the BES in March 2019, which included measures of each of the 'Big Five' personality traits:

agreeableness, conscientiousness, extraversion, neuroticism, and openness to experience.[15] The outcome variable was measured through a question asking respondents for their trust in MPs. To ensure the robustness of any identified relationships, the regression model included controls for factors that may covary with both personality and trust, namely age, education, gender, political attentiveness, and feelings of personal efficacy.[16] The model also included a measure of partisanship.

The results are presented in Table 1.1. They show that three of the five personality traits are significantly associated with trust. Agreeableness (warmth towards others) is positively associated with trust, while neuroticism (low emotional stability and anxiousness) and openness (enthusiasm for new experiences and creativity) are negatively associated with trust. We can compare the effect sizes for each of the different explanatory variables on trust by examining the standardized coefficients. These show that the associations with trust of the three personality traits are somewhat smaller than the associations of age, education, gender, personal efficacy, and political attentiveness. On this evidence, trust judgements appear to only weakly reflect aspects of individuals' personality. This lends support to the idea that individuals trust or distrust other people and organizations based on those

Table 1.1 Association of personality traits with trust

	Coefficient	Standard error	Standardized coefficient
Personality			
Agreeableness	0.03	(0.01)*	0.04
Neuroticism	−0.03	(0.01)*	−0.04
Openness	−0.03	(0.01)*	−0.03
Conscientiousness	−0.02	(0.01)	−0.03
Extraversion	−0.01	(0.01)	−0.01
Political engagement			
Personal efficacy scale	0.13	(0.04)**	0.07
Political attentiveness	0.03	(0.01)*	0.05
Partisanship			
Party identification (ref: conservatives)			
Labour	−0.16	(0.06)**	−0.05
Liberal Democrat	0.04	(0.09)	0.01
Other party	−0.65	(0.07)**	−0.15
None	−0.60	(0.06)**	−0.18

Continued

Table 1.1 Continued

	Coefficient	Standard error	Standardized coefficient
Demographics			
Age (years)	−0.01	(0.00)**	−0.07
Female	0.15	(0.05)**	0.05
Education (ref: no formal qualifications)			
GCSE	0.24	(0.09)**	0.08
A level	0.25	(0.10)*	0.06
Sub-degree	0.34	(0.11)**	0.07
University degree and above	0.39	(0.10)**	0.14
Adjusted R^2		0.07	
F		18.10	
Prob > F		0.00	
N (unweighted)		3,972	

*$p \leq 0.05$; **$p \leq 0.01$ (two-tailed).
Source: British Election Study Internet Panel, wave 15 (2019).

actors' qualities or actions, not because of individuals' intrinsic make-up or features.

Cognition and affect

If personality traits do not strongly shape individual trust judgements, which other factors might do so? It is sometimes suggested that expressions of trust contain modest calculative or evaluative content, and instead comprise little more than gut reactions towards an actor (Hetherington, 2005: 51). Some analysts suggest that trust reflects a generalized faith in another person or object, in which cognitive evaluations play little role (Lewis and Weigert, 1985; Möllering, 2001; Li, 2015). Qualitative studies probing the basis of people's trust judgements suggest that these often reflect broad impressions of a political actor (for example, that politicians engage in 'a lot of talk'), rather than detailed information about them (Carnaghan, 2011; Dekker, 2011).[17] General perceptions—or stereotypes—have also been shown to affect people's trust in political institutions above and beyond people's ideological judgements and general worldviews (Johnson, 2020).

In seeking to identify the bases of trust judgements, a useful initial distinction is between beliefs that are primarily 'cognitive'—based on perceptions, information, and deliberation—and beliefs that are primarily 'affective'—based on feelings and values (Lewis and Weigert, 1985; McAllister, 1995). We might anticipate people being more inclined to affective judgements in cases where they hold little information about an object or where trust evaluations are complex to form and cognitively effortful. Thus, Rahn (2000) shows how, when faced with the tricky task of responding to survey questions on whether 'most people' can be trusted (a social, rather than political, form of trust), people's judgements are strongly influenced by their general mood (measured through feelings of worry, anger, upset, enthusiasm, frustration, and hope). Affective judgements may also predominate after events—such as threats—that stimulate emotional responses. Thus, in the aftermath of the 9/11 terrorist attack in the United States, people's confidence in government was shown to have been strongly shaped by general feelings of pride and hope (Gross, Brewer, and Aday, 2009).

Aside from feelings and emotions, there are other routes by which individuals might reach trust judgements, even if they do not possess extensive information about an object or are unwilling to engage in taxing cognitive processes. This is particularly relevant, given that many people hold little information about political actors and institutions (Carpini and Keeter, 1996). Yet they may be able to overcome such deficiencies by using simplified features of an object to support a trust judgement. For example, in a study of Californian farmers, the trust judgements of individuals facing an unfamiliar agency were found to rest more heavily on general impressions and stereotypes than were the trust judgements of individuals facing a more familiar agency about which they possessed greater knowledge (Lubell, 2007). In addition, individuals forming an impression of some objects may draw on those objects' traits—their perceived characteristics or qualities. Within the field of social psychology, various traits have been identified as central to judgements about political actors, notably competence, empathy, integrity or honesty, and reliability (Kinder, 1986; Funk, 1996). In assessing whether they trust a political actor, citizens are likely to draw on perceptions of such traits.

An alternative characterization of judgement formation involves distinguishing between different styles of object appraisal. Appraisals can be based on either a predetermined view of an object (a 'schematic' reaction) or on a constructed set of perceived positive and negative features of that object (a 'piecemeal' reaction). Individuals are likely to resort to schematic judgements if they hold strong feelings about, and resonant images of, an object. If, however, the individual has personal experience of the object, has not developed strong feelings towards the object, and has complex or conflicting views on the object, they are more likely to employ a piecemeal approach to judgement formation (Fiske, 1986; Fiske and Neuberg, 1990). Since people in Britain generally do not have direct personal experience with politicians (few people have met their MP, for example) yet usually possess some initial feelings about them, it is likely that individuals' trust judgements will often rest more on schematic appraisals than on piecemeal appraisals. In other words, trust is often likely to rest more heavily on feelings about, and images of, politicians than on more detailed, and continuously updated, appraisals of their behaviour and performance.

This does not mean, however, that individuals' trust judgements simply comprise routinized or knee-jerk reactions. A recent study on the formation of trust beliefs found that individuals take longer to evaluate other people's trustworthiness than to evaluate their own trustworthiness. This suggests that trust judgements of other people involve cognitive reflection rather than simply an automatic or immediate reaction (Neumann, 2016). Something of the same might well be true in the case of trust in political actors or institutions.

Thus, trust judgements are often likely to reflect generalized feelings and impressions of an actor rather than detailed consideration of their actions and behaviour, although there is likely to be some room for the latter. This is particularly the case for certain types of individuals, notably people who are politically informed. It has been shown that relative to their poorly informed counterparts, well-informed individuals are more likely to base trust judgements on an actor's behaviour and performance. For example, in her study on individuals' trust in other people, Rahn (2000) finds that general mood (measured by people's feelings about the state of the country) has a weaker association with trust among well-educated people than among their poorly educated counterparts. Similarly, Mondak and colleagues (2007) find that among politically knowledgeable Americans, evaluations of Congress are shaped more by assessments of policy performance and representation than are the evaluations of less knowledgeable Americans. The latter are more likely to base their evaluations on 'shortcuts' or indirect indicators of congressional performance, such as what they think of the president and of their own representative (see also Citrin and Luks, 2001: 18–19).

Along the same lines, a study of public trust in the European Parliament has shown that as people become more informed about EU institutions, their levels of trust in those institutions become less shaped by affective feelings towards the EU (measured by attitudes towards its unification) and more shaped by instrumental evaluations (measured by perceptions of the benefits brought by the EU) (Torcal, Muñoz, and Bonet, 2012). In addition, a study examining levels of public trust in national political institutions across

European countries found levels of economic performance and government corruption to be more strongly associated with trust among highly educated citizens than among poorly educated citizens (van der Meer and Hakhverdian, 2017). However, the argument that politically informed citizens employ different, and more cognitively demanding, criteria in forming trust judgements than their less informed counterparts is by no means universally accepted. For example, van Elsas (2015) finds trust to be no more shaped by judgements of politicians' competence or responsiveness among highly educated people than among poorly educated ones. I return to this topic in Chapter 5, when I review how far the level of political information serves to moderate the impact of cognitive and affective evaluations on British citizens' trust judgements.

Overall, we can think of individuals' trust judgements as resting on foundations that run from detailed information about an actor's behaviour and performance to more generalized feelings about the actor or even more broadly to an individual's general emotional state or mood. Different individuals may base their trust on different foundations. In particular, there is evidence that trust judgements among educated and politically informed individuals draw on information about actors' performance rather more than do the equivalent judgements made by less-educated and informed individuals, whose trust judgements rest more on affective feelings. Yet even among informed individuals, cognitive and time constraints might limit the amount of deliberation involved in evaluating political actors. After all, for most people, politicians and political institutions are distant objects with whom they have little or no direct contact. Many people also hold existing feelings—some of which will be strongly valenced—about those objects. This suggests that individuals' trust judgements may often be largely affective or impressionistic rather than cognitive or deliberative. In fact, when experimental studies have provided people with information about government policy performance, the impact of that information in stimulating individuals to 'update' their evaluations of government has often been found to be modest (James, 2011; James and Moseley, 2014). A recent study among Democrat and Republican partisans in the United States who were asked to engage in trust games with their partisan opponents found that providing objective information about the trustworthiness of those opponents (measured by the amount of money returned in a monetary allocation game) only partially changed participants' trust (Hernández-Lagos and Minor, 2020).

The implication of this is that the way individuals form trust judgements—often resting on feelings or impressions—makes trust resistant to change in the face of new information. Trust is therefore often 'sticky'. This means that any initiatives to stimulate levels of trust across the population might be advised to focus on how citizens feel about political actors rather than assuming that trust will necessarily respond to positive information about politicians' performance or behaviour.

Negative and positive information

Notwithstanding the role of feelings and impressions, people's trust judgements are likely to be at least partly shaped by the information they receive about actors and institutions. Such information may come in either positive or negative form. Negative information is often held to have a greater effect on individuals' trust than positive information. This insight is captured in the adages that trust 'arrives on foot but departs on horseback' and that trust 'is easily lost but only with difficulty regained'.

Social psychologists have long contended that people's evaluations of an object are shaped more strongly by negative information about that object than by positive information (e.g. Fiske, 1980). In the political sphere, a host of judgements have been shown to be driven predominantly by negative evaluations over positive evaluations (Soroka, 2014), including people's assessments of politicians (Lau, 1982). Trust in political institutions has been found to be asymmetrically related to positive and negative information, with negative information and performance appraisals having a stronger effect on trust than positive information and performance (Slovic, 1999; Kampen, Van De Walle, and Bouckaert, 2006; James and Moseley, 2014; Olsen, 2015).[18] Poor national economic conditions have been found to depress people's trust more than the boost received from good economic conditions (Hetherington and Rudolph, 2015: 66–69).[19] In a survey experiment conducted in the United States, the same authors (2015: 188–192) found that the decrease in trust triggered by providing research participants with negative information about government performance outweighed the increase in trust triggered by providing them with positive information about government performance. Studies of people's judgements about the police have found that levels of satisfaction and confidence are depressed more by negatively evaluated encounters with officers than they are stimulated by positively evaluated encounters (Skogan, 2006; Bradford, Jackson, and Stanko, 2009; Myhill and Bradford, 2012). Similarly, neurological studies have shown that information designed to convey an untrustworthy image (such as an untrustworthy-looking face) has a stronger effect on people's brains than does a trustworthy-conveying image (Winston et al., 2002). If negative information does have such a heightened effect, it may be unsurprising that citizens are routinely found to harbour little trust in political actors; indeed, low trust may be the 'default' for many citizens (Hardin, 2002: 90–93, 164–168).

We can test for the effects on trust of negative and positive assessments by drawing on data collected by the 2010 BES. Alongside questions on trust in various political actors and institutions, the BES survey also asked respondents for their feelings about various policy issues. Some of these feelings were positively valenced (feelings of happiness, pride, hope, and confidence), while others were negatively valenced (feelings of anger, disgust, unease, and fear). Comparing the effects of the two types of feeling, we find a stronger association with trust of negative feelings than of positive feelings. For example, among people who felt 'disgust' at the country's economic situation, 56 per cent manifested low trust in politicians, while only 19 per cent of people who were 'hopeful' about the economy manifested high trust.

Yet we might ask which way around is causation running: are people's negative feelings triggering lower levels of trust, or might people's existing low levels of trust be triggering negative feelings? To disentangle these competing causal effects, we can draw on BES panel data collected between winter 2016 and late spring 2019.[20] By measuring attitudes among the same individuals at different points in time, we can identify the net effects of positive and negative evaluations on trust by controlling for respondents' existing levels of trust. The model therefore estimates the effect on trust (measured in 2019) of a set of positive and negative evaluations (measured in 2019), net of existing levels of trust (measured in 2016), and also—since party identification is likely to shape both levels of trust and evaluations—of partisanship (measured in 2019). The evaluations relate to six different policy areas: the economy, the national health service, education, the cost of living, immigration, and crime. On each of these areas, BES respondents were asked whether the service had got better or worse or had stayed the same. For each policy area, I take those evaluating performance as 'staying the same' as the baseline or reference category and then identify the evaluations of those respondents judging performance as either 'getting worse' or 'getting better'. The negative or positive evaluations for each policy area are then entered separately into a regression model predicting trust.

The results (Figure 1.5) confirm that negative evaluations have a stronger association with trust than positive evaluations. None of the positive policy assessments has a significant (and positive) association with trust (represented by coefficients that fall to the right of the line positioned at 0 with

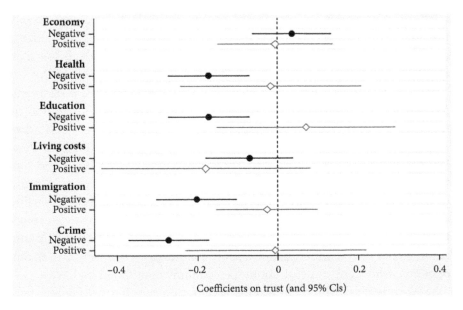

Figure 1.5 Negative and positive evaluations and trust
Source: British Election Study Internet Panel, Waves 10 and 16

confidence intervals that do not cross the line). By contrast, negative assessments on four policy issues—the health service, education, immigration, and crime—are significantly negatively associated with trust (represented by coefficients that fall to the left of the 0 line and with confidence intervals that do not cross 0). Thus, even when account is taken of people's existing levels of trust, negative evaluations of policy outcomes exert a downward drag on trust, while positive evaluations have no countervailing upward effect.

It is also worth noting the effect that trust itself has on how people interpret information. Studies have shown that people's existing levels of trust shape, or moderate, the effect of (positive and negative) information on subsequent trust (White et al., 2003). In one study of this effect, conducted among citizens in the United States, it was shown that negative information about food outlets had a stronger impact on people's trust in those outlets than did positive information. Moreover, this effect was particularly pronounced for outlets that were already the subject of low trust. This effect is reproduced in Figure 1.6. From this graphic, we can see that for trusted food outlets, the provision of either positive or negative information has only minimal effects on changes in people's trust. But for outlets that are not trusted, negative information has a markedly greater effect on trust than positive

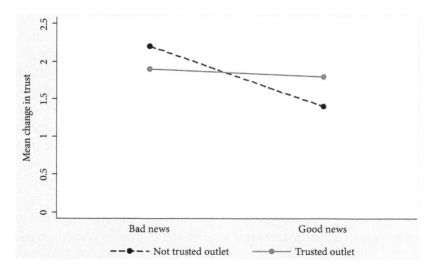

Figure 1.6 The impact of negative and positive information on trust in food outlets

Source: Cvetkovich et al. (2002: Figure 2)

information (Cvetkovich et al., 2002). This suggests that if attitudes towards an actor are already negative—as is the case with many people's feelings about politicians—further negative information may well have a substantial additional eroding effect.

In sum, there is clear evidence that negative information and evaluations affect trust more than do positive information and evaluations. Trust appears to be easily lost but only with difficulty regained. Moreover, the impact of negative information may be particularly acute among people who are already distrustful. If that is the case, politicians must be careful to avoid giving further grist to the mill of those who already think ill of them.[21]

1.5 Conclusion

This chapter has explored various aspects of trust in an attempt to shine more light on the concept's nature. It has not done so via the usual route of abstract, or 'top-down', conceptual analysis. Rather, it has explored trust via a more 'bottom-up' approach, focusing on the ways in which individuals express their trust and form trust judgements. This concluding section summarizes some of the main findings and their implications for our understanding of trust.

At its core, trust comprises a judgement by an individual that another person or organization is likely to act in their (the individual's) interests. Trust may lead an individual to engage with, or make themselves vulnerable to, the object of trust, although in the political realm citizens often have little choice over whether to engage with state actors and institutions. The judgements that underpin an individual's trust may arise from calculative or deliberative reasoning based on information about an actor; trust judgements may also draw on more impressionistic, trait or stereotype-based, or even affect-driven reasoning that contains little information about the actor. Trust may thus rest on various different evaluatory processes, involving particular balances of cognitive and affective inputs. Trust is often treated in the academic literature (particularly by political scientists, it must be said) primarily as a cognitive evaluation, reflecting an individual's deliberative appraisals of an actor's behaviour or performance. However, psychologists' emphasis on individuals' cognitive limitations and unwillingness to engage in effortful information processing suggests that expressions of trust may often rest on more immediate and impressionistic bases, along with more general feelings.

Two broad implications follow from this. The first is that if expressions of trust often contain minimal amounts of information, there must be some doubt about the utility of these expressions. These doubts feed through into concerns over the way we usually measure trust (explored further in Chapter 3). They also raise questions about whether minimally informed or ritualistic expressions of trust are likely to have major consequences for people's attitudes and behaviour. Expressions of trust that possess only shallow bases are unlikely to provoke strong behavioural responses among citizens, and thus the kind of serious civic and political challenges identified in the Introduction. This insight is pursued more fully in Chapter 7, which considers the consequences of trust. The second implication is that trust might be resistant to new information, and thus to change. As we have seen, people's trust in political institutions tends to be quite stable over time. Individuals do not appear to compute wholly new judgements every time they are asked about their trust; instead, existing beliefs and feelings seem to strongly condition subsequent expressions of trust.

Moreover, if trust evaluations do change, this may primarily be in a negative direction. The evidence points to trust being shaped more strongly by negative information than by positive information. This is not to say that conditions of low trust are fated to endure. In the Conclusion, I explore the issue of whether trust levels can be raised, and present evidence that such a positive outcome can be achieved. Yet the evidence presented in this chapter suggests that low levels of trust across the population may be tricky to shift. Where trust is low, people may be more willing to accept confirmatory negative information about political actors than more challenging positive information. Indeed, many citizens appear to hold negative impulses—or 'implicit attitudes'—towards public officials that shape their evaluations of these actors (Marvel, 2015, 2016).[22] Such implicit attitudes have been identified among American citizens, but also appear among British citizens, among whom one study found an overwhelmingly negative skew of attitudes towards politics. Asked for a word or phrase that they associated with politics, almost two-thirds of the British sample nominated a negative descriptor, while less than 5 per cent nominated a positive descriptor, the remaining descriptors being neutral (Stoker, Hay, and Barr, 2016). This ingrained negativity towards political actors among many citizens presents a high hurdle to be overcome if levels of trust across the population are to improve.

The final feature of trust to emphasize is the complexity of its nature, a complexity that often goes unrecognized in studies on the issue. It is unhelpful to think of people as being either trusting or distrusting of politicians and political agencies. Instead, people's attitudes are often more varied than this over-simplified binary distinction. An individual who is low in trust is not necessarily distrustful. They may believe an actor to be lacking in competence, benevolence, and integrity, and thus not worthy of trust. Yet they may not necessarily believe the actor to be incompetent, uncaring, and morally compromised. There is a distinction between lacking trust and actively distrusting, a distinction which unfortunately often goes elided in survey-based analyses of trust. Many individuals may inhabit the hinterland between trust and distrust, which some label 'mistrust' although which might better be labelled 'scepticism'. Individuals may also be ambivalent about political actors, perceiving them to manifest both virtues and vices. Shoehorning individuals into either the 'trust' or 'distrust' camp fails to acknowledge that many individuals—perhaps well over half the populations in Britain and the United States—hold more varied, and complex, attitudes towards their political rulers.

The complexity of people's trust judgements makes it important to explore in detail how trust is measured (a task undertaken in Chapter 3), which factors shape trust (Chapter 6), and what kinds of outcomes trust gives rise to (Chapter 7). It is also important to identify the position or status of trust; to clarify where trust sits as a measure of citizens' orientations towards their political leaders and the political system. This task is taken up in Chapter 2.

Chapter 2
Why focus on trust?

Trust is an important concept because it captures some key aspects of the vertical relations between citizens and their political rulers. By focusing on trust, we seek to understand more clearly how citizens relate to those rulers. Yet what is it about these relations that is captured by the concept of trust? How do these relations differ to those captured by alternative concepts? What are the particular virtues of studying the associations between citizens and governments through the lens of trust? After all, trust is but one aspect of the vertical relations between citizens and governments that fall under the broad label of 'political support'. Political support denotes the various orientations that citizens have towards political actors, institutions, and the system as a whole. Trust represents one such orientation, and we need to be clear which particular aspects of political support it captures and what we learn about citizens' relations with political actors by focusing on it.

This chapter builds on the previous one by extending its coverage from the *nature* of trust to the *status* of trust. The chapter explores what kind of orientation is represented by trust, and where trust sits in relation to other forms of political support. In pursuing this task, the chapter responds to Levi and Stoker's (2000: 497) plea for 'scholars [...] to develop a clear sense of how trust differs from other kinds of judgments about political actors or institutions'.

Determining the status of trust requires us, first, to identify whether trust captures appropriate and useful evaluations that citizens form of political actors and institutions. In particular, does trust move beyond citizens' evaluations of specific political actors to capture their broader orientations towards the political system? Second, we need to establish in which other ways these orientations can be captured, and how trust relates to these alternative forms of political support. Third, we need to identify whether evaluations of trust have particular associations with individuals' behaviour—notably their engagement in civic and political life—compared with other forms of political support. In pursuing these three tasks, the goal of this chapter is to provide a firmer conceptual and empirical basis for our focus on trust as a gauge of the vertical relations between citizens and their political rulers.

2.1 The nature of political support

Political support represents the mixture of positive and negative orientations that citizens have towards the principal actors, institutions, rules, and norms that structure the political system. In the hands of its chief analyst, David Easton, political support is argued to consist of 'specific' and 'diffuse' types of judgement (Easton, 1965, 1975). Easton suggested that specific forms of political support reflect citizens' perceptions that the political system is delivering favourable outputs, while diffuse forms of political support rest on broader judgements about the appropriateness and propriety of political actors and processes. Specific support thus comprises evaluations of the day-to-day decisions and outputs of individual governments and should adjust as one set of political office-holders is replaced by another. Specific support is thus liable to short-term fluctuation. Diffuse support, however, rests on broader judgements about democratic institutions and practices and is thus less susceptible to short-term change. Diffuse support comprises a deep 'reservoir of favourable attitudes' (Easton, 1965: 273) towards the political system, less easily affected by day-to-day events than specific forms of support, but with more damaging and enduring consequences when weakened.

Easton further categorizes different forms of political support by identifying particular objects of support, namely political 'authorities', the political 'regime', and the political 'community' (Easton, 1965). This threefold categorization was extended by Dalton (1999), who subdivided the political regime into three additional categories, representing regime 'principles' (denoting the values or norms underpinning a political system), regime 'performance' (denoting the generalized operation of a political system), and regime 'institutions' (denoting evaluations of particular institutions).[1] Empirical validation for this conceptual distinction has been provided by studies conducted across the world, which highlight significant variations in political support, namely distinctive individual orientations towards the political community, regime principles, regime performance, regime institutions, and political actors (Dalton, 2004: 57–62; Booth and Seligson, 2009: chapter 2; Norris, 2011: 43–46).

This distinction between specific and diffuse forms of support, and the position within this continuum of citizens' evaluations of different objects, suggests that political support comprises various types or forms. We can map these along a 'specific-diffuse' spectrum, in which evaluations of particular politicians are positioned at one end and judgements about the political community and political principles are positioned at the other (Figure 2.1). This spectrum of orientations thus runs from incumbent evaluations, or specific support, at one end, to judgements about the nature and desirability of the wider political order, or diffuse support, at the other.

In the main, studies of political support have focused on orientations in the middle of the spectrum and not on those at either extreme. Very specific forms of support (i.e. evaluations of incumbent political actors) are likely to be strongly shaped by partisanship, and may well be transient, subject to short-term changes in policy performance and political personnel. Yet very diffuse forms of support (i.e. assessments of political principles) are too abstract and general to tell us much about how citizens evaluate political actors and agencies. Analysts' focus has quite reasonably been on the middle portion of the spectrum, comprising citizens' evaluations of the performance of key political actors and institutions.

Yet in narrowing down the types of political support for analytical focus, we should avoid demarcating boundaries too precisely. While he distinguished between specific and diffuse forms of political support, Easton also acknowledged the porous nature of the dividing lines; different forms of support, he said, 'may well shade into each other at some point' (Easton, 1975: 448). Thus, specific support might reflect perceptions of general government performance—usually associated with diffuse support—as well as evaluations of immediate outputs (Easton, 1975: 438–439, 441–442). In turn, diffuse support might draw on judgements about immediate outputs cumulated over time, or alternatively on people's responses to a particular 'shock' to the system (Easton, 1975: 445).[2] Empirical studies have indeed suggested that generalized measures of political support may sometimes be shaped by evaluations of incumbent actors and their performance (Muller and Williams, 1980; Magalhães, 2014; Lu and Dickson, 2020).

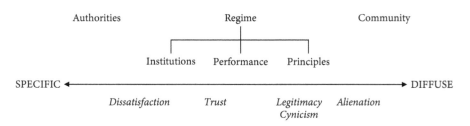

Figure 2.1 The spectrum of political support

2.2 The status of trust

Some scholars claim that citizens' expressions of trust primarily reflect evaluations of incumbent political actors rather than more generalized evaluations of the political system (Citrin, 1974; Citrin and Green, 1986). As such, it is argued that trust has only limited use as a gauge of how citizens relate to the wider political system. Thus, for example, an early empirical study of people living in West Germany found that the distribution of trust cleaved more closely to evaluations of incumbent political actors than it did to evaluations of the political system as a whole (Muller and Jukam, 1977). More recently, an analysis of attitudes towards the United States Supreme Court found that a survey item measuring trust tapped attitudes towards the day-to-day performance of the Court rather than to a broader judgement of its legitimacy (Gibson, 2011).

Trust does indeed appear to partially reflect people's evaluations of incumbent governments. We can see this in Figure 2.2, which shows trends in British people's trust in their government, broken down by whether they identify with the governing party or main opposition party.[3] As the graph shows, levels of trust often vary significantly between these two groups, by almost 30 percentage points at times. These results suggest that people's expressions of trust may owe as much to their feelings about the party in government as to their general evaluations of the political system

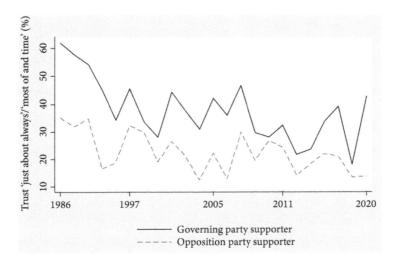

Figure 2.2 Trust among government and opposition supporters
Source: British Social Attitudes

(for similar evidence from the United States, see Keele, 2005; Theiss-Morse, Barton, and Wagner, 2015: 176).

Note, however, that levels of trust among opposition party supporters do not always rebound when their party retakes government office. In fact, as the data show, the trend over the period is towards lower trust across all partisans. So while at any one point in time, levels of trust are coloured by partisan evaluations, over time these immediate—or specific—evaluations appear to aggregate into more generalized—or diffuse—appraisals of the political regime. Citizens' immediate evaluations of political actors may well form 'running tallies' that contribute towards broader assessments of political performance (Hibbing and Theiss-Morse, 1995: 13). This would reflect Easton's claim about the porousness of specific and diffuse forms of political support. Over time, judgements about incumbent political actors may well translate into more generalized judgements about the operation and performance of the political system.

The overlap between people's trust judgements and their evaluations of the broader political system can also be seen at particular points in time. In Britain, we can observe this by drawing on data from the European Social Survey, whose 2012 wave included measures of both specific and diffuse evaluations. Specific evaluations were tapped through appraisals of the incumbent government ('how satisfied are you with the way the government is doing its job?') and of policy outcomes ('how satisfied are you with the present state of the economy?') Diffuse evaluations were tapped through appraisals of the quality of national democracy ('how democratic do you think Britain is?' and 'how satisfied are you with the way democracy works in Britain?'). Trust was measured in relation to politicians and parliament (responses were combined to form a single trust index). Simple (zero-order) correlations show that people's trust judgements were closely tied to their feelings about incumbent political actors. The correlation between trust and perceptions of government performance is 0.62, while trust is also closely tied to satisfaction with the state of the economy (correlation = 0.53). At the same time, trust judgements are also closely associated with perceptions of how democracy is seen to work (= 0.58) and of how democratic the country is seen to be (= 0.51).

Similar evidence can be seen in the United States and Canada. In both countries, the 2019 wave of the Americas Barometer survey asked respondents about trust and, in addition, about their respect for the country's political institutions, their satisfaction with democracy in the country, and their assessments of the country's political leader (President Trump in the United States and Prime Minister Trudeau in Canada) and, in the United

States, of Congress. In Canada, people's trust (measured in relation to the legislature and political parties, combined in a single scale) was closely related to their assessments of prime ministerial performance (correlation = 0.54), but also with their satisfaction with democracy (= 0.54) and even more strongly with respect for political institutions (= 0.76). In the United States, trust (measured in the same way) was modestly correlated with democratic satisfaction (= 0.35), yet more strongly correlated with institutional respect (= 0.58). Trust was also related to evaluations of political actors, but only in the case of Congress (= 0.62), not of President Trump (= 0.03).

Hence, while trust is substantially associated with how people evaluate incumbent political actors and policy outputs, it is also associated with wider assessments of the functioning of the political system. Trust captures not only how people feel about incumbent political actors but also more generalized judgements about the nature and operation of the political system (see also Miller, 1974; Gabriel, 1995; Dalton, 1999; Booth and Seligson, 2009: chapter 2; Parker, Parker, and Towner, 2015).[4] As Levi and Stoker (2000: 491) have claimed:

> judgments about the trustworthiness of government or of politicians are more than ideological or partisan reactions to specific incumbent administrations. They are generalized judgments that influence whether citizens endorse or reject existing authorities and public policy or institutional reform.

If trust comprises elements of both immediate (or specific) and generalized (or diffuse) evaluations, the question then arises of whether these evaluations are distinctive. How do evaluations of trust differ from other types of evaluation falling under the heading of 'political support'? Maybe one of these other evaluations captures citizens' relations with political actors and institutions better than does trust. We can only identify whether this is so by identifying the different forms of political support and considering how they relate to trust.

2.3 Forms of political support

There are numerous concepts or labels used in the academic literature to describe or capture different aspects of citizens' vertical orientations towards the political system. A small sample of a large population includes concepts such as alienation, legitimacy, cynicism, trust, and dissatisfaction. But what aspects of the relations between citizens and political rulers does each concept capture, and what—if anything—might be particularly appropriate about describing these relations in terms of trust?

Among the different forms of political support, the most deep-rooted and broad orientation is represented by *alienation*. To be alienated is to experience a 'relatively enduring sense of estrangement from existing political institutions, values and leaders' (Citrin et al., 1975: 3). As a concept, alienation emphasizes feelings of distance or separation from the political system. These feelings go beyond perceptions that political actors are untrustworthy; to be alienated, individuals must also feel detached from the political system (Citrin et al., 1975: 4). Such detachment might be manifested in attributes like a lack of national pride, a feeling that politicians are fundamentally self-serving not public-serving and that politics has no clear meaning and a rejection of accepted social and political norms (Finifter, 1970; Citrin et al., 1975). Conceptually and empirically (Mason, House, and Martin, 1985; Citrin et al., 1975), distrust in political actors and institutions might contribute to a state of alienation (and indeed is sometimes held to define alienation; Macke, 1979), but nonetheless the elements, referents, and consequences of alienation are broader than those relating to trust.

Closely linked to alienation is the concept of *legitimacy*. Feelings of alienation and legitimacy both reflect assessments of the principles and practices of political decision-making and are thus primarily directed at political institutions and the political regime rather than at particular political actors. Alienation and legitimacy thus both tap 'diffuse' forms of support in Easton's terms. Legitimacy refers to the view 'that authorities, institutions and social arrangements are appropriate, proper and just' (Tyler, 2006: 376; also Easton, 1965: 278). Legitimacy may involve various appraisals, covering such features as the accountability and efficiency of governments, the fairness of the decision-making process, and the equity of its outputs (Weatherford, 1991, 1992). While trust is often seen as an element within legitimacy (e.g. Tyler and Degoey, 1996; Weatherford, 1992), appraisals of legitimacy are usually held to comprise broader judgements than those of trust (Easton, 1975: 453; Dogan, 1997). In the context of judgements about the police, for example, trust has been argued to reflect individual assessments of officers' intentions and competence, while legitimacy is argued to reflect assessment of officers' power and authority (Hough, Jackson, and Bradford, 2013: 333; see also Jackson and Gau, 2016).

The criteria underpinning political alienation might also be employed in individual feelings of political *cynicism*. Although cynicism is sometimes seen as the antonym to trust, it really comprises a deeper negativity towards political authority (Agger, Goldstein, and Pearl, 1961; Baloyra, 1979). Cynicism reflects a 'generalized suspiciousness and pessimism' towards political life that stems as much from social disadvantage and dislocation as from critical evaluations of the political process (Citrin and Muste, 1999: 476). Nonetheless, cynicism also involves critical evaluations of politics, notably perceptions of politicians being motivated by personal gain and of political institutions facilitating such behaviour. These evaluations overlap with elements that underpin trust,[5] although cynicism reflects a more deeply held antipathy to politicians and politics than does distrust. Eisinger (2000: 55) suggests that 'cynicism is more than mild distrust. Cynicism entails intense, antagonistic distrust of or contempt for humanity'. Pattyn et al. (2012) measure cynicism through survey items that tap a belief that there is something fundamentally rotten about politicians (indicative survey item: 'no man can hope to stay honest once he enters politics'). They measure trust, however, through items that focus on more specific aspects of behaviour ('politicians usually try to keep the promises they have made during the election'). These measurement choices reflect scholars' belief that cynicism comprises a broader and deeper negative orientation to the political system than does distrust.

A form of support that reflects more specific judgements about political actors and institutions is *(dis)satisfaction* (Oliver, 2014: 7–8). An individual experiences satisfaction with a politician or political agency in the case of a positively evaluated output or outcome; dissatisfaction arises if that output is negatively evaluated (Easton, 1975; Oliver, 2014). Dissatisfaction is a specific form of political support, shaped by the particular actions and outputs of incumbent governments.[6] Negative or positive evaluations can therefore be transient if a government's subsequent actions are judged differently.

There are thus various ways of capturing—via different concepts or labels—the nature of citizens' relations with the political system. Some of these concepts tap broad orientations to politics, others tap more specific evaluations. Alienation and cynicism tap people's general sense of their position vis-à-vis the political process, while legitimacy taps their sense of the normative status of a country's political regime and rulers. On the other hand, dissatisfaction taps people's evaluations of political actors' day-to-day decisions. The various forms of political support thus capture different aspects of the relations between citizens and the political system (they also have somewhat different associations with individuals' wider attitudes and behaviours, an issue I explore below). Drawing on the distinction between specific and diffuse evaluations, we can place the different forms of support on a spectrum ranging from immediate evaluations to broader and more generalized appraisals (Figure 2.1). Specific orientations—represented by dissatisfaction—do not provide a useful gauge of citizens' deeper feelings towards the political order. Citizens may manifest dissatisfaction with an incumbent government without protesting against its authority or denying its right to make decisions. On the other side of the spectrum, orientations like alienation, cynicism, and legitimacy capture citizens' broad evaluations of the political system but tell us little about their more routine reactions to political actors.

Trust appears to sit somewhere in-between these two poles, capturing both specific judgements about political actors (Is the government acting in the public interest?) and more diffuse evaluations of the political system (Are decision rules fair and equitable?). Yet this conclusion arises from conceptual reasoning and delineation; what evidence is there that it also reflects the way citizens think in practice?

2.4 Is trust distinctive?

One difficulty in distinguishing between different forms of political support and identifying the place of trust within these various judgements is that few opinion surveys carry many questions tapping citizens' attitudes towards different aspects and features of the political system. One survey that has carried evaluations of different objects of support is the World Values Survey (WVS). Drawing on WVS data from the mid-1990s, Klingemann (1999: 37) was able to distinguish between attitudes towards democratic principles, the political community, and the political regime. Again using WVS data from the same period but utilizing a wider set of indicators that opened up attitudes towards the political regime, Dalton (2004: 59) found that attitudes towards political institutions were largely distinct from attitudes towards political authorities and democratic principles. Most recently, Klingemann (2014) has shown that levels of confidence in legal and political institutions are substantially unrelated to people's views about the importance of democracy (see also Norris, 2011: 44–46; Bellucci and Memoli, 2012; Martini and Quaranta, 2020: 36).

There is thus some evidence that people's attitudes towards different levels or tiers of the political system are mutually distinct. However, the WVS on which Klingemann and Dalton drew lacked any items on political trust; instead, attitudes towards the political regime and institutions were tapped through items referencing 'confidence' in political organizations. Analysis by Booth and Seligson compensates for this by utilizing surveys conducted in various Latin American countries that include items referencing political trust. Their findings suggest that in some cases, trust in

Why focus on trust? 57

political actors and institutions comprises a distinctive form of political support. For example, among a sample of Costa Rican citizens, expressions of trust in various institutions—such as political parties, parliament, and the Supreme Court—are found to be empirically distinct from evaluations of the effectiveness of the political system or agreement that the political system should be supported (Booth and Seligson, 2009: 31–32, 62, 203–207; see also Mason, House and Martin, 1985; Seligson, 1983; Weil, 1989). This suggests that evaluations of trust may tap qualitatively different judgements to appraisals of the wider political system.[7] Broadly similar results were also obtained by a study among American students, which showed that expressions of political trust, legitimacy (measured by feelings of duty to obey the law), and cynicism (measured by believing the law only works for some people) overlapped to an extent, but were, nonetheless, distinguishable from one another (Hamm et al., 2011, 2013a; see also Pattyn et al., 2012). Even in authoritarian countries like China, studies have identified a distinction between people's trust in national institutions and their broader feelings about the political system, captured, for example, by indicators of whether the political system is capable of solving national problems (Lu and Dickson, 2020).

When it comes to Britain, there are unfortunately few surveys that contain measures tapping different forms of political support. One survey that did carry such a range of indicators was the 1997 British Election Study (BES) which, in addition to measuring trust, also explored people's evaluations of the democratic system and of representative bodies like political parties. Drawing on the BES, Pattie and Johnston (2001) found that these forms of political support did not lump together in citizens' minds but were instead differentiated. To be precise, people's attitudes across the eleven measures of political support showed four structuring points, or 'dimensions'. These related to the perceived responsiveness of political parties, the democratic quality of the political system, political trust, and the effectiveness of voting for different political parties. In other words, people's trust in government and politicians was found to be distinct from their evaluations of how well democracy functioned and of the responsiveness and effectiveness of political parties.

One potential shortcoming of these results from Britain and elsewhere is that they rely on a statistical technique called factor analysis to identify the nature and structure of political support. Yet the use of factor analysis is appropriate only for variables that are continuous in scale and follow a normal distribution (Curran, West, and Finch, 1996). When variables are measured on an ordinal scale and/or manifest a skewed distribution, the correlations between them are likely to be attenuated (Finney and DiStefano, 2006). In turn, this can produce an apparently distinctive, or multi-dimensional, structure to people's responses rather than a singular or unidimensional structure. In the present context, this would mean that different forms of political support are more likely to appear as distinctive, rather than as similar to one another.

To overcome these problems, I analyse responses to various survey measures of political support—derived from the British Social Attitudes survey of 2005—using Mokken scale analysis, a technique more suited to data that manifest a non-normal distribution (Van Schuur 2003, 2011). The measures I use are (full question wordings and response options are provided in Appendix 2.1):

1. Democracy is better than any other form of government (mean = 0.75)
2. Importance to democracy of right to protest (mean = 0.84)
3. Present system of governing Britain (mean = 0.44)
4. Satisfaction with the way democracy works in Britain (mean = 0.59)
5. Trust in British governments (mean = 0.33)
6. Trust in MPs (mean = 0.18)
7. MPs lose touch with people (mean = 0.31)
8. Parties are only interested in people's votes, not their opinions (mean = 0.32)
9. Government has done a good or bad job (mean = 0.52).

Mean levels of agreement with each of these statements are shown in brackets (which use normalized variables, with values ranging from 0 to 1). These show that people are more strongly supportive of democratic principles than they are trusting or likely to evaluate government performance in positive terms. When a Mokken scale analysis is applied to these measures, the results show that responses do not fall on a single scale. The final seven items comprise a moderately strong scale (H_S = 0.43). But the first two items do not fit onto this scale, although they do not comprise their own scale. This shows us two things. First, there is a distinction between people's evaluations of the political system's performance—including their trust in government and in politicians—and their views about the desirability of democracy and the importance to democracy of the right to protest. Second, there is no substantial differentiation when it comes to people's evaluations of different aspects of the political system. Feelings of trust overlap with people's appraisals of public officials' representativeness ('MPs lose touch with people') and responsiveness ('Parties are only interested in people's votes, not their opinions'). Unlike the results reported in some of the studies identified above, the results from this analysis—which employs a more robust statistical technique—suggest that people's judgements about the quality and performance of the political system are largely undifferentiated.

We see a similar pattern in people's attitudes by examining survey data collected among other national populations. One survey containing different measures of political support, and which is thus suited for the current purpose, is the Americas Barometer. This asks respondents for their attitudes towards various features of the political system, ranging from assessments of incumbent governments to evaluations of democratic principles. Ordered from the most specific to the most general, these measures are:

1. How would you rate the job performance of [prime minister/president]?
2. How would you describe [country's] economic situation?*
3. To what extent do you trust [institutions]?
4. To what extent do you respect the political institutions of [country]?
5. How satisfied or dissatisfied are you with the way democracy works in [country]?
6. To what extent do you think that one should support the political system of [country]?
7. To what extent are you proud of being a [nationality]?*
8. To what extent do you feel proud of living under the political system of [country]?
9. Democracy may have problems, but it is better than any other form of government.
(* indicates questions not asked in the United States.)

As with the analysis reported earlier, I use data drawn from samples of the population in Canada and the United States in summer 2019. A Mokken scale analysis on the US data identified a single scale (H_S = 0.54) covering people's trust (in the legislature and parties, combined in a single scale) and pride in institutions, their respect and support for those institutions, and their satisfaction with democracy. This scale did not include responses to assessments of President Trump's performance (judgements about such an unusual president appear to be *sui generis*); nor did attitudes to democracy fit closely onto this scale. As with Britain, then, it appears as though people's judgements about trust are largely distinct from their evaluations of democratic principles. The same is not the case, however, in Canada, where responses across each of the various measures are found to form a single, unidimensional scale ($H_S = 0.52$).

These results suggest that trust is not a particularly distinctive form of political support. People's trust judgements are closely related to their evaluations of other aspects of the political system, even if they do not strongly overlap—in Britain and the United States at least—with appraisals of democratic principles.

Yet this conclusion may partly reflect the way that different forms of political support are typically measured in surveys. If trust and other forms of political support are measured in general terms, it is not terribly surprising that survey respondents often answer these questions in similar ways. What if trust is measured in a more specific way, to more closely capture the content of the concept identified in Chapter 1? We can test this in Britain using an online survey fielded in summer 2019 on a sample of participants drawn from the recruitment platform Prolific Academic. This survey asked the participants (totalling 1,180 people) to indicate their agreement or disagreement with various statements designed to tap four different forms of political support: dissatisfaction, scepticism, distrust, and cynicism. In turn, distrust was seen to comprise three distinct dimensions: competence, benevolence, and integrity. In all, 21 measures were fielded to tap the different forms of political support (the question wordings are provided in Appendix 2.2). To test whether people's responses matched the postulated structure, a higher-order four-factor model was fitted to the data. In this model, the lower-order factors of competence, benevolence, and integrity are explained by a higher-order (latent) variable tapping distrust, alongside separate (latent) variables tapping dissatisfaction, scepticism, and cynicism. The hypothesized structure to the data is shown in Figure 2.3.

A confirmatory factor analysis showed that the model fitted the data well (CFI: 0.970; RMSEA: 0.04).[8] In other words, people's distrust in politicians comprises a distinct evaluation to feelings of dissatisfaction, scepticism, and cynicism.[9] Thus, when we use survey measures that more specifically and precisely tap different forms of political support—in particular probing people's feelings of trust in a more detailed way—we find greater distinctiveness in people's orientations towards the political system. Bear in mind that the sample on which this survey was fielded does not comprise a representative cross section of the British population, meaning we should be cautious about generalizing these results. Yet the findings at least suggest that when citizens' orientations towards the political system are measured more precisely than is often the case, we find a clearer distinction between trust and other forms of political support.

Why focus on trust? 61

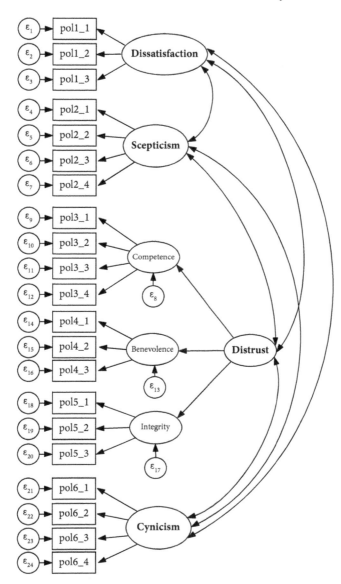

Figure 2.3 Structural model of different forms of political support

2.5 The relevance of trust

If, as we have just seen, citizens' trust judgements sometimes overlap with their evaluations of other aspects of the political system, what do we gain by focusing on the concept of trust? Does studying trust provide us with distinctive insights that might be missed by studying these other evaluations?

One way of answering this question is to consider what consequences might arise from different forms of political support among citizens, and to identify whether any of these effects might be particular to their judgements of trust.

There are solid reasons for thinking that they might. If an individual lacks trust in an actor, they are unlikely to engage with them and to comply with their edicts. Yet if an individual is merely dissatisfied with that actor, they are more likely to limit their behaviour to seeking to replace them, perhaps at the ballot box. Feelings of alienation or cynicism are likely to encourage broader behaviours, such as support for anti-system parties and a rejection of state authority (Booth and Seligson, 2009: chapter 5; Pattyn et al., 2012; Christensen, 2016; Van Assche et al., 2019). In other words, different orientations towards the political realm might be expected to translate into somewhat different behavioural responses among citizens. Specifically, we might expect people low in trust to be particularly likely to shun voting or engaging with policymakers and to limit their acceptance of, and compliance with, collective obligations. People who are dissatisfied with incumbent actors might be expected to be particularly likely to vote against these actors in elections. People who believe the democratic system to be working poorly might be anticipated to engage in 'unconventional' forms of political participation and to favour reform of the political system. More alienated or cynical individuals might be more likely to support anti-system parties and to reject political actors' authority.

To date, rather few attempts have been made to test these expectations. One exception is a set of studies by Gunther and colleagues that explores the consequences of different forms of political support (Gunther and Montero, 2006; Gunther, Montero, and Torcal, 2007). In analyses of citizens' attitudes in fledgling democracies in Latin America and Central and Eastern Europe, these authors find that different forms of political support are, indeed, associated with particular forms of behaviour. Thus, for example, 'political discontent' (comprising evaluations of the country's political and economic situation and operation of the democratic system) is found to increase levels of anti-incumbent voting. Yet 'political disaffection' (comprising appraisals of the responsiveness of the political system) has no such effect. Instead, disaffection is found to reduce membership of organizations such as political parties, rates of political discussion, and reported interest in politics.

Another attempt to identify the behavioural effects of different forms of political support was conducted by Booth and Seligson (2009), drawing on data collected from samples of the populations in various Latin American countries. These authors find that evaluations of regime principles, institutions, and performance are more closely associated with levels of political participation than are either very specific forms of political support (such as assessments of incumbent actors) or very diffuse forms of support (such as feelings of political community). On the other hand, diffuse forms of support (notably feelings of political community) are more closely associated with people's attitudes towards democracy, in the form of opposition to armed rebellion and to violent protest (Booth and Seligson, 2009: 234–240).

To explore whether different forms of political support are similarly associated with particular forms of civic and political behaviour in Britain, I draw on evidence from two surveys. The first is the Citizen Audit, conducted in 2001.[10] This survey is one of the few conducted in Britain that meets our needs since it carries measures both of different forms of political support and of different forms of civic behaviour. The measures of political support comprise satisfaction with the way democracy works, trust in government, and appraisals of how the government is managing public services.[11] These measures thus tap a general evaluation (satisfaction with democracy), a mid-level evaluation (trust in government), and a more specific evaluation (appraisals of government performance). The civic behaviours comprise vote choice (for or against the incumbent governing party), political participation (likelihood of voting and of engagement in different forms of protest activity), and adherence to various civic duties (for example, complying with tax rules).

The results appear in Table 2.1, which shows the (zero-order) correlations between the three measures of political support and the various behavioural outcomes. Evaluations of government performance are, as expected, associated with voting for/against the incumbent government. Trust is also associated with incumbent voting, although evaluations of democratic performance are not. The latter, broader, evaluations are more closely associated with participation; democratic satisfaction is positively associated with electoral turnout and negatively associated with willingness to protest. The strongest association with electoral engagement is with trust, however. Moreover, trust is most extensively associated with a range of civic behaviours, including willingness to serve on a jury (albeit that the correlations here are weak).

The second source of data draws on a sample recruited via Prolific Academic in 2019, discussed above. Participants in this study ($N = 1,180$) completed a survey that posed questions on different forms of political support—dissatisfaction, scepticism, distrust, and cynicism (see Appendix 2.2 for the relevant survey indicators)—and also on different forms of political and civic behaviour. These behaviours are related to the way citizens deal with information provided by politicians (e.g. by seeking to verify it or reject it), their propensity to complain about political decisions and to seek

Table 2.1 The behavioural correlates of different types of political support

	Trust	Democratic satisfaction	Government performance evaluations
Voting behaviour			
Anti-incumbent voting	−0.23	–	−0.24
Political participation			
Likelihood of voting	0.23	0.17	0.10
Would contact a politician	0.04	−0.06	−0.04
Would go on demonstration	–	−0.13	−0.09
Civic engagement			
Importance of complying with rules on tax	0.11	0.14	0.10
Importance of obeying the law	0.09	0.15	0.08
Would inform Inland Revenue of a mistake	0.10	0.09	0.10
Would not claim undue state benefit	0.04	0.07	–
Would serve on jury	0.05	–	–
Would give blood	–	–	–
Minimum N (weighted)	2,425	2,586	2,646

Bivariate correlations. All entries are significant at the 5 per cent level (two-tailed test); dashes indicate non-significant correlations.
Source: Citizen Audit 2001.

alternatives to existing politicians, and their acceptance or rejection of politicians' authority. These categories of behaviour were selected to represent a spectrum, ranging from relatively inconsequential actions (such as verifying externally provided information) to more consequential actions (such as denying the authority of politicians). The utility of these measures is that they enable us to capture not necessarily how people would behave in practice but rather any differences in the behaviours associated with trust compared to the other forms of political support.

The (zero-order) correlations between each form of political support and each type of behaviour are laid out in Table 2.2. The results show that distrust does not have consistently distinctive associations with people's reported behaviour. Expressions of distrust are not associated with very different behaviours to expressions of dissatisfaction, scepticism, or cynicism. However, there are some behaviours that are more closely associated with trust than with these other forms of political support. Distrust has a rather stronger association with accepting or rejecting information from politicians

Table 2.2 The behavioural correlates of different types of political discontent

	Dissatisfaction	Scepticism	Distrust	Cynicism
Verification of information				
It is ok to accept what politicians tell us without checking whether they are right*	0.22	0.28	0.15	0.03
It is too risky to automatically accept the advice of politicians; people should always check this advice for themselves	0.31	0.36	0.24	0.13
When a politician tells me anything, I always double-check to make sure it is true	0.31	0.31	0.28	0.21
When a politician tells me something important, I typically try to get a second opinion	0.27	0.33	0.24	0.16
Rejection of information				
When politicians tell me something, I tend to listen*	0.22	0.15	0.33	0.24
I tend not to accept information provided by politicians, even when that information is supposedly factual	0.26	0.25	0.32	0.27
I usually accept what politicians tell me on important issues*	0.31	0.32	0.36	0.22
People should always follow the advice given to them by politicians*	0.30	0.31	0.28	0.12
Complaining				
If my MP provided poor service, I would complain about them	0.17	0.18	0.14	0.06
If politicians are not providing the service people expect, we should complain so they can improve things	0.28	0.26	0.21	0.10
Seeking alternative providers				
When it comes to politics, we should look to politicians to help resolve the big issues*	0.28	0.21	0.30	0.18
When it comes to issues facing the country, I prefer to look for information online rather than rely on what politicians say	0.32	0.33	0.33	0.23
I would be willing to vote for one of the non-mainstream parties in a future election	0.20	0.19	0.13	0.07

Continued

Table 2.2 *Continued*

	Dissatisfaction	Scepticism	Distrust	Cynicism
Rejection of authority				
It would be much better if ordinary people had greater say over policy decisions, not just politicians	0.30	0.20	0.36	0.29
People should obey the laws the government lays down*	0.12	0.08	0.14	0.10
When it comes to policy issues, people should rely on politicians' judgements rather than deciding things on their own*	0.23	0.21	0.19	0.08
It is fine if people do not accept what politicians say	0.26	0.26	0.21	0.13

Bivariate correlations. All entries are significant at the 5 per cent level (two-tailed test).
Minimum *N*: 1,179. * Item reverse-coded.
Source: Prolific Academic survey, 2019.

than does cynicism, for example. The same is true in the case of accepting politicians' authority. Trust is also more closely associated than other forms of political support with a desire to increase popular input into policy decisions ('It would be much better if ordinary people had greater say over policy decisions, not just politicians') and a belief in adhering to rules ('People should obey the laws the government lays down').

The results summarized in Tables 2.1 and 2.2 capture associations between attitudes and behaviours and make no effort to establish causality. Nor do they control for other factors likely to shape these associations. Both of these limitations are addressed more fully in Chapter 7, where the consequences of trust are examined more systematically. What these results suggest, however, is that people's trust in political actors does not appear to be associated with behaviours that are very different to those associated with other orientations to the political system. As a result, our focus on trust should not be rationalized because this way of capturing citizens' relations with their political rulers provides a unique insight into what people think and how they behave. The modest variations in the associations with citizens' civic attitudes and behaviours that we have identified between trust and other forms of political support suggest that trust is not necessarily a better or more useful concept for analytical focus. They merely suggest that trust captures a somewhat different perspective on the way that citizens relate to their political rulers.

2.6 Does it make sense to 'trust' government?

Having devoted space to establishing where trust sits as a measure of citizens' political support, and of its distinctiveness in relation to other measures, I end the chapter by considering a broader challenge to the status of the concept, namely that relations between citizens and political rulers do not merit the label of 'trust'. As discussed in Chapter 1, trust involves an individual's evaluation of whether an actor is likely to behave in a manner consistent with their interests. This evaluation depends on the individual having sufficient knowledge of the actor to judge them worthy of trust or not.

For this reason, many analysts have suggested that information is a precondition for trust. As Offe (1999: 55) argues, 'Trust is a thoroughly cognitive phenomenon. It depends upon knowledge and belief'. Ignorance about an object stands as a barrier to judgements about whether that object is trustworthy or not (Hardin, 2002: 151–172; Ullmann-Margalit, 2004; Saunders, Dietz, and Thornhill, 2014). The requisite level of information to support trust is sometimes suggested to exist only in relations between individuals—who enjoy extensive mutual knowledge—and not in relations between individuals and organizations—which tend to be marked by scant knowledge and little or no personal contact (Zmerli et al., 2007). Where citizens lack good knowledge of a political actor, how can they appraise that actor's intentions, competence, and integrity, the cornerstones of trust? Faced with large and remote institutions like government, says Hardin (2002: 151–172, 2006: 29–30, 67–70, 2013), citizens' trust must rest on the less cognitively demanding, and more cognitively realistic, base of observing past patterns of behaviour and extrapolating from these to predict future behaviour. Yet judgements based on an institution's future behaviour are best characterized as 'confidence', argues Hardin, not as 'trust', which is informationally more demanding. Trust involves a belief that another actor intends to act in one's interests; confidence drops any assumption of motivation and simply involves an expectation—based on extrapolation from past actions—that the actor will behave in a particular way (see also Luhmann, 1979: 18–23, 1988).

A related point is made by Warren (1999). While contemporary citizens are more educated and have access to more information than in the past, the requirements necessary to evaluate the trustworthiness of political actors have expanded. Earlier generations, brought up in less socially diverse societies, may not have required extensive knowledge of elected representatives to assess their trustworthiness. Instead, strong bonds of identity between constituents and representatives would have provided sufficient information for the former to judge how well the latter were serving their interests. Deep and stable social gradations—such as social class in early twentieth-century Britain—helped individuals to assess whether an actor was 'one of us', and therefore trustworthy (see also Newton, 1999a: 179). In today's more diverse society, however, identities cannot so readily be used to infer others' trustworthiness. Instead, politicians forge 'communities of interest' around policy proposals, administrative competence, and personal character. One problem is that these are artificial constructs, lacking the solidity of the 'thick' trust relationships of earlier periods. Because of their flimsiness, forged communities of interest provide a weak basis for representation, liable to unravel under the demands of government (Warren, 1999: 314–317). An additional, and for our purposes more important, problem is that trust requires a more complex range of information than previously. The social background of an actor no longer provides a simple shortcut for an individual wishing to appraise their trustworthiness. Absent such ready and simple cues, a more detailed palette of information must be considered in evaluating trustworthiness.

We may doubt how many citizens possess such extensive information. Clearly, very few individuals hold knowledge of government actors that they do of friends or work colleagues. As a result, expressions of trust in a friend or colleague usually involve a far richer base of information than expressions of trust in a politician or government agency. Yet this weaker informational base does not negate the place of trust in characterizing the vertical relations between citizens and rulers. This is because trust can rest on more limited, and even secondary, sources of information. Citizens do not necessarily need to know whether the actors holding political office are motivated to serve people's interests; instead, all they require is knowledge of whether the general character of those individuals, along with the incentives and constraints they face, is such that the actors are likely to serve the public interest or not. Trust can arise 'when one party to the relation believes the other party *has incentive to act in his or her interest* or to take his or her interests to heart' (Cook, Hardin, and Levi, 2005: 2; emphasis added). An individual need not believe that (or even know whether) an actor is concerned to behave in a way consistent with their individual interests. Trust may nonetheless arise because the actor is perceived to be constrained from behaving in a self-interested way and is instead perceived as likely to serve public goals through the provision of appropriate incentives.

Hence, when it comes to trust in actors such as governments, it is awareness of the institutional arrangements surrounding decision-makers, rather than detailed knowledge of the personalities and characteristics of particular actors, that underpins most citizens' judgements.[12] A citizen may trust a political actor even if they cannot observe that actor's motivations, provided that appropriate incentives exist (such as any claim made by the actor being subject to independent verification or, in the case of a lie, to a penalty) that encourage the agent to act in a trustworthy manner (Lupia and McCubbins, 1998). Trust thus rests on, or 'implies procedures for selecting and constraining the agents of institutions so that they are competent, credible and likely to act in their interests of those being asked to trust the institutions' (Levi, 1998: 80). Or if incentives and constraints establish particular roles for public officials, then trust 'refers to perceptions about the motivations and capabilities of specific individuals, who may or may not be known personally, with regard to their *roles* [...] in situations where wrong decisions can lead to negative consequences for members of the public' (White and Eiser, 2006: 1188, emphasis in original).

Trust, then, can realistically rest on the various arrangements and structures that induce public officials to behave in responsive and responsible ways. These structures enable citizens to step back from the task of constantly monitoring their elected representatives and of gathering extensive information about their agents' actions. Gamson's (1968: 54) definition, quoted in Chapter 1, is therefore apposite. This definition equates trust with a judgement about the 'probability ... that the political system (or some part of it) will produce preferred outcomes even if left untended'. On this view of trust, the relevant question about trust an individual should pose is not, in Parry's (1976: 142) pithy example, whether they should buy a second-hand car from a particular seller but whether protective legal sanctions exist should the seller pass on a dud.

2.7 Conclusion

Trust is often assumed to be an important feature of the relations between citizens and political rulers in democratic states, but this assumption is rarely explored and tested. Analysts often dive into discussions of trust without pausing first to consider whether trust is as relevant as assumed. This chapter and the previous one have sought to establish firmer foundations for the concept by exploring which aspects of citizens' relations with political actors and institutions are captured by trust. These foundations have been constructed both conceptually and empirically. The conceptual foundations were established in Chapter 1, where I argued that it makes sense to characterize the vertical relations between citizens and their political rulers in terms of 'trust', where this involves a judgement about whether a political actor is likely—by virtue of their character and/or the incentives and sanctions they face—to serve one's interests.

In empirical terms, the findings presented in this chapter suggest that citizens' expressions of trust do not capture either immediate assessments of incumbent political actors ('specific' support) or generalized appraisals of democratic norms ('diffuse' support) but rather a mid-range evaluation that extends across the performance of particular governments and the practices involved in political decision-making. In this way, trust—at least as it is usually measured in population surveys—appears to capture both immediate and more generalized forms of political support. Moreover, this helps account for the utility of the concept of trust over that of related forms of political support, such as dissatisfaction, cynicism, alienation, and legitimacy. Trust captures important features of the relations between citizens and political decision-makers (How likely is a politician to pursue my interests?) that more specific concepts (e.g. dissatisfaction) and more generalized concepts (e.g. cynicism) arguably do not.

Trust is not a wholly stand-alone, or wholly distinctive, orientation of citizens towards the political system. It is a form of political support and shares many of the meanings and implications of other forms of support. Yet trust also captures some particularly salient features of those orientations and is closely associated with particular civic and political behaviours among citizens. To that extent, trust is important and worthy of study.

Chapter 3
Measuring trust

The previous two chapters have highlighted the importance of analysing trust, but also the complexity of the concept and thus the potential difficulties in measuring it. Unless one treats trust as revealed in people's actions (an assumption questioned in Chapter 1 and considered in more detail in this chapter), we must conclude that the concept is not directly observable. Attitudes cannot, of course, be directly observed; instead, we ask people—via surveys, interviews, focus group discussions, and the like—to reveal their thoughts and beliefs. Some of these thoughts can be straightforwardly, and directly, measured. Thus, for example, if we want to know what people think about the state of the economy, we can straightforwardly ask our survey respondents a question like: 'In the past year, do you think the economy has got stronger or weaker?' If we want to know what people make of the incumbent prime minister, we can ask them a question like 'Do you think [individual] is doing a good job or a bad job as prime minister?' In both cases, aside from issues of interpretation (what constitutes a 'strong' or a 'weak' economy? What comprises a 'good' or a 'bad' job?), we can treat survey respondents' answers to these questions pretty straightforwardly as representing their evaluations of the national economy and of the incumbent national leader. However, trust is a more complex concept than either economic evaluations or incumbent appraisals. This complexity creates difficulties for measurement that, unfortunately, are often wished away in empirical studies. Yet unless we pay attention to these difficulties, we potentially weaken our ability to accurately measure—and thus to understand—trust.

3.1 Practices and problems in the measurement of trust

Political trust was first measured on a nationwide survey in the form of a battery of questions fielded on the United States' National Election Study (NES) in 1958 (item 2 dates from 1964). This battery comprised the following items:[1]

1. How much of the time do you think you can trust the government in Washington to do what is right?
2. Would you say the government is pretty much run by a few big interests looking out for themselves, or that it is run for the benefit of all people?
3. Do you think that the people in government waste a lot of the money we pay in taxes, wastes some of it, or don't waste very much of it?
4. Do you think that quite a few of the people running the government are a little crooked, not very many are, or do you think hardly any of them are crooked?

These items are still used by the NES to measure trust, albeit that the wording of the fourth item has been altered, with 'corrupt' replacing 'crooked'. However, although widely assumed to measure political trust, the items were originally designed to tap people's 'basic evaluative orientations toward the national government' (Stokes, 1962: 64), and in particular their assessments of officials' honesty, competence, and procedural correctness. There was no justification of the questions' status as measures of trust, and indeed no reference to the concept, in Stokes' (1962) explanatory account. Outside the United States, and in cross-national surveys, trust is more typically measured through single-item survey measures worded along the following lines: 'How much do you trust [institution]?'

In the United States, scholars have explored how far the NES measures tap generalized evaluations of the political system, as opposed to evaluations of incumbent political actors (Citrin, 1974; Hill, 1981; see the discussion in Section 2.2, Chapter 2). Outside the United States, however, little attention has been paid to the adequacy of the single-item measure. The assumption—rarely made explicit—is that trust is adequately captured by a single survey item that directly references the concept. As we saw in Chapter 1, however, these survey items tend to focus on trust and ignore the measurement of active distrust among citizens. Yet even if we focus on trust, assumptions about the measurement capability of single-item measures are questionable, for five principal reasons:

1. There is little way of knowing how far the measure fully captures the concept.
2. The measure risks tapping incumbent evaluations as opposed to a more generalized assessment of the political system.
3. The measure is vague and thus open to different interpretations and understandings among respondents.

4. The measure fails to capture the presence of both negative and positive evaluations among respondents; it thus ignores trust 'ambivalence' among individuals.
5. The measure risks encouraging 'impressionistic' responses as opposed to more deliberate or considered responses.

The bulk of this chapter is devoted to reviewing these issues. I then consider whether trust is properly measured as an attitude ('stated trust') as opposed to a behaviour ('revealed trust'). The chapter concludes by identifying how analysts might overcome some of the main problems identified here and measure trust more effectively.

Problem 1: Does the measure capture the concept?

The first problem concerns whether the concept of trust is capable of direct measurement. Single-item survey measures assume a one-to-one correspondence between the indicator and the background concept. This assumption usually remains implicit and is only occasionally made explicit. In cases where the correspondence between indicator and concept is made explicit, Selnes (1998), Metlay (1999), and Lang and Hallman (2005) argue that trust is a unidimensional construct that is—as Selnes (1998) argues—directly accessible to survey respondents.[2] Yet even if a concept is found to be unidimensional (i.e. containing a single defining core element or meaning), this does not mean that it can be adequately measured through a single survey item. This would require showing that the item fully encapsulates the concept's meaning and nature.[3]

Moreover, theoretical and empirical analyses of trust usually suggest that the concept is not unidimensional but instead contains various dimensions (relevant studies from the fields of political science, risk management, organizational science, public policy, and health studies include: Citrin and Muste, 1999; Grimmelikhuijsen and Knies, 2017; Johnson, 1999; Earle, 2010; McEvily and Tortoriello, 2011; PytlikZillig et al., 2016; Ozawa and Sripad, 2013). If trust comprises different components or dimensions, it would seem unlikely that any single-item indicator is able to fully encompass all of their meanings.[4] As two prominent analysts have recently argued, 'The concept of political trust has many dimensions and it is likely that few of our "workhorse" measures are sufficient to explain all of them' (Wilson and Eckel, 2017: 137). Moreover, not only are single-item indicators unlikely to fully 'map' the concept of trust, but their reliability is also difficult to assess, while they are also prone to measurement error (deVellis, 1991; Spector, 1992: 4–5; Fabrigar, Krosnick, and MacDougall, 2005; 27).[5]

Many other concepts closely linked to trust are deemed by scholars to be multidimensional and hence capable of measurement only through a range of survey indicators rather than through a single indicator. This list includes: trust in risk management (Poortinga and Pidgeon, 2003; Allum, 2007), the healthcare system (Egede and Ellis, 2008) and natural resource management agencies (Hamm et al., 2013b; Smith et al., 2013), confidence in the legal system (Gibson, Caldeira, and Spence, 2003; Hamm et al., 2011; Jackson et al., 2011) and the political system (Keller et al., 2011), interpersonal trust (Yamagishi and Yamagishi, 1994), dispositional trust (Frazier, Johnson, and Fainshmidt, 2013), political efficacy (Morrell, 2003), political cynicism (Cheng et al., 2012; Pattyn et al., 2012), democratic norms[6] (McClosky and Zaller, 1984), democratic support (Magalhães, 2014), legitimacy (Tankebe, 2013), legal cultures (Gibson and Caldeira, 1996) and system justification (Kay and Jost, 2003; Rutto, Russo, and Mosso, 2014). Indeed, early efforts to measure concepts like political cynicism (Agger, Goldstein, and Pearl, 1961), political alienation (Finifter, 1970), and political trust itself (Craig, Niemi, and Silver, 1990) employed multi-item indicators in their analysis. The assumption behind these efforts was that the concepts being studied comprised different features or dimensions, which could only be captured by using a range of measurement indicators. Yet, more recently, this insight has not been widely applied to the analysis of trust.

To demonstrate the merit of treating trust as a multidimensional construct, I refer the reader back to Figure 2.3 in Chapter 2. This graphic laid out a model which posited three different dimensions—competence, benevolence, and integrity—to trust. Using data collected from a sample of British respondents, this model provided a more satisfactory fit to the data than a model containing a single trust factor.[7] We can further explore the claim that trust is, in empirical terms, a multidimensional construct as opposed to a unidimensional one with the help of another survey I conducted in 2019 using a different sample of British participants (again collected via Prolific Academic). This survey posed respondents with the following set of indicators, selected to capture particular aspects or dimensions of trust:

1. Most politicians do not know much about the issues they have to deal with.
2. Most politicians do not do a capable job.
3. Politicians waste a lot of public money.
4. Politicians rarely show good judgement when making decisions.

5. Politicians don't care much about ordinary people.
6. Politicians rarely listen to what their constituents tell them.
7. Politicians tend to look after their own interests rather than trying to help others.
8. Politicians are out of touch with what people want.
9. Politicians will usually mislead you about things.
10. Politicians distort the facts to make their decisions look good.
11. Politicians promise things at elections but forget them afterwards.
12. I sometimes feel as if politicians treat me less well than other people.

We could have measured trust by simply combining respondents' scores on each item into a single aggregate scale. After all, people's responses to the items show a high level of internal consistency (the Cronbach's alpha for the twelve items = 0.91). Yet this does not mean that the items all measure the same underlying or unidimensional concept. We can explicitly test for a unidimensional scale, using confirmatory factor analysis, by forcing each of the items to load onto a single trust factor. The resulting model shows a modest fit to the data, however (χ^2 = 299.73, p < 0.000; CFI = 0.931, RMSEA = 0.07). These results show that respondents' replies to the different items do not adequately reflect a singular pattern consistent with the items tapping substantively similar issues. We can then test for a multidimensional scale, with trust comprising three distinct factors relating to competence (measured by the first four survey items), benevolence (the next four survey items), and integrity (the remaining four survey items). Fitting this three-factor model to the data produces a stronger, and indeed acceptable, fit (χ^2 = 115.53, p < 0.000; CFI = 0.979, RMSEA = 0.04).

What this modelling shows is that people's responses to the various survey questions on trust in politicians accord more closely to a three-dimensional structure of trust than to a unidimensional structure of trust. People's evaluations of politicians' competence are not the same as their evaluations of politicians' motives or benevolence which, in turn, are not the same as their evaluations of politicians' integrity.[8] This conclusion mirrors those drawn from similar exercises conducted in different countries, such as the United States. These studies show that people assess politicians' benevolence rather differently from their competence or integrity; these assessments are not explained or accounted for by a single generalized assessment of trust (Hamm, Smidt, and Mayer, 2019).

The Prolific Academic survey also assessed levels of trust using a more traditional measure of the concept. It asked respondents how much they trusted a range of actors, with scores measured on a scale from 1 ('distrust completely') to 10 ('trust completely'). These measures enable us to test how far such single-item measures of trust overlap with the more specific multi-item measures of trust that are disaggregated into separated competence, benevolence, and integrity scales. The correlations between people's expressed trust in government ministers and their appraisals of politicians' competence, benevolence, and integrity are fairly strong (competence = 0.55, benevolence = 0.51, and integrity = 0.60). The correlations between expressed trust in politicians and appraisals of the three dimensions of politicians' activities are stronger still (competence = 0.63, benevolence = 0.60, and integrity = 0.67). These results tell us two things. First, single-item generalized measures of trust appear to be answered by respondents with a broad range of politicians' qualities or characteristics in mind, with associations particularly close in the case of integrity appraisals (this issue is explored further in Chapter 6). Second, and more important for the present purpose, single-item generalized measures of trust cover some, but by no means all, of the more specific trust evaluations. Even a correlation of 0.67, for example, means that only 46 per cent of the variance in people's appraisals of politicians' integrity is explained by the generalized measure of trust in politicians. Thus, while generalized survey questions may offer a proxy for assessing people's trust in actors and institutions, these results suggest they leave plenty of the content of that trust unmeasured.

Problem 2: Does the measure capture generalized evaluations rather than incumbent evaluations?

The previous chapter suggested that trust represents a 'middle-level' judgement that sits between the specific and diffuse poles of political support. Trust judgements may contain elements of general or diffuse evaluations, but also appear to reflect more specific appraisals of particular actors and governments. As a 'running tally' of government evaluations, trust is likely to contain a mixture of generalized and more specific judgements. Yet if trust is found to reflect little more than judgements about incumbent politicians, this reduces its value as a measure of how citizens relate to the wider political system.

It is precisely this concern, however, that hangs over single-item measures of trust of the form 'How much do you trust [institution]?' For example, a study of American citizens' attitudes towards Congress found that measuring congressional approval in a single-item form ('Do you approve or disapprove of the way the US Congress has been handling its job?') attracted a stronger influence of evaluations of the incumbent president than did multi-item measures of congressional approval that tapped the various dimensions of legislative support (Mondak et al., 2007: 41). Single-item questions on attitudes towards a specific institution risk tapping judgements that are contaminated by people's feelings about incumbent personnel. As Margaret Levi (2022: 9) notes, single-item survey measures of trust 'seldom distinguish between favorable affect and perceptions of trustworthiness'.

Multi-item measures that direct respondents towards the specific aspects or dimensions of a concept appear less prone to such incumbency contamination. In Chapter 4 (see Figure 4.4), I reproduce data showing that over time, people's feelings of political discontent (a concept that is closely related to trust) do not change in line with their judgements about incumbent political actors. Part of the reason for this may be that discontent is measured through a range of indicators tapping different features or dimensions of the underlying concept. Multi-item measures allow for questions probing people's attitudes to particular features of the political system, shifting evaluations away from feelings about the incumbent government. Single-item measures of concepts like trust are, by contrast, more generalized and may encourage respondents to use their feelings about incumbent politicians as a heuristic, or shortcut, in forming a judgement.

Problem 3: Does the measure have an invariant meaning?

Survey questions that explicitly reference potentially complex concepts like trust might attract different understandings of that concept among respondents. One survey respondent might understand trust in a particular way and respond to a survey question with this interpretation in mind, while another might hold a different understanding and thus provide a different interpretation. Studies of interpersonal or social trust have suggested that single-item indicators provide imperfect measures where the meaning of the concept is imprecise or variant between individuals (Miller and Mitamura, 2003; Sturgis and Smith, 2010; Bulloch, 2013; Crepaz et al., 2014). We know from qualitative research that complex terms such as 'democracy' are interpreted in different ways both across and within populations (Canache, Mondak and Seligson, 2001; Carnaghan, 2011; Schaffer, 2010). Yet one principle underlying the design of survey questions is that they should be understood in comparable terms by different individuals (Fowler, 2009: 91–94). Where survey questions are potentially understood and interpreted differently by respondents, we cannot rule out the possibility that any variations in the distribution of responses—between groups or over time—might reflect differences in comprehension and interpretation rather than differences in substance (Sturgis and Smith, 2010: 89).

Problem 4: Does the measure suppress ambivalent attitudes among respondents?

Survey items that squeeze a range of potential evaluations into a single expressed opinion risk understating the level of uncertainty and ambivalence in people's attitudes. The same individual may harbour both positive evaluations of an actor or institution ('the government is competent') and negative evaluations ('the government is not concerned about people like me'). As we saw in Chapter 1, American citizens appear to manifest high levels of ambivalence in their attitudes towards political institutions. Thus, between 50 and 70 per cent of Americans have been found to hold attitudes towards Congress, the Supreme Court, and the incumbent president that contain both positive and negative feelings (McGraw and Bartels, 2005; Gainous et al., 2008). Data from Britain, again reported in Chapter 1, showed a similar proportion of people (64 per cent) holding positive and negative views of politicians; only 36 per cent of British people were found to hold consistently positive or consistently negative attitudes.

Qualitative research has suggested that one reason people find it difficult to answer generalized questions about broad concepts such as 'confidence' or 'trust' is that they feel unable to summarise competing positive and negative feelings about an object (Charlton, Morton, and Ipsos MORI, 2011). While some studies have suggested that individuals may be able to reconcile positive and negative evaluations of an organization (Walls et al., 2004), many are likely to find this cognitively challenging. Surely it would be preferable if ambivalent feelings could be recorded rather than being suppressed by limiting responses to a single survey question.

Problem 5: Does the measure encourage 'impressionistic', as opposed to considered, responses?

Although population surveys are the pre-eminent source of data on public attitudes in advanced democracies, their results are often imperfect guides to people's beliefs. In the case of trust, particular concerns arise over whether survey questions accurately and reliably capture individuals' evaluations of political actors and institutions.

For a start, there is the suggestion that people's self-reported trust might lack much substance due to ignorance of the actor or organization being evaluated. To provide an example of this, take people's attitudes towards a rather obscure organization: the Office for National Statistics (ONS), the agency responsible for providing official data in the United Kingdom. In 2018, the British Social Attitudes survey asked its sample whether they had heard of the ONS; 73 per cent of respondents said they had, while 27 per cent said they had not. Yet among the latter group (which amounted to 528 people), 45 per cent were willing to offer a view when asked in a subsequent question how much they trusted the ONS. Moreover, not only did these respondents proffer an evaluation of an agency they confessed not to have heard of, but these evaluations were more negative than those proffered by respondents with some knowledge of the agency. Among those lacking knowledge of the ONS, 23 per cent expressed distrust in it, while among those with some familiarity with the ONS the proportion of distrusters was just 10 per cent.

It could well be that respondents who confessed not to having heard of the ONS but who nonetheless offered a trust evaluation inferred trustworthiness from something in the agency's title ('is something to do with government'; 'is involved in controversial official statistics'; 'sounds authoritative'). Studies of people who express attitudes on made-up, or 'fictitious', policy issues suggest that such 'pseudo-attitudes' may arise from survey respondents' tendency to infer meaning from questions when they lack any knowledge of the topic (Bishop, 2005: chapter 2). Yet such inferences are likely to be based on weak foundations and, as such, are unlikely to strongly predict other important attitudes and behaviours among individuals.

A related concern is that survey questions probing an individual's trust in some distant political actor or institution might induce rapid or impressionistic responses rather than more considered or deliberative responses, which would be more cognitively demanding and thus potentially off-putting (Kampen, Van De Walle, and Bouckaert, 2006). Single-item trust questions taking a generalized form ('How much do you trust [institution]?') might encourage individuals to engage in 'schematic' reasoning based on general feelings and impressions that are instantly called to mind, over 'piecemeal' reasoning based on consideration of specific positive and negative assessments (the distinction between 'schematic' and 'piecemeal' reasoning was introduced in Chapter 1). Hence, generalized single-item survey measures of trust risk picking up routine or even superficial feelings, while more considered judgements are only likely to be triggered by more focused and specific questions (Citrin, 1977: 384; Citrin and Muste, 1999: 468–469).

Routine feelings may be even more pronounced when the dominant social discourse stresses the prevalence, and even utility, of distrust over trust. The risk here is the reverse of that encountered when survey researchers ask people for their attitudes towards democracy. Here, social desirability norms may artificially inflate levels of support, as people consider democracy to be a socially valued good (De Jonge, 2016). Yet where citizens encounter a continual stream of messages—from sources like the media and populist politicians—that people in authority are not to be trusted, the very mention of 'trust' in a survey question might be enough to exert a negative priming effect, serving to artificially depress individual responses.[9] What happens, though, when attitudes to government are measured without giving people the time to consider their response and thereby potentially taking into account social desirability norms? In an exercise where trust in government was assessed implicitly—by pairing on a computer mention of the word 'government' with trustworthy or untrustworthy descriptors and by measuring how quickly respondents paired government with each descriptor—researchers found levels of trust to be significantly higher than where trust was assessed via a standard survey question (Intawan and Nicholson, 2018; see also Murtin, Fleischer, and Siegerink, 2018: 32–33). The researchers concluded that, as was suggested above, many individuals hold ambivalent attitudes towards government; they may *express* negative sentiments, but they *feel* more positive sentiments. The negative sentiments recorded in traditional survey measures may reflect an inability among individuals to accurately access the warmer sentiments they often harbour towards government.[10]

Summary

Analysts have chosen to measure trust overwhelmingly via surveys that pose respondents with single-item questions that directly reference the concept. However, there are various problems with this way of measuring trust. Underlying these problems is the potential gap between a complex and multidimensional *concept* and a simple and singular *measure*. Ideally, we would reduce the risk of such a gap by closely linking the concept of trust (as discussed in Chapter 1) with its measurement. Yet within political science, such explicit and careful linkages are rarely made. Efforts by scholars in the

1960s and 1970s to operationalize and empirically measure concepts such as 'political support' and 'political alienation' have not been followed up and built on. In his discussion of political legitimacy, Weatherford (1991: 252) lamented that:

> After flourishing in the 1960s and 1970s, survey-based research on legitimacy has been notable more recently for its lack of progress at building on earlier theoretical conceptions and advancing to cumulate new insights.

As he goes on to note, the reason for this stuttering progress is not a lack of attention paid to theorizing concepts such as legitimacy, political support, or trust (as we saw in Chapter 2) but a reluctance to devise empirical instruments capable of accurately and fully measuring these concepts.

3.2 Is trust an attitude or a behaviour?

In her 2002 Reith Lectures, the political philosopher Onora O'Neill argued that trust 'talk' is 'cheap' and that people's expressions of trust are often unreliable guides to whether they truly trust or not. Where an individual has the choice over whether or not to engage with a public actor or service provider, their actions (i.e. whether they engage or use the service) constitute a more accurate barometer of their trust than what they say. Drawing on examples of such actions, O'Neill claims 'the evidence suggests that we still constantly place trust in many of the institutions and professions we profess not to trust' (2002: 13). But what is this evidence? Do people *place* their trust in organizations, by engaging with them, even when they *state* they do not trust them?

This is a tricky question to answer since there is a paucity of data on different manifestations of trust. Various studies have been conducted in which behavioural measures of trust (for example, how much money players in a 'trust game' pass on to other participants) have been compared to attitudinal measures of trust. The conclusion is that the two measures do not correlate particularly strongly (Twyman, Harvey, and Harries, 2008; Ermisch et al., 2009).

Yet this finding arises from analyses of horizontal, or social, forms of trust. When it comes to vertical, or institutional, trust, there is some evidence of greater consistency between behavioural and attitudinal measures. Yet this evidence is only tentative since it is difficult to directly compare people's expressions of trust with their manifested trust behaviours. In the examples provided, behaviour is measured by what individuals say they would do, not by what they have actually done.

The first example concerns engagement with the police and is drawn from the Citizen Audit survey of 2001, conducted among a sample of the British population.[11] This survey carried questions on whether people trusted the police and also on the actions they would take in the event of witnessing a robbery in the street. These actions included contacting the police, either anonymously or not. The reported likelihood of contacting the police and giving one's name was greater among people with high trust in the police (at 89 per cent) than among people with low trust in the police (at 70 per cent).[12] People with low trust in the police were more likely than high trusters to contact the police but avoid giving their names.

A second example concerns a situation in which citizens may have less choice over engaging with an organization. The British Social Attitudes survey in 2002 asked people whether, in the course of the past year, they had visited their local doctor (general practitioner or GP) or a National Health Service (NHS) hospital outpatient department. It also asked about levels of trust in GPs and hospital doctors. People who fall sick have the option of looking after themselves, visiting a private medical practice, or visiting their GP or local hospital of which, in Britain, the latter option is by far the most common. Yet even though the level of choice here is limited (sick people need medical care, and the most widespread provider of such care in Britain is the NHS), we find that people who do not trust medical practitioners are less likely to report engaging with doctors than people who do trust them. Among people with high trust, 35 per cent reported having visited their GP and 29 per cent their hospital, while among people with low trust, 26 per cent reported having visited their GP and 24 per cent their hospital.

There remains a question over whether an individual's trust is best measured by what they do or by what they say. Onora O'Neill is undoubtedly right to argue that even people who profess not to trust an organization still often engage with that body. Still, professed trust does seem to have some association with people's behaviour. The behavioural indicators reviewed here point to rather less engagement among people who report being low in trust than among people who report being high in trust. People who profess a lack of trust in a public service might still engage with that service but at a lower rate than people who profess a greater degree of trust. Attitudinal measures therefore seem to have some virtues as barometers of people's trust in public actors and institutions.

3.3 Conclusion: Moving on with measurement

Trust is an important feature of citizens' relations with political leaders, with potentially significant consequences for civic and political life. Yet the importance of trust has arguably not been sufficiently recognized and supported when it comes to measuring the concept. Researchers have settled into a practice of gauging trust through single-item questions that assume the concept possesses a clear and unified meaning. Faced with the pressing tasks of identifying where trust comes from and what effects trust has, analysts seem to have forgotten—or more likely to have ignored—the equally important, but rather duller, issue of how the concept should be measured. Yet amnesia and suppression carry risks since they may undermine attempts to accurately capture levels of trust and to identify associations with important outcomes. Other scholars share these concerns. Gershtenson and Plane (2011: 132), for example, having noted the way scholars rely on single-item indicators of trust, go on to observe:

> there is a dearth of serious evaluations of alternative trust measures. Without empirical evidence that one measure is better or worse than others, political science research on trust is likely to remain fragmented, and thereby limited in its ability to truly understand the relationship between political trust and other variables.

At present, most of our measures of trust derive from population surveys, and most of these are based on single-item indicators of the concept. Researchers studying the topic (including the current author) are thus reliant on this conventional way of gauging how people feel about their political rulers. This is not to say that conventional measures are necessarily wrong. Rather, it is to urge analysts to exercise greater caution in extrapolating from a measure whose validity is unclear. The distribution of trust at any particular point in time, and in relation to particular objects, may be imprecisely captured if survey questions serve to suppress conflicting evaluations among individuals, trigger appraisals of incumbent actors, and invoke routinized or knee-jerk responses. In addition, conventional measures of trust often fail to distinguish between respondent trust and distrust, which may imperil our ability to detect the consequences of trust. The knock-on effects of citizens' attitudes may be limited if recorded negativity among citizens merely taps an absence of trust rather than the presence of active distrust. As we will see in Chapter 7, expressions of low trust often have rather modest associations with attitudinal and behavioural outcomes. It is difficult to determine whether this modesty arises because trust is genuinely not consequential or, instead, because the concept is being misdiagnosed in the first place. The suspicion remains that conventional survey-based measures of trust may not tap considered evaluations of political actors and institutions as much as ritualistic negative reflexes that may not be deeply felt nor have significant effects on individuals' behaviour (Citrin, 1974; Citrin and Muste, 1999: 468–469). At present, we have few tools with which to test this suspicion. Yet if trust is such an important commodity in contemporary politics, we surely should.

SECTION 2
WHAT IS GOING ON? LEVELS AND CAUSES OF TRUST

Chapter 4
Is there a problem of trust?

The previous chapters were devoted to clearing a path through some of the undergrowth: identifying what trust means and consists of (in Chapter 1), exploring where trust sits as a measure of political support (in Chapter 2), and analysing how trust is measured (in Chapter 3). Having dealt with these important issues, we are now in a position to examine levels of trust in Britain and to identify whether there is a 'problem' of low trust, and if so what this problem consists of. This chapter focuses on people's trust in different institutions, on how levels of trust have changed over time, and on how levels of trust among the population in Britain compare with those among populations in other advanced democracies.

4.1 Levels of trust

Few, if any, readers will be under the misapprehension that British people trust their political representatives and rulers. As we shall shortly see, they do not. Yet followers of the news might also wonder whether trust is any higher in the personnel holding other high-profile offices? After all, in recent years, Britain has witnessed high-profile scandals involving the police (for example, the numerous recent controversies over London's police force), healthcare workers (over various incidents of clinical negligence and mishandling of patients), private enterprises (notably the actions of the banks in contributing to the 2008 financial crisis), charities (over claims of sexual exploitation by aid workers), and the media (notably over some newspapers' hacking of phones belonging to private individuals).[1] Might these incidents have contributed to a general crisis of trust in key civic and social institutions?

In fact, there is little evidence of any such general crisis of trust. The most extensive evidence on trust in different professional groups derives from surveys conducted by the market research company Ipsos. These surveys ask people whether they trust various groups to tell the truth. The most recent survey, conducted in autumn 2022, found that eight in ten or more of the population trusted doctors, teachers, and judges, while more than six in ten

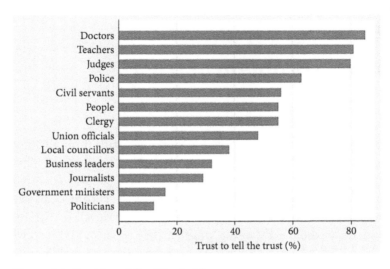

Figure 4.1 Trust in public office-holders
Source: Ipsos Veracity Index

trusted the police, and well over half trusted the clergy and civil servants (Figure 4.1). Towards the lower end of the scale, just over three in ten people expressed trust in business leaders. Propping up the scale are journalists, government ministers, and politicians.

These figures do not suggest a general crisis of trust in key public actors. Even among office-holders closely attached to the state, there is often substantial public trust: in judges (in whom 80 per cent of the population express trust), the police (63 per cent trust), and civil servants (56 per cent trust). Among state office-holders, low trust is limited to political or partisan actors.

4.2 Trust within the population

How far do these levels of trust vary within the population? Are some types of individuals more or less trusting than others? Most analyses find that trust tends to distribute fairly evenly across the population, with minor variations between different social groups (on the UK, see Pattie and Johnston, 2001; Clarke et al., 2009: 300–303; Schoon and Cheng, 2011; on the US, see Alford, 2001).

We find a similar picture when we examine levels of trust among different social groups, using a measure of trust fielded on the British Election Study in May 2022. This survey asked respondents about their trust in Members of Parliament, with responses recorded on a scale from 1 (no trust) to 7 (a great deal of trust). The results highlight some variations in trust between individuals in different demographic and socio-economic groupings (Table 4.1). Trust is higher among men than among women, and among the young (those aged 18–25) and the old (those in their mid-60s and above) than among the intermediate age groups. Trust is higher among people located in 'core' regions (London and the South East) than among people in more 'peripheral' regions (Scotland, Wales, and the North East and North West of England). Trust is also higher among minority ethnic groups (e.g. people expressing a black African or Caribbean ethnicity) than among white British individuals.[2] Finally, levels of trust are greater among people within higher socio-economic groups, although differences in trust by education are

Table 4.1 Levels of trust among population sub-groups

	Mean	Sig		Mean	Sig
Gender			*Years in education*		
Male	2.57		20 years or more	2.54	
Female	2.49	<0.01	17–18 years	2.55	
N	(29,681)		16 years	2.48	
			15 years or less	2.52	<0.02
Age			N	(26,732)	
18–25	2.47				
26–35	2.23		*Occupation/class*		
36–45	2.32		Professional; manager	2.63	
46–55	2.34		Supervisor	2.56	
56–65	2.51		Small employer	2.56	
66+	2.81	<0.01	Intermediate	2.54	
N	(29,687)		Technical	2.46	
			Routine	2.39	<0.01
Region			N	(23,716)	
North East	2.44				
North West	2.42		*Ethnicity*		
Yorkshire and the Humber	2.53		White British	2.54	
East Midlands	2.55		White other	2.40	
West Midlands	2.58		Mixed	2.30	
East of England	2.53		Indian/Pakistani/	2.75	
London	2.70		Bangladeshi/other Asian		
South East	2.62		Black African/Caribbean	2.88	<0.01
South West	2.57			(27,599)	
Wales	2.40				
Scotland	2.32	<0.01			
N	(28,711)				

Significance measures the difference in mean scores between groups in each category.
Source: British Election Study internet panel (wave 23; May 2022).

marginal.[3] In all cases, however, the magnitude of these variations is fairly small. The results confirm that levels of trust do not differ greatly within the population.

4.3 Trends in trust

As we have seen, people in Britain today appear to have rather little trust in core political actors and institutions. Yet is this contemporary picture very different from that of the past? Consider, for example, this opening to a study on the topic:

> The extent to which people hold *politicians* and *politics* in disrepute, the extent to which these words symbolise something negative rather than something positive, is a matter of some concern to political theorists concerned with the relationships of the governed to the governors as well as to political reformers and professional politicians interested in changing or maintaining the relationships.

The date of the study? 1961 (Agger, Goldstein, and Pearl, 1961: 477). Analyses in the United States have pointed to numerous examples of public scepticism of, and even antipathy towards, politicians dating back to the 1940s and 1950s (Bennett, 2001).[4] Similar attitudes from those decades have also been recorded in Britain (Jefferys, 2007). Stoker (2017: 37–38) reports Gallup polls from the 1940s that capture people's discontent with features of election campaigns, while Mass Observation from the same decade recorded public discussions about politicians' perceived self-serving nature and lack of honesty. To give a couple of examples from early opinion polls, asked in 1945 whether the government was keeping people informed about its policies, far more people answered in negative terms (50 per cent) than in positive terms (29 per cent), while a year earlier, almost as many people believed British politicians were mainly out for themselves (with 35 per cent agreeing) as believed they were serving the country as a whole (36 per cent) (Gallup, 1976).[5] In similar vein, Mass Observation reported just after the end of the Second World War that:

> In the political sphere, as in other spheres, people are losing faith in the goodwill and potentialities of authorities. 'Whatever you do you get the same thing.' It does not mean that they are apathetic in their minds, that they don't *care* what happens. Probably more care today than ever before. But they feel they're out of the picture, that all the great hierarchies of organisation by which lives are increasingly ordered aren't really *concerned* with them and their wants and needs. It is

not chiefly that people are losing faith in ideals and objectives, but they are losing hope of the capacity and desire of those in prominent positions to help realise those desires. *Apathy is the apathy of frustration more than of thoughtlessness.*

(Hart, 1978: 58; italics in original)

In Britain, the longest set of consistently worded survey measures of political trust began with the Protest, Dissatisfaction and Change survey conducted in 1973 and continued with the British Social Attitudes survey, from 1986. The wording of the question on trust asked by each survey was: 'How much do you trust a British Government of either party to place the needs of this country and the people above the interests of their own political party?' (1973) and 'How much do you trust a British Government of any party to place the needs of this country above the interests of their own political party?' (1986 onwards).

Each survey offered identical response options to these questions, namely a four-point scale comprising 'just about always', 'most of the time', 'only some of the time', and 'almost never'. As discussed in Chapter 3, this way of asking about trust is not ideal. It directs respondents to a specific criterion of trust (namely responsiveness to popular demands) and thus ignores other criteria that may be involved in trust judgements. It also assumes that parties in government should serve popular demands rather than partisan interests. Yet whatever the question's shortcomings, its value lies in its longevity; it has now been asked in a consistent format for almost five decades, allowing us to gauge the dynamics of trust over an extended period of time.

I show these trends in two forms: by overall mean (Figure 4.2a) and by distribution on each of the four response options (Figure 4.2b). The results show how levels of trust often fluctuate. Some of these fluctuations—particularly around the national elections in 1997, 2001, 2005, and 2010 and around the changes in prime minister in 2007, when Gordon Brown replaced Tony Blair—involved increases in trust. Other fluctuations involved pronounced declines in trust, in particular around the controversial decision to take Britain to war in Iraq in 2003, the 'Cash for Peerages' controversy in 2006, and the MPs' expenses scandal in 2009.[6]

Aside from short-lived fluctuations, however, we can see a clear decline in trust over the period. Compared to 1986, mean levels of trust among British citizens declined by almost one quarter by 2009 (Figure 4.2a). Although levels of trust subsequently picked up a little, they ended significantly lower than they started. Moreover, levels of trust fell from a modest base; even in the early 1970s, trust across the population was below the midpoint of 2.5.

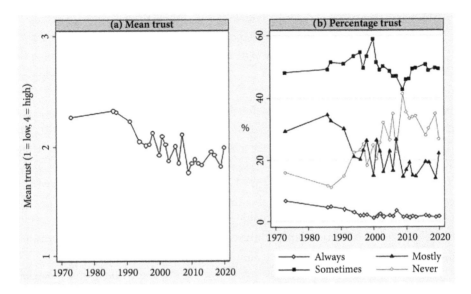

Figure 4.2 Trust in government in Britain, 1973–2020
Source: Protest, Dissatisfaction and Change; British Social Attitudes

The major changes in levels of trust have occurred principally among people who say they trust government 'most of the time' or 'almost never' (Figure 4.2b). Among people who cautiously trust (trust government 'some of the time') or fully trust (trust government 'just about always'), the distributions have changed little over the period. Changes in trust across the population instead reflect a marked decline in the number of people with high trust (trust government 'most of the time') and a marked increase in the number of people with low trust (trust government 'almost never').

Unlike with government, however, people's trust in other public actors and organizations has not fallen (Figure 4.3). Over almost four decades, there has been no decline in people's trust in judges, the police,[7] or business leaders, while their trust in civil servants has actually risen.[8]

As noted earlier, sporadic opinion surveys and participant interviews suggest that people's discontent with politicians in Britain extends back over a long period of time. Using a method of amalgamating different measures of political support into a summative score of 'political discontent', Jennings et al. (2017) show that discontent rose from the mid-1960s to the 1980s—extending across the 50 per cent threshold—and has since continued to increase, peaking in 2016 (Figure 4.4). Alongside political discontent, the graph also shows trends in people's approval of the government, which

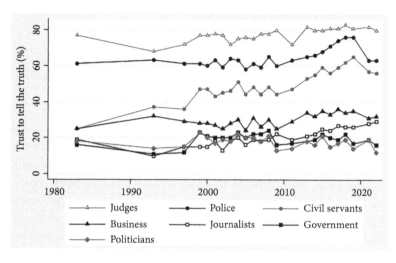

Figure 4.3 Trust in public actors, 1983–2022
Source: Ipsos Veracity Index

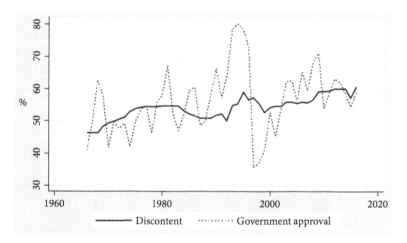

Figure 4.4 Trends in political discontent, 1966–2016
Source: Jennings et al. (2017: Appendix, Table A4)

show markedly greater fluctuations. This reinforces the distinction made in Chapter 1 between people's appraisals of incumbent political actors and their broader political discontent or distrust. More relevant for our purposes here, however, is the picture the data show of a clear and long-standing decline in people's regard for political actors and institutions.

4.4 Trust in Britain compared

How does this picture of trust in Britain compare with the situation in other, comparable, countries? To provide a wider perspective, I draw on data from the European Social Survey collected in 2018–2019. This survey asked respondents across a range of European countries for their trust in various institutions, with responses recorded on a scale from 0 (no trust at all) to 10 (complete trust). The results show that levels of trust among British citizens fall towards the lower end of the range. Britons sit alongside the Irish in their limited trust in representative institutions like parties, politicians, and parliament, a little above the French and a little below the Germans (Figure 4.5). Across Western Europe in general, citizens place more trust in law-enforcing institutions (notably the legal system and the police) than in representative institutions. The trust 'gap' between the two is particularly noticeable in Germany, Spain, Britain, Ireland, and France (also in Finland, where trust in the police is particularly high), while lower in Norway, Sweden, and the Netherlands.

Extending the coverage beyond Western Europe, we find that levels of trust in government and civil servants among British citizens fall towards the mid-point of the global distribution (Figure 4.6).[9] Levels of trust in Britain are lower than in the Scandinavian countries but higher than in the United States and Japan.

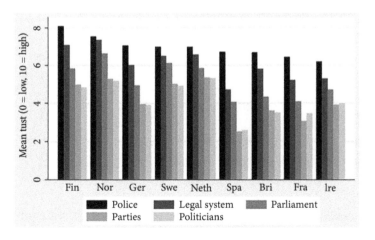

Figure 4.5 Trust in core political institutions in nine Western European countries

Source: European Social Survey 2018. Weighted data

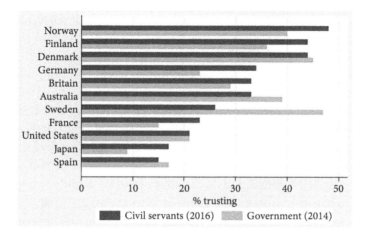

Figure 4.6 Trust in two core institutions in eleven advanced democracies
Source: International Social Science Programme. Data unweighted

While, as we have just seen, there has been a significant decline over time in Britons' trust in partisan and political actors, it is unclear how far the same is the case in other countries. An early pessimistic picture was painted by Dalton (2004: chapter 2; 2005; see also 2017a), who pointed to declining rates of trust in many advanced industrial democracies. More recent studies tend to be less pessimistic, finding little evidence of a general decline in trust across countries (Marien, 2011; Van De Walle, Van Roosbroek, and Bouckaert, 2008; Andeweg, 2014). Drawing on European/World Values Survey data over three decades, Norris (2022: 121–126) shows that declines in trust in some advanced democracies have been matched by increases in trust in others. Other studies similarly identify cases where popular trust in government has declined (including in France, Italy, Luxembourg, the Netherlands, and the United States, as well as Britain), yet also others in which trust has increased (including in Belgium, Germany, and Sweden) (Van Ham and Thomassen, 2017: Appendix 2C; Martini and Quaranta, 2020: 90; see also Torcal, 2017: 424–429).

We can see the over-time trends in levels of trust in selected countries in Figure 4.7, which draws on data from various international surveys (details of which are provided in Appendix 4.1). Among Western European countries, levels of trust in government have stayed broadly constant over time in seven: Austria, Belgium, Denmark, Finland, the Netherlands, Ireland, and Portugal (the latter two both suffered declines of trust after the financial crash in 2008 but increased levels of trust thereafter). Levels of trust increased in two countries, namely Germany and Sweden. Trust fell back in France and Italy, alongside a particularly sharp fall in two of the countries hardest hit by the 2008 financial crash: Greece and Spain. Note, however, that in most cases, any declines in popular trust in government have not been mirrored by declining trust in the justice system. Figure 4.7 also highlights declining levels of trust in Australia and the United States. Recent data collected by the Pew Center show that trust in the United States has declined even further from the low level recorded by the American National Election Study (ANES) in 2012. That year, the ANES found that 24 per cent of the US population trusted the federal government 'most of the time' or 'always'. By 2019, the proportion had fallen to just 17 per cent (Pew Center, 2019a; see also Citrin and Stoker, 2018).

Britain is therefore not alone in experiencing a decline in trust. Citizens in other countries have also become less trusting of their governments. Yet some of these cases—notably Greece, Italy, and Spain—were particularly hard hit by the 2008 financial crisis. If we exclude these examples, there are fairly few cases of declining trust among advanced industrial countries. Britain is therefore something of an exception in the way that over the last few decades, its citizens' regard for their political representatives has fallen away.

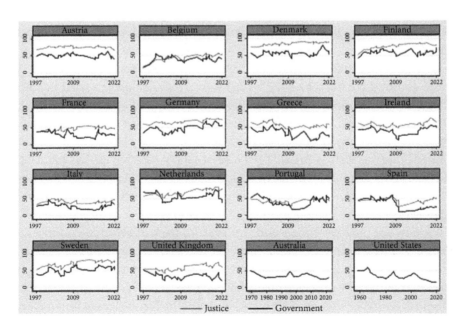

Figure 4.7 Trends in trust in advanced democracies

4.5 Conclusion

The evidence presented in this chapter does not point to a general or universal 'crisis' of trust. True, in some countries, levels of trust are low and have declined. Yet in others, rates of trust are still fairly high and have maintained over time. At least as measured by opinion surveys, there is little evidence of a crisis of trust across western countries. Any problems of trust are, instead, more specifically located.

One of these locations is Britain, where public trust in politicians is low and has declined significantly over time. Going back to the immediate aftermath of the Second World War, we can find ready evidence of British citizens holding negative views about politicians and governments. This suggests that Britons have never been fully supportive of, or trusting in, political elites. But as documented in various long-running surveys, that public regard has become more negative over time. Britain is thus one of the countries in which recorded levels of trust might represent a 'problem', if not necessarily a full 'crisis' (the task of determining the seriousness of low trust through an analysis of its effects is taken up in Chapter 7.) Even in Britain, though, low and declining rates of trust are specific, not general. There are plenty of public actors the public professes to trust, and has done so consistently over a period of time. This public regard even extends to office-holders closely attached to the state, such as judges, the police, and civil servants. If there is a problem (or a crisis) of trust, it relates specifically to partisan actors within the political system.

The low and declining levels of trust in Britain highlighted in this chapter raise questions of reasons and causes. Why have levels of trust declined over the past four or so decades? And what explains why people trust, or more obviously do not trust, political actors? These questions are taken up in the following two chapters. Chapter 6 explores the reasons for people's trust at particular points in time. Before then, Chapter 5 seeks to explain why that trust has fallen over time.

5
Why has trust declined?

Chapter 4 highlighted how, in Britain along with countries like Australia, France, and the United States, levels of trust have fallen over the past five decades or so. While this decline in trust is a source of concern for policymakers, for scholars, it provides valuable conditions enabling analysis of the reasons for the fall-away in the public's regard for its political rulers. The purpose of this chapter is to explore why citizens in Britain are less trusting of their political rulers today than they once were.

The dynamics of trust in Britain have, as we saw in Chapter 4, been marked by significant fluctuation, with levels of trust rising and falling quite sharply over short periods of time (see Figure 4.2). This suggests that people's trust in government responds to specific events. Trust often increases following elections and declines after events that call into question politicians' competence, honesty, and integrity. In Britain, such trust-depressing events include the controversial decision in 2003 to go to war with Iraq, the 'Cash for Peerages' controversy in 2006, and the 'MPs' expenses' scandal in 2009.[1] Part of the explanation for declining trust thus lies in the impact of particular events (Newton, 2006). Moreover, as we saw in Chapter 1, the negative information conveyed by such events is likely to have a particularly strong depressive effect on trust.

Yet underlying the effect of particular events are deeper causal processes whose impact is to reduce levels of trust among the population and to limit the potential for trust to rebound after dips (Dalton, 2004: chapter 4). In the following sections, I explore some of these processes (although note that coverage is dependent on the availability of appropriate longitudinal data, and is thus necessarily selective). The chapter begins by analysing whether declining levels of trust reflect lower public regard for political actors among particular groups within the population. It compares trends in trust among economically and educationally well-resourced individuals (the 'haves') and their less resourced counterparts (the 'have nots') and identifies a growing trust gap between the two groups, not only in Britain but in other countries too. The analysis also explores the evidence for any ageing and generational effects on the decline in trust.

Having examined how far declining trust might be accounted for by people's social and demographic characteristics, the chapter then explores the role of their beliefs and attitudes. Particular attention is paid to whether waning trust reflects citizens' evaluations of government performance, their expectations of what government should deliver, and whether politicians are seen to represent their needs. Given that most citizens receive information about politics via the media, attention is also paid to the role of newspaper exposure in shaping the dynamics of trust. The chapter concludes by summarizing the reasons behind the slump in British citizens' regard for political actors and institutions.

5.1 Changes of trust within the population

There is some suggestion in the literature that the decline in trust has been concentrated among particular social groups. In particular, Dalton (2004, 2005) has argued that trust has fallen predominantly among affluent, well-educated, and younger citizens. While the first two groups have reaped material benefits from the political system, all groups have begun to demand more of the political system which has failed to deliver outputs to match citizens' rising expectations. The net result, according to Dalton, has been a particular decline in trust among affluent, educated, and younger individuals within the population.

The evidence Dalton presents to support this claim derives primarily from the United States, although it also extends to countries like Britain. Dalton's data suggest that in the mid-1970s, educated individuals were more favourably inclined to the political system than their less educated counterparts. Thirty years later, however, these positions had reversed with educated individuals being less favourable in their regard for the political system (Dalton, 2004: 86–91). Dalton also claims that more affluent individuals have become less supportive of the political system, although the figures to support this claim are limited to the United States. Comparative data are also drawn on to argue that recent generations are less supportive of the political system than are older generations. However, there is some doubt over whether Britain fits this pattern since the relevant coefficients from Dalton's empirical models fail to achieve statistical significance (Dalton, 2004: 94).

This claim about declining political support among affluent, educated, and young individuals has been challenged by other studies that suggest support is higher, not lower, among people benefitting from the political system. In particular, levels of trust have been found to be significantly lower among economically disadvantaged individuals than among their more affluent counterparts (Miller and Borrelli, 1991; Patterson, 1999; Zmerli, 2012; Brandt, 2013; OECD, 2022: section 3.1).[2] We also saw some evidence of this for Britain in the data presented in the previous chapter (see Table 4.1).

To investigate whether declines in trust have been concentrated among the economic and educational 'haves' or 'have nots', I adopt a similar analytical approach to that used by Dalton. Within each population sub-group of interest, I identify levels of trust stretching back over the past thirty to forty years.[3] For each category within the population sub-group, I express levels of trust as the deviation (positive or negative) from the mean figure for the overall population. This way, the data capture how levels of trust for each category have changed *relative to the population as a whole.*

I begin with education, where I divide the population into two key groups: those with no qualifications and those with university degree-level qualifications.[4] In Figure 5.1, I plot the deviation from mean trust for each of these groups over the period 1973–2017. We can see that at any one point in time, those holding university degrees (denoted by the grey dots) tend to be more trusting than those with no qualifications (denoted by the black dots). The key result, however, is that the gap between the two has increased over time. This can be seen in the two fitted trend lines, which show how, over time, degree holders have become more trusting relative to the population as a whole, while those holding no qualifications have become less trusting.[5]

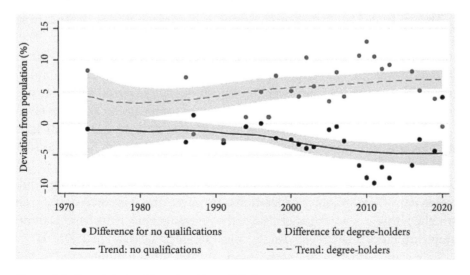

Figure 5.1 Trends in trust by education—Britain

Trend lines using a polynomial smoother. Shaded areas show 95% confidence intervals.
Source: Protest, Dissatisfaction and Change; British Social Attitudes

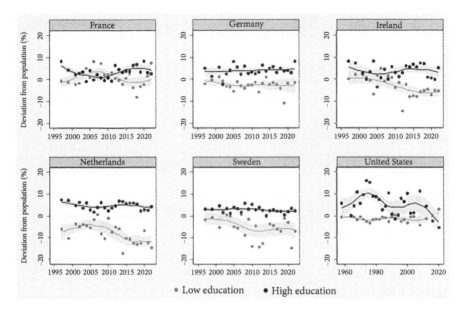

Figure 5.2 Trends in trust by education—selected countries
Source: Eurobarameter, ANES

A growing educational divide in trust is also apparent in other Western European countries. Figure 5.2 shows a similar pattern to that identified in Britain among populations in France (at least until very recently), Germany, Ireland, the Netherlands, and Sweden.[6] The one country where the decline in trust has not been concentrated among low educated citizens is the United States, where the decline of trust has been more marked among people educated to college level than among people educated to below college level.

Growing trust divides are not limited to education, but also extend to individuals' economic status. To show this, I draw on various economic indicators fielded on the British Social Attitudes (BSA) survey, notably self-reported household income, social class, and economic feelings.[7] For each indicator, I distinguish between high economic status individuals (income: the highest tercile income group; social class: those holding a salariat or professional occupation; economic feelings: those reporting living 'really comfortably' or 'comfortably' on their present income) and low economic status individuals (income: the bottom tercile income group; social class: members of the working class; economic feelings: those reporting 'struggling' or 'really struggling' on their present income). The deviations from mean levels of trust across the population for low and high economic status individuals are shown in Figure 5.3.

Trust: How Citizens View Political Institutions

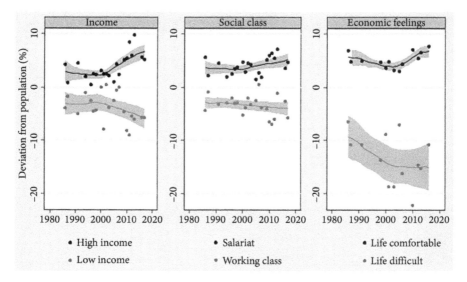

Figure 5.3 Trends in trust by economic status
Source: British Social Attitudes

The results show that levels of trust among high economic status individuals are greater than among low economic status individuals. Moreover, over time, high economic status individuals have become more trusting relative to the population as a whole, while low economic status individuals have become relatively less trusting.

Finally, what evidence is there that declining rates of trust might reflect 'generational effects'? Dalton has shown that in the United States, levels of trust among recent generations have fallen faster than those among older generations. When the 'baby boomers' of the 1950s came of age in the 1970s, Dalton showed they were more trusting in government than were previous generations. Yet he found more recent age cohorts to be less trusting than their older counterparts (2004: 91–94).

To explore the dynamics of trust among different age groups and age cohorts in Britain, I report data collected across nine time-points between 1973 and 2020. For each time-point, I show mean levels of trust averaged across five-year age groups (starting with those aged 18–22 years, then those aged 23–27 years, and so on). The results are presented in Table 5.1. The next to bottom row ('Mean') shows the decline in levels of trust across the population, from an average of 2.27 in 1973 to an average of 1.99 in 2020. Within each year (reading down each column), older age groups are usually more trusting than younger age groups. The bottom row ('Age gap') captures how

Why has trust declined? 103

Table 5.1 Levels of trust, by year and age cohort

	1973	1986	1991	1996	2001	2006	2011	2016	2020
Age									
18–22	2.08	2.23	2.08	2.08	2.15	1.85	1.96	2.15	1.80
23–27	2.25	2.27	2.27	2.01	2.03	1.94	1.94	1.79	1.94
28–32	2.31	2.26	2.17	1.93	1.98	1.82	1.95	1.97	1.78
33–37	2.26	2.36	2.28	1.90	2.15	1.95	1.90	2.01	1.91
38–42	2.33	2.28	2.26	1.93	2.08	1.84	1.93	1.89	1.87
43–47	2.27	2.28	2.23	1.95	2.11	1.90	1.82	1.93	1.88
48–52	2.26	2.46	2.25	2.05	1.96	1.64	1.84	1.82	1.98
53–57	2.23	2.36	2.25	1.97	2.02	1.72	1.89	1.98	2.04
58–62	2.24	2.45	2.32	1.99	2.06	1.81	1.78	2.01	2.03
63–67	2.37	2.15	2.42	2.21	2.17	1.87	1.92	1.87	2.05
68–72	2.35	2.40	2.17	1.96	2.09	1.89	1.80	1.97	2.14
73+	2.49	2.43	2.27	2.17	2.24	1.98	1.88	2.02	2.21
Mean	2.27	2.32	2.23	2.01	2.10	1.85	1.88	1.95	1.99
Age gap*	+0.26	+0.17	+0.05	+0.02	+0.08	+0.04	−0.11	+0.03	+0.30

Figures show mean levels of trust (4pt scale: 1=low trust 4=high trust)
* 'Age gap' is, for each survey year, the summed trust score for the two oldest age groups minus the summed trust score for the two youngest age groups, divided by 2.
Minimum number of respondents for any cell = 40
Source: 1973: Protest, Dissatisfaction and Change survey; thereafter: British Social Attitudes surveys.

much more trusting the oldest two age groups are than the youngest two age groups. The figures show that with some exceptions (notably 1973 and 2020), the age gap in trust is small.

The data provide little evidence of a decline in trust arising from the replacement of older age cohorts by newer ones. Take, for example, people born in the late 1940s and early 1950s, who came of political age in the early 1970s (and are represented in the 1973 survey by the 18–22 and 23–27 age groups). Reading along the rows, we can see that levels of trust among these cohorts are similar to those among more recent cohorts, up to 2006 and 2011 when levels of trust among the newest age cohorts fall away. But this is hardly evidence of a cohort effect (nor does it help to explain earlier declines in trust, in the mid-1990s for example). This can be seen more clearly if we trace the progress of different age cohorts over time (by reading the cells diagonally from top-left to bottom-right). Take people born in the early 1950s, for example (denoted by the light grey-shaded boxes). Individuals in this group were aged 18–22 in 1973 and showed a mean level of trust in that year of 2.08. By 1986, individuals in this group were now in their early-mid-30s and showed a level of trust of 2.36. By the end of the time period, in 2020, individuals in this cohort were in their mid-late 60s. At this point, their level of trust had fallen to 2.14. Or take an earlier age cohort, those born in the 1930s (denoted by the dark grey-shaded boxes). In 1973, this cohort was aged 38–42 and showed a mean level of trust of 2.33. By 2006, the mean level of trust for this group—now in their early-mid-80s—had fallen to 1.98.

Hence even among older cohorts who came of age holding high levels of trust, their experience of politics over time has served to depress previously rosy views of government. The declines in trust seen in the mid-1990s and 2000s can be observed among the older age cohorts as much as among the younger cohorts. There is little evidence of the generational effects that Dalton identifies in the United States. Instead, in Britain, the trends over time are more consistent with 'period effects', in which particular events induce a change in attitudes across the population. A similar picture—stressing the role of period effects over generational effects—has also been identified in studies of trust in other western countries (on the United States, see Twenge, Campbell, and Carter, 2014; on the Netherlands, see van der Brug and van Praag, 2007; on Italy, see Segatti, 2006; on Switzerland, see Widmer and de Carlo, 2010; across Western Europe, see Dustmann et al., 2017 and Wuttke, Gavras, and Schoen, 2022; on Australia, see Dassonneville and McAllister, 2021).[8] There is thus convincing evidence that declines in trust across the population are not triggered by the replacement of older generations by younger ones as much as by particular events and experiences that affect all age groups alike.

This section has shown how the overall decline of trust among the population has been particularly pronounced among certain social groups. While not the case for different age cohorts, there is clear evidence for such an effect among individuals in different socio-economic groups. In particular, there has been a particularly sharp decline in trust among poorer and less educated individuals, opening up a growing trust gap between the socio-economic 'haves' and 'have nots'.

5.2 The role of political beliefs and engagement

People's willingness to trust their political rulers is shaped by various perceptions and evaluations of those rulers and the institutions they inhabit. The range and effects of these beliefs are explored more systematically in Chapter 6. The focus here is on whether some of these beliefs might help explain not only whether an individual trusts a political actor at a particular point in time but also whether they explain changes in trust and more specifically the decline in levels of trust in Britain over the past few decades.

The beliefs and behaviours explored in this section are confined to those for which there exist suitable data extending back over time, and for which we can thus explore relationships with the dynamics of trust. These beliefs and behaviours fall into four camps:

1. Appraisals of how well the government is performing and expectations of what governments should deliver.
2. The degree of policy representation offered by political representatives to citizens.
3. The provision of information to citizens via the media.
4. The degree to which citizens are engaged with politics.

Government performance and expectations

People's trust in government is likely to be strongly shaped by how effectively governments are seen to deliver desired social outcomes. Readers interested in the nature of these performance perceptions, and the evidence from prior studies on their effects, are directed to the more extensive discussion in Chapter 6, Section 6.2. Here, I simply review how far perceptions of government performance might help us understand the decline of trust over the past four or more decades.

In 1973, 85 per cent of the British population judged government provision of medical care to be 'good' or 'very good'.[9] By 2002, the proportion judging the government to be 'very successful' or 'quite successful' in providing good healthcare for all citizens had fallen to 36 per cent, although this figure subsequently increased to 52 per cent in 2006, 59 per cent in 2012, and 60 per cent in 2016.[10] When it comes to looking after the elderly, 67 per cent evaluated government performance as effective in 1973, while by 2002, only 21 per cent felt the same. Again, assessments of performance rebounded more recently, with 29 per cent of people providing positive assessments of government performance on elderly care in 2006, 31 per cent in 2012, and 40 per cent in 2016. Thus, over the past four or more decades, there is evidence that people's appraisals of government performance have declined, although by no means in a linear fashion.

Not only have people become more critical of government performance, but the relationship between performance appraisals and trust has strengthened. The correlation between trust and evaluations of government performance on health was a modest 0.17 in 1973 but a rather stronger 0.29 in 2006 and 0.25 in 2016.[11] Thus, not only do people assess government performance more negatively than they did in the past, but these negative assessments appear to contribute more strongly to their judgements of trust.

Are today's governments also labouring under the pressures of higher popular expectations of what they should deliver? Earlier, we saw the argument made by Dalton that trust has declined principally among social groups whose expectations of politics outrun the system's ability to deliver. More generally, it has been argued that citizens expect more of their elected representatives today than in the past. Faced with these demands, and with more complex and tricky policy issues to resolve, governments almost inevitably fall short, resulting in widespread popular disappointment and distrust (Norris, 2011; Hardin, 2013).

One way of interrogating such claims is by examining trends in people's expectations of government. To do so, I draw on the BSA which, since 1985, has included questions measuring people's support for the government taking responsibility for providing jobs, healthcare, care for the elderly, and support for the unemployed. The distributions reported in Figure 5.4 (which shows the proportions who say it 'should definitely be' the government's responsibility to provide these services) show that public expectations of government are higher when it comes to the provision of adequate healthcare and elderly care than for the provision of jobs and a decent standard of living for the unemployed. Yet on all these areas of government responsibility,

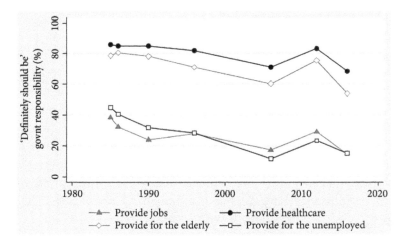

Figure 5.4 Public expectations of government, 1985–2016
Source: British Social Attitudes

expectations have declined somewhat over the past thirty years. On these measures, at least, the public seems rather less, not more, demanding of government today.[12]

To explore any changes in the relationship between trust and what people expect of government, I draw on the BSA question about government responsibility to provide jobs for all who want them. I contrast people who say this 'definitely should be' the government's responsibility (capturing high expectations) and those who say this should 'probably' or 'definitely not' be the government's responsibility (capturing low expectations).[13] Mean levels of trust among people with high or low expectations are presented in Figure 5.5. The figures show that among people holding high expectations of government, trust levels are usually lower than among people whose expectations of government are more modest. This fits with the hypothesis that high expectations are corrosive of trust. But over time, as the fitted trend lines show, levels of trust have declined almost as much among people holding low expectations as among people holding high expectations. There is little evidence here that inflated expectations of government have contributed to declining rates of trust.

Measuring expectations solely in terms of desired policy outcomes may, however, represent a rather narrow approach. There is evidence that when it comes to politicians' personal qualities and features, people are more demanding today than they were in the past. Using Mass Observation data, Clarke et al. (2018: 207–209) argue that people today expect politicians to

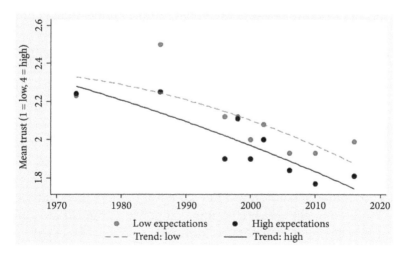

Figure 5.5 Trends in trust, by expectations of government

Source: Protest, Dissatisfaction and Change; British Social Attitudes

be more representative of them than did their predecessors in the 1950s. In that earlier period, the authors suggest, people primarily looked to politicians to serve their interests. Today, however, people also expect politicians to be 'normal' and 'in touch'. Politicians are therefore judged on how *like* or *of* the people they are, not just on whether they deliver *for* the people. Expectations may thus be important for feelings of trust, not so much in terms of what people expect politicians to do but in terms of what they expect politicians to be.

Policy representation

Politics concerns not only whether governments provide citizens with appropriate policy outputs but also how closely politicians represent citizens' views. The decline over time in levels of trust may thus arise from changes in how well the political system represents, or is seen to represent, citizens' opinions. There are various ways we can test the impact of policy representation on trust and to assess whether this impact has changed over time.

We can start by distinguishing the different types of policy preference held by individuals. Some individuals hold centrist or moderate preferences, while other people hold more radical or extreme views. The majoritarian political system in Britain is widely believed to encourage politicians and parties to crowd into the centre of the political spectrum to attract votes (Dow, 2001). This leaves individuals holding more distinctive views to be less closely represented, and thus to be less trusting in politicians and governments.

To test levels and trends of trust among people falling outside the political centre or mainstream, we can draw on the Protest, Dissatisfaction and Change survey from 1973 (which included a question asking respondents to self-position on a ten-point left–right scale) and the BSA from 1986 (which carried questions measuring people's attitudes to inequality and redistribution).[14] Policy extremity is captured by people locating at the ends of the left–right scale (1973) and by people strongly agreeing or disagreeing with the ideology statements (1986 onwards). The 10–20 per cent of the samples located at each end of the scale are taken as holding extreme views, while the remaining 80–90 per cent of the samples are taken as moderates. Mean levels of trust for each group are shown in Figure 5.6. In more than half the time-points captured by the surveys, we find that policy extremists are more, not less, trusting than policy moderates. Moreover, trust declines equally among both groups. There is no evidence here that even in a political system like Britain, declining rates of trust reflect negative judgements among people holding ideologically distinctive or extreme views.

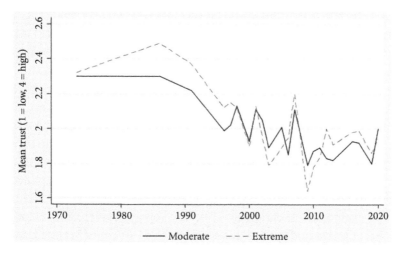

Figure 5.6 Trends in trust, by policy positions
Source: Protest, Dissatisfaction and Change; British Social Attitudes

While majoritarian political systems might incentivize politicians to cleave to the centre of the political spectrum and to represent the 'median voter', even citizens holding moderate political views may feel unrepresented by politicians and political parties. To explore the link between feelings of policy representation and trust, I draw on survey data that measure voters' own preferences on the balance between government taxation and spending and the policy positions they attribute to the two main parties: the Conservatives and Labour. Surveys conducted by the British Election Study (BES) in 1997, 2005, 2010, 2015, 2017, and 2019 asked people to place themselves on a scale anchored at one end by the option 'government should cut taxes a lot and spend much less on health and social services' and at the other end by the option 'government should raise taxes a lot and spend much more on health and social services'. By identifying where respondents position themselves and where they position each of the two parties, we can calculate the distance between voters' ideal points and the points they locate each of the two main parties at. The greater the distance, the lower the degree of policy representation.

Using these measures, we find that in 1997, levels of policy representation were fairly low, largely because the Conservatives were seen as being located well away from the average voter's ideal point. From 2005, levels of policy representation declined yet further. Measured on an 11-point scale, the distance between voters and the Conservative party increased from 2.02 points in 2005 to 2.65 points in 2015, and to 3.24 points in 2017, before narrowing to 2.66 points in 2019. The distance to Labour increased from 1.51 points in 2005 to 2.13 points in 2015 before declining to 2.08 points in 2017 and 2019. Over the past two decades, then, citizens in Britain have generally seen themselves as less well represented by the two main political parties.

Moreover, gaps in political representation are negatively associated with people's trust. In Figure 5.7, I show levels of trust (trust in government in 1997; trust in politicians thereafter) for each survey, broken down by the size of the representation gap.[15] For each year, as the representation gap increases, levels of trust are lower. The patterns are particularly noticeable in 2015 and 2017, when trust falls away more sharply as the representation gap increases.

These findings comport with those from other studies on the association between trust and perceived policy representation and responsiveness. Quantitative and qualitative analyses from Britain (Brandenburg and Johns, 2014; Osuna, Kiefel, and Katsouyanni, 2021) and countries like the United States (Cramer, 2016; Wuthnow, 2018: chapter 4) and the Netherlands (Noordzij, de Koster, and van der Waal, 2021a) have shown that low trust among many citizens stems from perceptions that their interests and identities are being ignored or passed over by political elites.

Politicians are often acutely aware of such perceptions, and in many cases have made efforts to close the representation gap. In the Netherlands, for example, MPs have been asked on various occasions whether their decisions should be guided by what voters want or by what they, personally, think is the right thing to do. In 1972, the overwhelming majority (71 per cent) of

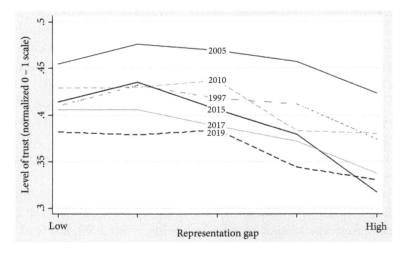

Figure 5.7 Levels of trust, by representation gap
Source: British Election Study

MPs believed they should be guided by their own judgement, while just 7 per cent felt they should follow voters' wishes. By 2006, the proportion of MPs favouring their own judgement had fallen to 49 per cent and the proportion privileging voters' views had risen to 19 per cent (Thomassen, 2013: 18). If this survey was repeated today, I suspect the swing towards privileging voters' views would be even greater.

Not only have many politicians attempted to represent voters more closely, many have also succeeded. A second study in the Netherlands has shown that the difference between the policy preferences of voters and of MPs has narrowed since the 1970s. Whether this outcome has arisen because unrepresentative MPs have been voted out of office or because MPs have become more sensitive to public preferences, the 'congruence' between voters and politicians has increased over the past four decades.[16] Yet, at the same time, the Dutch public has become more, not less, critical of politicians (Andeweg, 2011). It appears that perceived representation has not kept step with Dutch MPs' efforts and that these perceptions shape trust rather more than the reality.

Media coverage

A part of any negativity felt by citizens towards political actors may reflect the information about politics they receive. Much of this information is derived from the media, and it is often suggested that the media's negative content and tone—in denigrating politicians and highlighting their foibles and follies—serve to depress people's feelings of trust (Cappella and Jamieson, 1996). The coverage of politics in British newspapers has been shown to be particularly negative compared to that of newspapers in other countries.[17] Accordingly, we might anticipate that people's exposure to the media, particularly to newspapers, will be an important factor in accounting for declining rates of trust. However, previous empirical studies have found little evidence of such an effect (Norris, 2011; chapter 9; Newton, 2019: chapter 8).[18]

To explore the effects of media exposure, I compare rates of trust among readers both of upmarket or 'broadsheet' newspapers and of downmarket or 'tabloid' newspapers, in both cases relative to rates of trust among people who report not reading a newspaper at all.[19] I present the results in the form either of a positive differential (where broadsheet or tabloid readers are more trusting than people who do not read newspapers) or a negative differential (where broadsheet or tabloid readers are less trusting than people who do not read newspapers).[20] The results—presented in Figure 5.8—show two things.

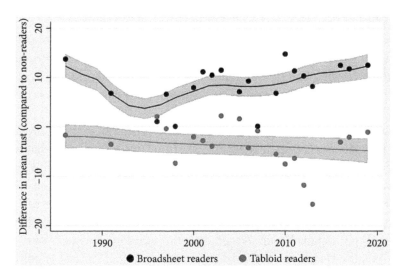

Figure 5.8 Differences in trust, by newspaper readership
Source: British Social Attitudes

First, levels of trust are mostly lower among tabloid readers than among people who do not read newspapers (reflected in difference scores in most years of lower than zero). Second, this negative differential with trust has increased somewhat over time, as shown by the slightly downward sloping (polynomial) best-fit line. Among readers of broadsheet newspapers, by contrast, the best-fit line slopes upwards in a positive direction. Thus, compared to people who are not exposed to newspapers on a regular basis, readers of broadsheet titles have become rather more trusting over time. But among people who are exposed to tabloid news coverage, levels of trust have declined slightly.

Political engagement

Might levels of trust in politicians have declined because people are no longer as concerned or engaged with politics as they once were? This is a tricky question to answer, as it is not easy to identify indicators tapping the relevance or importance of politics for citizens. A surrogate, if somewhat basic, indicator is people's reported interest in politics. Based on this measure, people's engagement with politics appears to be increasing, not decreasing. Data from the BSA show that levels of political interest have slightly increased since 1986.[21] In Figure 5.9, I plot mean levels of trust among people who, when asked about

Why has trust declined? 113

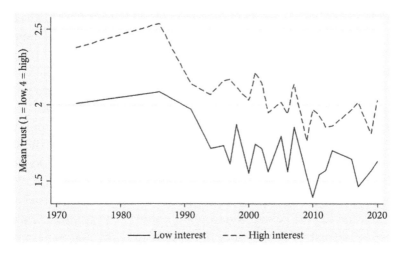

Figure 5.9 Trends in trust, by interest in politics
Source: Protest, Dissatisfaction and Change; British Social Attitudes

their interest in politics, report either 'a great deal' (signifying high interest) or 'none at all' (signifying low interest). Unsurprisingly, people who profess an interest in politics manifest higher rates of trust than people who profess no interest. But the trends over time among the two groups are fairly similar; declining levels of trust are not concentrated only among people with little interest in politics. Hence, at least as measured by political interest, there is scant evidence that trust is declining in Britain because people are disengaged from politics.

5.3 Modelling the impact of demographic and political factors

So far, we have considered how far declining levels of trust can be explained by individuals' demographic characteristics and socio-economic status, their evaluations and expectations of government policy performance, their assessments of policy representation by political parties, their exposure to the media, and their general engagement with politics. To identify the effects of these factors when considered together, I construct a longitudinal multivariate model of trust. This involves pooling data across various waves of the BSA survey between 1986 and 2016.[22] Since the BSA does not include measures of each factor across different surveys, the model of trust only includes variables measuring individuals' demographic characteristics and socio-economic status, their expectations of government delivery, the extremity of their policy position, their exposure to the media, and their levels of political interest.

To begin with, I simply model the effects of time on trust, via the inclusion of a set of year or time variables (full results from the models are provided in Appendix 5.2). The coefficients for the time variables are all negative, reflecting the fact that trust has declined since 1986. The second model includes individuals' cohort or age. Compared to those born at the start of the twentieth century (the 1900s–1920s), those born in the middle decades (the 1940s–1960s) manifest significantly lower rates of trust. Among people born more recently (the 1970s onwards), however, rates of trust are no lower. Reinforcing the conclusion from the cohort analysis presented above, the decline of trust in Britain does not appear to reflect the replacement of older 'deferential' age cohorts by younger 'cynical' age cohorts.

The third model includes measures tapping people's socio-economic status. When it comes to education, the results show lower rates of trust among people with no formal educational qualifications relative to people with university degrees. In the case of economic status, the results show lower rates of trust among economically hard-pressed individuals (those saying they are 'struggling' on their household income) than among their economically stable counterparts (those saying they are 'comfortable' on their household income).[23] The key question is whether—as suggested in Figures 5.1 and 5.3—the relationship between socio-economic position and trust has changed over time. To assess this, I include in the fourth model interaction terms that enable us to identify the dynamic (i.e. over time) effect on trust of economic feelings and education levels. A negative coefficient on these interaction terms signifies that the core group is getting less trusting over time relative to the reference category; a positive coefficient signifies that the core group is getting relatively more trusting (Firebaugh, 1997: 43–63).

The results show significant negative interaction terms for both economic feelings and education. This suggests that people who are economically struggling and people with low educational qualifications have become less trusting over time than their economically comfortable and educationally well-qualified counterparts, even when period and generational effects are taken into account. These dynamic patterns can be seen in Figure 5.10, which shows how levels of trust have fallen particularly sharply among those struggling to cope economically and among the poorly educated.[24]

We can use the same technique to assess whether changes in trust over time are associated with the extremity of people's policy views, their level

Why has trust declined? 115

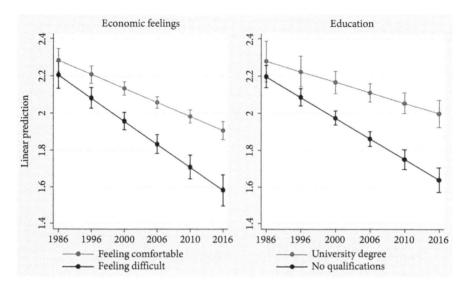

Figure 5.10 Impact of economic feelings and education on trust over time
Source: Figures derived from Model 4, Appendix 5.2

of interest in politics, their newspaper readership, and their expectations of government. The results appear as the fifth model in Appendix 5.2. Note that the inclusion of these factors serves to eliminate the significant associations with trust of both time and generation. Thus, the features that made people born in decades from the 1940s onwards less trusting of government than their older predecessors appear to reflect individual differences in political interest, expectations of government, and media exposure.

In turn, lacking interest in politics and holding high expectations of government are associated with low rates of trust. However, neither of these factors (nor holding politically extreme views) shapes the dynamics of trust over the period; for each of these factors, the interaction with the time variable does not reach statistical significance. There is a hint that people's exposure to certain media forms might have contributed to the decline in trust. The interaction coefficients for newspaper readership suggest that readers of 'middle market' and 'tabloid' newspapers have become less trusting over time relative to people who do not read a newspaper. However, these effects are not strong, as can be seen from Figure 5.11, which shows how readers of tabloid newspapers have gone from holding very slightly higher rates of trust than non-newspaper readers at the start of the period to holding very slightly lower rates of trust at the end of the period.[25]

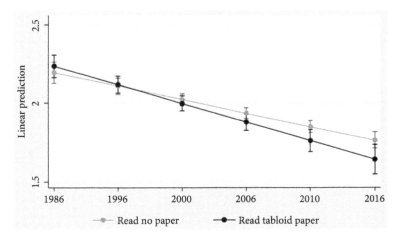

Figure 5.11 Impact of newspaper readership on trust over time
Source: Figures derived from Model 5, Appendix 5.2

5.4 Conclusion

The principal conclusion of this analysis of changes in trust among the British population over the past four or more decades is that declining public regard for political actors is concentrated among society's 'have nots' rather than among its 'haves'. As noted earlier, Dalton (2004) argues—on the back of data from the United States and other advanced democracies—that declining rates of trust reflect more critical attitudes primarily among affluent and well-educated citizens. The results presented here tell a different story. They show that the decline in trust has primarily taken place among people who are struggling economically and who lack formal educational qualifications.[26] Falling levels of trust in Britain can partly be explained by people at the economic margins no longer believing that politicians and the political system are providing for them or representing their interests (see also Thomassen, 2015).

Concluding his analysis of the way that social changes in western societies have contributed to a diminishing popular respect for politicians, Dalton (2004: 96) observes:

> democracies are not losing support from those at the margins of politics, but from the young, better-educated and upper-status citizens who have benefited most from social progress.

Dalton's claim is theoretically plausible and appears to be confirmed by data from the United States. However, as shown here, the evidence from Britain—and from other Western European countries (as shown in Figure 5.2)—suggests the opposite conclusion. The decline in trust has been concentrated primarily among less economically and educationally advantaged individuals within society. Citizens endowed with economic and educational resources may trust government today rather less than they used to. But their trust has dwindled at a slower rate than people at the economic and social margins.[27]

At the same time, declining public trust also reflects a set of attitudes and beliefs among British citizens. Drawing on the best sources of longitudinal data, we have found little support for the idea that trust has declined because people today expect more of their government than they did in the past, because politicians are failing to represent people with more radical views than theirs, or because politics is less important to people today than it used to be. Instead, trust appears to have declined because people are more critical of government performance and feel that political parties are less representative of their policy preferences and views. These findings provide clues about which elements of political life might shape citizens' judgements of trust. To go beyond such clues, and to identify more fully what kind of appraisals shape citizens' trust, is the central task of the next chapter.

6
Why do citizens trust (or not)?

The clues about the sources of individuals' trust provided in the previous chapter arose from longitudinal data collected over a forty- to fifty-year period. While such data are valuable in helping us to understand why levels of trust might have changed over time, there are plenty of potential determinants of trust that are not covered by good longitudinal data. We often lack extensive survey measures stretching back in time that enable us to gauge people's evaluations of how government has performed and how political actors have behaved. This limits our abilities to appraise a wide range of evaluations and to determine their relevance for people's feelings of trust. However, fuller sets of measures are often available at particular points in time—because a more extensive and detailed survey has been conducted—providing opportunities for a fuller analysis of the causes of trust. This chapter examines what such data tell us about the sources of trust in Britain.

The analysis that follows is devoted to two key tasks. The first is to identify as comprehensively as possible the types of consideration that individuals draw on when deciding whether a political actor is worthy or not of trust. As shown in previous chapters, trust is a broad judgement that potentially encapsulates a number of considerations. The first part of this chapter identifies these considerations and assesses the contribution of each to individual judgements of trust. A second task is to explore uniformities and differences in these relationships. Existing studies often suggest that trust reflects a particular set of considerations, without exploring whether these considerations are consistent across different objects of trust, different individuals making trust judgements, and different points of time at which trust judgements are formed. Yet the considerations people draw on in making trust judgements might well vary depending on the object under evaluation, the nature of the trustee, and the time-point or context in which that evaluation is taking place. The sources of trust may thus show important variations as well as consistencies.

6.1 What shapes trust?

Judgements about whether or not to trust an actor or institution potentially call on a wide range of evaluatory criteria. In identifying such criteria, we can draw on studies conducted not only in political science but also in academic disciplines such as psychology, sociology, risk studies, management, and business and information studies. To provide some order to the numerous criteria for trust identified in these studies, we can organize them under various broad headings (see Figure 6.1). One fairly basic feature suggests that individuals are likely to trust an actor if the decisions they make fit with their personal preferences or values. Alongside the substance of a decision, trust may also be responsive to its distributional qualities. Thus, trust is likely to be forthcoming if an actor's decision is seen to represent a fair distribution of benefits across affected parties. Moreover, trust is likely to be shaped not only by what an actor delivers but also by the way they operate, for example, how fair their decision-making procedures and processes are seen to be.

At a very general level, then, we might distinguish between three broad considerations in judgements of trust, namely the perceived *outcomes*, *distributive justice*, and *procedural qualities* (notably fairness) of a decision-maker (Tyler, Rasinski, and Griffin, 1986; Tyler, 1988; Brockner and Wiesenfeld, 1996).[1] Trust judgements may reflect evaluations of relevant decision-making outcomes particularly in situations where an individual 'wins' or 'loses' from a policy decision, or holds strong opinions about the issue involved. Hence trust in a public organization responsible for a significant policy issue (e.g. the siting of a nuclear facility) is likely to reflect an

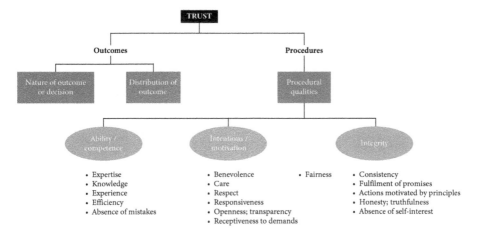

Figure 6.1 Typology of factors shaping trust judgements

individual's attitudes on that issue (in this case, their beliefs about the merits, or dangers, of nuclear power). Where evaluations of trust lack a substantive reference, however, considerations about outcomes may be less important and perceptions of procedural qualities—fairness, for example—may become more important (Tyler, Rasinski, and Griffin, 1986: 975; Brockner and Wiesenfeld, 1996: 189–190; Earle, 2004).

Another important distinction when it comes to trust is between a decision-maker's concern with an individual's interests, on the one hand, and their competence to act on those interests, on the other. This reflects a basic distinction in the way people form impressions of others, involving perceptions either of an object's warmth or of their competence (Fiske and Durante, 2014). Similarly, trust is often seen to reflect evaluations of an actor's *intentions* and of their *abilities* (Johnson, 1999; Hardin, 2002, 2006; Levi and Stoker, 2000: 476; Colquitt, Scott, and LePine, 2007; Earle, 2010). Other studies have added a third broad antecedent of trust, namely *integrity* (Mayer, Davis, and Schoorman, 1995; PytlikZillig et al., 2016).[2] Although these three antecedents of trust overlap to some extent (e.g. an actor's virtuous intentions share some features with their integrity), they also are held to provide distinctive foundations for trust.

Within each of these three broad criteria, a set of more specific factors may be employed by citizens in assessing an actor's trustworthiness (Butler, 1991; Mayer, Davis, and Schoorman, 1995; McKnight and Chervany, 1996; Johnson, 1999; Colquitt, Scott, and LePine, 2007; Earle, 2010; McEvily and Tortoriello, 2011).[3] Within the criterion of *ability* or *competence*, citizens may assess an actor's expertise or knowledge, along with their experience, efficiency, and avoidance of mistakes. Within the criterion of *intentions*, citizens may assess the extent to which an actor is deemed to be benevolent, caring, and respectful of other people's interests. Within the criterion of *integrity*, citizens may assess whether an actor behaves in a manner consistent with their promises and in conformity with suitable ethical principles. In the following sections, I use this threefold typology to identify what the extensive and multidisciplinary empirical literature tells us about the sources of trust.

6.2 What do we know about the sources of trust?

Competence

It is often assumed that people will trust politicians if they deliver the outputs that citizens desire. Trust as a bond between citizens and governments—the former entrusting the latter with powers to act on their behalf—involves judgements about whether governments are responsive to citizens' needs and capable of delivering the demanded level of economic, political, and social outputs. Hence it is suggested that people are likely to evaluate political actors against their delivery of desired outcomes.

Analyses of the impact of government performance on trust have typically taken one of two forms. The first measures performance in objective terms, and considers whether citizens in political units marked by high levels of economic and social performance are more trusting of governments than their counterparts in units marked by low levels of performance. The second measures performance in subjective terms, and considers whether citizens who perceive economic and social performance to be good are more trusting than citizens who perceive performance to be poor.

In objective terms, studies have shown a positive link between countries' levels of economic development and aggregate levels of trust and democratic satisfaction among national populations (Weatherford, 1987; Wessels, 2009; Norris, 2011: chapter 10; Armingeon and Guthmann, 2014; van Erkel and van der Meer, 2016). Analyses using longitudinal data suggest that changes in economic conditions (such as rates of GDP growth and unemployment) have a significant impact on people's evaluations of political actors (Patterson and Caldeira, 1990; Bellucci and Memoli, 2012; Martini and Quaranta, 2020: 115–123). Subjective measures of government performance have also been found to correlate closely with measures of political trust. Studies have shown a strong relationship between trust and individual perceptions of their own, or of their country's, economic situation (Citrin and Green, 1986; Keele, 2007; Whiteley et al., 2013: 260–266; Magalhães, 2016).[4] Trust has also been found to be shaped by government performance in areas other than the economy. Thus, changes in levels of trust in the United States during the 1980s and 1990s have been linked to changing perceptions of government performance on issues like crime (Chanley, Rudolph, and Rahn, 2000). Other studies have also shown a strong association between individuals' trust and their assessments of government performance on issues like education and health (Grönlund and Setala, 2012; Kestillä-Kekkonen and Söderlund, 2015).

Yet the relationship between trust and economic evaluations is sometimes found to be limited. Using individual-level data, Dalton (2004: 115–125) shows the relationship between economic evaluations and trust to be modest. Thus, peaks and troughs in people's feelings of economic confidence are not strongly related to changes in people's trust in government. Popular reluctance to trust elected officials even during periods of economic optimism can be seen in data collected in the United States from the late 1970s. These data show the proportion of people who report trusting the national government alongside the proportion of people reporting satisfaction with the state of the country. During periods of economic boom, such as the mid-1980s and the late-1990s, people sometimes felt positively about the state of the country without this optimism translating into higher rates of trust in government (Pew Center, 2015: 25). Comparative analyses also suggest that variations in economic conditions between countries are sometimes only weakly associated with differences in levels of trust (van der Meer and Hakhverdian, 2017). This may be because people do not always attribute responsibility for economic outcomes to politicians; blaming government for bad economic times or rewarding them for good ones (Citrin and Green, 1986). Indeed, some scholars have suggested that citizens in rich countries are more demanding of politicians, and so less likely to trust governments even when the countries they rule over are performing well compared to other, poorer, states (McAllister, 1999).

Going beyond government performance, how far is trust affected by perceptions of politicians' competence and ability? Some studies have suggested that people are prone to trust government when they believe that officials are 'smart' and 'know what they are doing' and less likely to trust government when they view officials' competence more negatively (Ulbig, 2002). Studies conducted by psychologists have also shown that people trust institutions if key personnel are seen as competent, for example, by having relevant experience or a track record of providing accurate information (Terwel et al., 2009). People may also form trust judgements on the back of assessments of efficiency; levels of trust have been found to be particularly low where governments are deemed to be inefficient and wasteful of public funds (Hetherington, 2005: 16–35; see also Owen and Dennis, 2001).

However, there is some doubt about how far trust is shaped by perceptions of actors' abilities and competence. For a start, studies show that politicians are often rated quite highly on their competence; it is other aspects of their performance—for example, their benevolence or integrity—where public ratings tend to be lower (Fiske and Durante, 2014). We can see this among British citizens by drawing on the sample collected from the online crowdsourcing platform Prolific Academic described in Chapter 3. This sample completed a survey which included various statements tapping people's evaluations of politicians' competence, benevolence, and integrity. Summing the responses to each into single scales (where 1 = negative evaluations and 6 = positive evaluations), we find that citizens rate politicians' competence more highly (mean = 2.89) than their benevolence (mean = 2.63) which, in turn, is rated more highly than their integrity (mean = 2.50).

Studies of citizens in the United States show similar results. A study conducted in 2015 found Americans to believe that the key fault of elected officials lay less in their competence than in their honesty. When asked about the traits of various groups of people, 67 per cent of the sample labelled elected officials as 'intelligent', the same proportion as for the typical American, although a little lower than the proportion for business leaders. However, politicians were rated more negatively on 'honesty', where just 29 per cent of elected officials were seen to possess this trait, against 45 per cent for business leaders and 69 per cent for the typical American (Pew Center, 2015: 75). When the same respondents were asked about the major problem with national politicians, their most frequent gripes related to a lack of responsiveness to the public (politicians were instead seen to be influenced by interest groups, to care primarily about their own careers, and to be out of touch with ordinary citizens) and to dishonesty; there was less criticism of their competence or their wise use of government funds (Pew Center, 2015: 74). A more recent study by the RAND Corporation found that the feature of the US Congress that respondents identified as most important for judgements of trust was politicians' honesty, followed by their concern with national interests. Politicians' skills and knowledge came a distant third (Kavanagh et al., 2020: 67). In short, politicians appear to attract negative evaluations not so much for their perceived lack of competence but for their perceived lack of integrity and concern with citizens' needs (see also Hibbing and Theiss-Morse, 2002: 109–110; Bertsou, 2019b).

Benevolence or concern

Empirical analyses tend to show that trust is more strongly influenced by people's perceptions of whether politicians are motivated to look after their interests than by perceptions of politicians' competence. Studies conducted in the United States and across various European countries have found that popular discontent primarily reflects feelings that political elites are weakly concerned with, and attuned to, citizens' problems and concerns (Owen and Dennis, 2001; Hibbing and Theiss-Morse, 2002: chapter 3; Farnsworth, 2003; Catterberg and Moreno, 2005; Jones and McDermott, 2010; van Wessel, 2010; Dekker, 2011; PytlikZillig et al., 2016; Noordzij, de Koster, and van der Waal, 2021a).

Using data from surveys of Swedish citizens, Grimes (2006) showed how changes in people's trust of a state institution (the Swedish rail authority) reflected how far they thought that body has taken local people's views into account. An analysis of the law-making process in the United States showed that people's legitimacy assessments were more strongly shaped by perceptions of lawmakers' intentions than by perceptions of the neutrality and representativeness of the decision process (Gangl, 2003). Studies have found that politicians are more trusted, or the objects of greater satisfaction, when they are seen as being aligned, or congruent, with voters' own policy preferences than when they are seen as holding incongruent preferences (in Britain, see Brandenburg and Johns, 2014; for other countries, see Werner, 2016; André and Depauw, 2017).[5] Studies of trust in other public bodies, like the police, also show that public support is heavily dependent on whether those bodies are seen as acting with people's priorities and concerns in mind (van Craen and Skogan, 2015).

Yet if trust is closely associated with judgements about decision-makers' concern with other people, few people perceive politicians to be motivated in this way. Studies in the United States have shown that citizens see politicians as more responsive to the concerns of interest groups than to the concerns of voters (Hibbing and Theiss-Morse, 2002: 95–106, 121–124). Analyses in Britain have similarly found that people distrust politicians because they are seen as motivated by their own goals and ambitions, rather than by the interests of the citizens they serve (Graham et al., 2002). A survey conducted in 2012 found that Britons' low opinions of politicians arose from a perception that MPs did not understand or share the concerns of ordinary people (Wallis, 2012; Wright, 2013). One reason politicians are seen as unresponsive to public concerns might be because they are seen as different to most other citizens. Studies have found that levels of trust in public institutions are higher where the composition of these bodies is seen as representative of the wider population, for example, in terms of their gender balance (Riccucci, Van Ryzin, and Lavena, 2014; see also Arnesen and Peters, 2018). Other studies have shown that satisfaction with democracy is higher when people feel that legislators share the same experiences of crime, public services, and the economy as they do (Allen and Sarmiento-Mirwaldt, 2015). If people feel that public officials look different or experience life differently, to them, the less trusting they seem to be.

Integrity

Most studies exploring the association between citizens' trust and the behaviour of political elites have focused on the role of misconduct or corruption. When these behaviours are measured through perceptual indicators on surveys, an obvious directional issue arises; perceived political misconduct may shape feelings of trust, yet existing feelings of trust may also shape perceived misconduct (Wroe, Allen, and Birch, 2013). Yet studies designed to overcome this chicken-and-egg problem have identified an independent, and causal, effect of political misconduct and lack of probity on trust. Thus, experimental and quasi-experimental studies—which provide conditions in which the effects of misconduct on trust can be more robustly identified—show that people's trust in politicians declines when politicians are presented as behaving dishonestly (Faulkner, Martin, and Peyton, 2015) or when incidents of political corruption are made public (Ares and Hernández, 2017). Levels of trust among individuals also pick up when politicians are presented as acting with probity (Martin et al., 2020). Cross-national and longitudinal studies that employ objective, rather than more problematic subjective, measures of political misconduct similarly find these to correlate fairly well with trust (Chanley, Rudolph, and Rahn, 2000; van der Meer, 2010; van der Meer and Hakhverdian, 2017).[6]

Beyond corruption or misconduct, other ethical qualities of politicians' behaviour may also contribute to popular feelings of trust. One such quality is the extent to which policy decisions are seen to reflect principled, as opposed to partisan, motivations. Public support for decision-makers has been found to be higher when their choices are seen to reflect objective reasoning rather than partial or partisan reasoning (Ramirez, 2008). Acting for partisan reasons also depresses trust compared to acting on constituents' needs (Bøggild, 2020). Similarly, trust has been found to be low if people believe politicians lack principle and engage in ritualistic behaviour—such as point-scoring—while trust has been found to rise when politicians are seen to pursue value-driven goals (Dekker, 2011). Likewise, trust in politicians is lower when politicians are perceived to seek an electoral advantage rather than taking decisions on a more dispassionate basis (Bøggild, 2016). This reflects a pattern that is particularly prominent in the United States, where citizens appear to dislike bickering and conflict between different political parties; public approval of Congress has been shown to decline when the parties are in conflict with one another (e.g. by engaging in heated debate or by voting against one another) and to increase when the parties act more harmoniously and cooperatively (Funk, 2001; Ramirez, 2009; Jones, 2015).[7] In fact, approval of Congress has been found to fall when it engages in its core function—of debating and passing legislation—since this role tends to involve disputes between the parties and conflict with the President (Durr, Gilmour, and Wolbrecht, 1997).

Another feature of politicians' ethical qualities that is important for trust relates to consistency and the keeping of promises. Here, studies—drawing on both quantitative and qualitative data—have shown that people react negatively to politicians when they fail to keep their word and to fulfil their promises (Graham et al., 2002; Naurin, 2011: chapter 6; Rose and Wessels, 2019; Ipsos, 2019: 81). Experimental research in the United States has found that people's trust in political representatives declines if those representatives alter their policy stance as opposed to remaining consistent (Sigelman and Sigelman, 1986; Doherty, Dowling, and Miller, 2016).

One factor that does not fall squarely into any of the three procedural features just outlined (and identified in Figure 6.1)—namely competence, benevolence, and integrity—is fairness. This factor involves a decision-maker treating the views and claims of everyone affected by their decision with equal consideration and weight. Fairness may arise either in relation to the outcome of a decision ('distributive fairness') or to its processes ('procedural fairness'). Numerous studies have shown that people's feelings of trust or satisfaction are shaped by whether they feel a decision-making process is fair or not; indeed, trust is often found to be shaped more by the fairness of the process than by its substantive outcome (Tyler and Caine, 1981; Lind and Tyler, 1988; Esaiasson, 2010; van Ryzin, 2011; Herian et al., 2012).

Summary

An individual's judgement of whether a political actor can be trusted or not is likely to rest on one or more of three broad bases: (i) whether the actor is deemed *competent*, (ii) whether the actor is perceived as *concerned* with other people's interests and needs, and (iii) whether the actor is seen to behave ethically and with *integrity*. In practice, there is considerable overlap between these bases, and so it is often difficult to separate them (e.g. an absence of self-interest might indicate that a politician is responsive to public demands, while also suggesting that they manifest clear moral principles and personal integrity). Yet to the extent that the three bases can be separated, the evidence from existing studies suggests that competence is a weaker determinant of trust than benevolence and integrity.

6.3 How do we know about the causes of trust?

In assessing the potential causes of trust, scholars have employed a variety of methods and sources of data. One way of identifying what drives people to trust or distrust political actors and institutions is simply to ask them.

This approach can be adopted either in large-scale opinion surveys or in smaller-scale qualitative exercises. Another way of identifying causes is to compare citizens located in different units (e.g. regions within a country or different countries themselves), and to trace back any variations in trust to differences between units in factors likely to shape and explain trust. A third way of identifying causes is through experimental designs, in which participants are randomly assigned to different treatments hypothesized to shape trust, with any subsequent variations in trust between groups taken to indicate the causal effect of the treatment.

Taking these methods in reverse order, experimental research designs are increasingly employed to analyse trust, although the majority of such experiments focus on trust between individuals (horizontal or 'social' trust) rather than on trust between individuals and organizations (vertical or 'political' trust) (Wilson and Eckel, 2011). There are fairly few experimental studies on the factors shaping political trust; as yet, this research design provides a limited amount of data from which to construct an understanding of causal factors. Yet experimental designs are highly effective at identifying causal relationships, even if they suffer from concerns over generalizability or 'external validity'.

The second type of research design, using a comparative approach, may also help us to identify the sources of trust if we can trace variations in trust across units to differences between those units in a hypothesized causal factor. Comparative analyses have been widely employed to study trust, often focusing on the impact of such factors as economic conditions, levels of corruption, and degrees of policy representation. Yet because many of the hypothesized causes of trust lack measurement instruments across units, comparative analyses tend to be limited in the range of factors they can explore. In addition, even though the 'logic of comparison' may, in theory, enable researchers to isolate the effects of a specific factor on trust, questions remain about whether this variable is genuinely causal or whether some other (unobserved) difference between units is shaping the observed variations in trust.

The bulk of the studies seeking to identify the causes of trust draw on survey data—collected nationally or cross-nationally—measuring different evaluations of political actors. Surveys often allow researchers to assess the effects on trust of a range of potential causal factors since they often have the space to field indicators tapping a variety of attitudes that might covary with trust. Yet surveys often manifest features that hinder our ability to analyse trust. One such feature, identified in Chapter 1, is that surveys tend to employ closed-ended questions—that limit the response options available to survey respondents—rather than open-ended questions—that allow respondents more scope to identify their own choices. Occasionally, citizens' perspectives on trust are identified through qualitative research designs such as focus groups, in-depth interviews, and analyses of citizens' newspaper correspondence (Graham et al., 2002; van Wessel, 2010, 2017; Dekker, 2011; Kemmers et al., 2015; Bertsou, 2019b; Noordzij, de Koster, and van der Waal, 2021a). The sources of trust identified in such studies are often richer and more extensive than those covered by batteries of survey questions. Qualitative exercises also highlight how some people's trust judgements rest on highly personalized judgements and inferences (van Wessel, 2017). Surveys cannot mirror the breadth and detail of the sources of trust identified in such qualitative exercises. It is as well to recognize at the outset that even well-designed and spacious surveys may enable analysts to capture only a fraction of the reasons people have for trusting their political rulers.

Another potential problem arising from survey data collected at a single point in time is the well-known issue of causal inference. When cause and effect are measured at the same point, it becomes difficult to identify the causal ordering between the two. Studies—such as those cited above—that claim to identify an effect of politicians' behaviour or degree of responsiveness on trust may well have the story the wrong way round; rather, existing feelings of trust may induce people to perceive politicians as behaving unethically (Dancey, 2012; Wroe, Allen, and Birch, 2013) or as being unresponsive (Chanley, Rudolph, and Rahn, 2001). It is often the case that solid theory provides a good guide to the direction of a causal relationship; at a conceptual level, the effect of X on Y might make sense, while a reverse effect of Y on X might not. Where theory does not provide such guidance, however, other forms of data can help to verify findings obtained from cross-sectional data. Over-time, or longitudinal, data can often help isolate causal relations more precisely, and in the analysis that follows, I complement where possible evidence gained from surveys undertaken at a single point in time with measures of people's attitudes gathered over a period of time.

6.4 Identifying the sources of trust in Britain

The most extensive source of survey data on trust in Britain is the British Election Study (BES), a high-quality population survey conducted at general elections since 1964. Unfortunately, recent BES surveys lack many good measures of trust. For these, we have to go back to earlier surveys conducted in 2005, which contain indicators both of trust and of the factors likely to shape trust. This reliance on older survey data is unfortunate, as it means the results of any analysis are somewhat dated. But this is unlikely to be a major problem since, in general terms, the factors shaping trust are unlikely to be strongly time-dependent. Specific events may sometimes have a particular effect on trust (as we will see in Section 6.5). Yet there is little reason to believe that the broad evaluations shaping people's trust change much over fairly short periods of time. The factors shaping trust are thus likely to be broadly similar whether the analysis takes place in the 2000s or in the 2020s.

The 2005 BES study comprised three main elements: a pre-election survey, a post-election survey, and a self-completion mailback survey. For reasons to be explained shortly, the first part of the analysis draws on the pre-election wave. This was conducted between February and April 2005 and involved interviews with 3,589 people. The measure of trust draws on two survey questions that asked for respondents' trust in parliament and in politicians. I sum the responses to these two questions into a single trust scale, whose values range from 0 (indicating 'no trust') to 10 (indicating a 'great deal of trust').

People's assessments of politicians' ability or competence are measured by BES survey items asking respondents how well they judge the government to have handled various policy issues, notably crime, asylum seekers, the health service, terrorism, the economy, and the level of taxation. I combined these judgements in an additive scale tapping people's assessments of government policy delivery, with high scores indicating positive assessments.[8] Politicians' abilities are also tapped through people's assessments of the state of the economy; in this case, how people believed the national economy was likely to perform over the coming year.

Some people may lack clear views on how well the government is handling issues like the economy and health. But they may have more generalized feelings about the state of the country, reflecting the fact that people's judgements often rest on gut-level feelings as much as on cognitive assessments (Kuklinski et al., 1991). The 2005 BES included questions that asked people for their feelings—both negative (e.g. 'disgust') and positive (e.g. 'happiness')—about the state of the economy and the health service. For each issue, the models test for the effects of negative policy feelings as against positive policy feelings.[9] Finally, since trust may well be shaped by people's assessments of high-profile policy actors, I include a measure of the perceived competence of the then prime minister, Tony Blair.

To gauge the effects on trust of people's perceptions of politicians' concern to serve public interests, or benevolence, the models draw on two measures. The first measure involves a question on whether people believed the prime minister to be responsive to voters' concerns. On an 11-point scale (where 0 = absence of the quality and 10 = presence of the quality), Tony Blair was seen as rather more competent (mean score: 5.73) than responsive (mean score: 4.85). The second measure of benevolence taps how well people feel represented by the governing party, Labour. Representation is measured by reference to where, on two ideological scales (one measuring preferences over whether to raise or lower taxation and public spending, the other measuring left–right preferences), people place themselves, and where they place the Labour party. Representation is deemed to be higher the smaller the distance between the two; where the gap widens, the degree of representation is lower. Modelling representation on both scales suggests that trust is shaped more by representation on the tax-spending scale than by representation on the left–right scale. I therefore limit the analysis to how responsive Labour is seen to be on the issue of taxation and public spending.

Alongside competence and benevolence, the model also includes a measure of whether the government is seen to be equitable, represented by a survey question that asked people whether they think the government treats people fairly.

The constructed model of trust is presented in Figure 6.2. Trust is hypothesized to be shaped by three features of trustworthiness: competence, benevolence, and fairness (unfortunately, the pre-election wave of the BES survey contained no measure of politicians' integrity, which therefore cannot be assessed). To ensure that any association between judgements on these

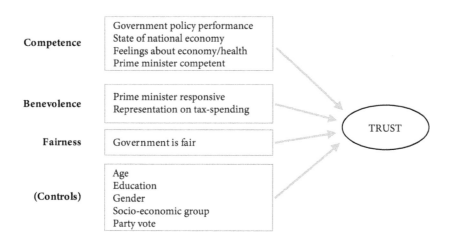

Figure 6.2 Relationship of different dimensions of trustworthiness with trust: cross section

features and trust is not shaped by individuals' personal characteristics, the model controls for a number of demographic, socio-economic, and political variables, notably age, gender, education level, socio-economic position (social class), and party vote (for space reasons, the results of these controls are not presented).[10]

The results showing the associations with trust of these different attitudes and evaluations are shown in column 1 of Table 6.1. These show significant associations with trust of assessments of policy delivery, the economy, and prime ministerial competence. People are able to link such cognitive appraisals to trust; once these assessments are accounted for, more affective feelings about the state of the economy and the health service do not have a significant association with trust. Evaluations of government fairness

Table 6.1 Associations between competence, benevolence, and fairness appraisals and trust

	(1) Pre-election wave		(2) Comparison of pre/post-election waves	
Competence				
Government handled policy issues well	0.46	(0.09)**	0.33	(0.08)**
National economic situation will get better	0.16	(0.05)**	0.02	(0.05)
Positive feelings about economy	0.09	(0.10)	–	–
Positive feelings about health	–0.02	(0.10)	–	–
Prime minister is competent	0.08	(0.03)**	0.04	(0.02)
Benevolence				
Governing party is responsive on tax-spending	0.05	(0.03)*	0.01	(0.03)
Prime minister is in touch with people	0.24	(0.03)**	0.10	(0.03)**
Fairness				
Government is fair	0.31	(0.06)**	0.18	(0.06)**
Trust at wave 1	–	–	0.36	(0.03)**
Constant	–1.30	(0.33)**	0.86	(0.32)**
F		44.73		114.50
Model significance (prob > F)		0.00		0.00
R^2		0.40		0.46
Weighted N		3,921		2,969

Figures show coefficients and associated standard errors. Models also control for age, education, social class, gender, and party vote (results not shown). *$p < 0.05$; **$p < 0.01$ (two-tailed test).
Source: British Election Study 2005. 2005 BES. Model 1: pre-election wave; Model 2: pre/post-election waves.

and prime ministerial responsiveness are also closely related to trust, as are people's perceptions of how well they are represented by the governing party.

The substance of these effects can be seen in Figure 6.3, which shows the predicted, or marginal, values of trust at different levels of each explanatory variable, holding constant the values of the other variables in the model. The strength of the effect can be measured by the degree to which values of trust change given shifts in the levels of the explanatory variable, or the steepness of the slope for each variable. The figures show that evaluations of government performance and perceptions of prime ministerial responsiveness both have substantively strong associations with trust. We can directly compare the effects of different judgements when it comes to appraisals of the prime minister. Judgements of Tony Blair's responsiveness have a stronger association with trust than judgements of his competence. An increase in perceived responsiveness (from the minimum to the maximum level) is associated with a rise in trust from 3.23 to 5.64 (on a 0–10 scale), an increase of 22 per cent. An increase in perceived competence is associated with a rise in trust from 3.94 to 4.73, an increase of 7 per cent. This is in line with the point made earlier that trust is affected more by judgements about an actor's motivations than about their competence.[11]

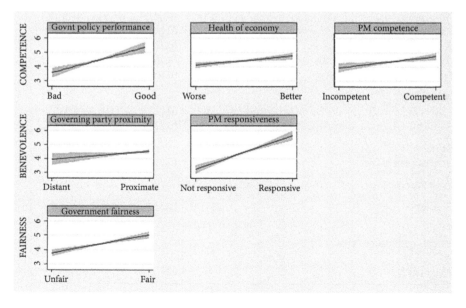

Figure 6.3 Association with trust of different judgements
Source: Model I, Table 6.1.

We should bear in mind, though, the point made earlier (Section 6.3) about the causal direction of identified associations. How can we be sure that judgements about an actor's responsiveness are shaping feelings of trust, and not vice versa? This reverse causal model is certainly plausible, yet cannot be ruled out in modelling exercises that rely on data gathered at a single point in time. To identify causal effects more accurately, we need observations gathered at different points in time. That way, we can identify how far evaluations of politicians measured at some preceding point are associated with levels of trust measured at a later point. This temporal ordering of the variables allows us to reduce, if not necessarily to eliminate, the risk of reverse causality.

We can introduce such a temporal sequencing using the 2005 BES since the pre-election wave of this study (conducted in February–April 2005) was followed by a post-election wave (conducted in May–July 2005). Of the sample interviewed in the pre-election wave, 2,959 people, or 82 per cent, were re-interviewed in the post-election wave. We can therefore draw on these two survey waves to explore how far changes in levels of trust between the pre-election wave and the post-election wave were affected by evaluations of politicians recorded in the pre-election wave.[12]

I estimate the same model as earlier, except that the variable being explained is now trust measured post-election. The explanatory variables are the same as shown in Figure 6.2, with three exceptions. First, they include a term for trust measured at the pre-election wave; its inclusion means that the model is now estimating the effects of the independent variables on *change* in trust between the two waves. Second, they omit the terms for policy 'feeling' since feelings about the economy and the health service proved insignificant predictors of trust in the first model. Third, since the model is based on the same respondents across the two waves, less care is needed in controlling for respondents' demographic and socio-economic characteristics. The revised model (Figure 6.4) therefore omits the control variables, with the exception of the measure of party voting.

The effect of modelling trust as a function of attitudes recorded at an earlier point in time (Model 2 in Table 6.1) is to reduce the independent effect on trust of some variables. In this model, trust is no longer significantly associated with people's judgements about the future health of the economy, by assessments of the prime minister's competence, and about their proximity in policy terms to the governing party. Yet trust remains associated with people's assessments of government policy management, by whether the government is seen as fair, and by whether the prime minister is seen as responsive to voters' concerns. Since these evaluations are measured before the final measure of trust, we can be more confident that these judgements are driving trust

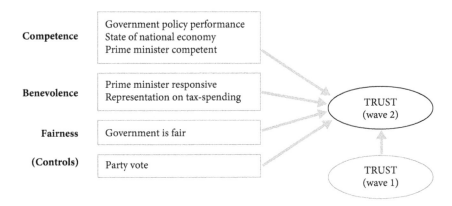

Figure 6.4 Relationship of different dimensions of trustworthiness with trust: over time

rather than vice versa. Having done so, we find that trust reflects people's assessments both of politicians' abilities and of their intentions.

The broad sources of trust—reflecting evaluations across various aspects of politicians' behaviour and performance—are further supported when we draw on the third part of the 2005 BES survey, the self-completion questionnaire. This survey included three measures of how people perceived the main political parties in Britain: as in touch/not in touch with ordinary people, as promise-keeping/promise-breaking, and as capable/incapable of strong government. These measures are helpful since they enable us to move beyond people's perceptions of politicians' ability (captured in the survey question about whether parties are capable of strong government) and intentions (whether people think parties are in touch) to also consider perceptions of politicians' integrity (captured in the survey question about whether parties keep their promises).[13] For each of these measures, I constructed variables comprising three levels: whether people felt neither of the main parties (the Conservatives and Labour) manifested virtuous qualities, (ii) whether people felt only one party manifested virtuous qualities, and (iii) whether people felt both parties manifested virtuous qualities.[14] The model also controls for the same attitudinal and demographic variables as the models reported in Table 6.1.

The results (which are reported in full in Appendix 6.1) highlight the importance of each type of judgement. Assessments of parties' responsiveness and fidelity are both strongly associated with trust, as can be seen in the sharply upward slopes of the lines shown in Figure 6.5 (which

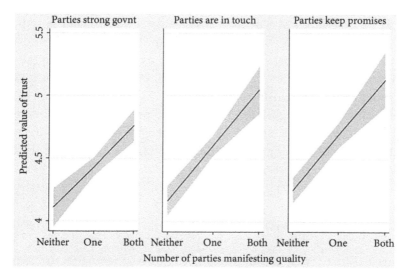

Figure 6.5 Association with trust of judgements about parties
Source: Model in Appendix 6.1

capture the effects on trust of how many parties are seen to manifest each quality). Assessments of parties' strength are also closely associated with trust, although the effect is slightly weaker (i.e. the slope is more shallow).

Summary

This section has explored the sources of citizens' trust against a broad range of evaluations and assessments of politicians' actions and behaviours. Three broad evaluations have been identified, relating to actors' competence, benevolence, and integrity. Evaluations of each have been shown to be associated with trust, particularly closely in the cases of assessments of politicians' integrity and concerns about other people. These results hold when trust is modelled in a dynamic way that takes more account of the causal ordering of variables.

6.5 Variations in the sources of trust: People, institutions, and contexts

Having established some of the broad factors underpinning individuals' trust judgements, we now turn to consider how far these sources might vary, depending on the nature of the trustor, the agency being reviewed, and the context or time-point at which trust is assessed. Such detail is important if we are to understand whether trust rests on broadly consistent or more distinctive sets of factors. This section thus extends the previous one by examining commonalities and particularities in the sources of trust. It starts with individuals and considers whether the sources of trust vary between people commanding higher or lower levels of political information. It then considers whether the sources of trust are consistent or variant across different institutions. Finally, it considers how far the sources of trust vary over time.

The specifics of trust: Individuals

It is argued that 'Trust is a thoroughly cognitive phenomenon. It depends upon knowledge and belief' (Offe, 1999: 55). We noted this claim in Chapter 1, where we also observed the argument (e.g. Rahn, 2000) that people who are well-informed about politics base their trust judgements on somewhat different—and more cognitively demanding—factors than people who are poorly informed. However, these judgements related to interpersonal or social forms of trust. Might there be similar differences when it comes to people's trust in political actors and institutions?

Previous studies have indeed suggested that politically informed and uninformed citizens employ rather different criteria in forming such trust judgements. In the United States, politically knowledgeable citizens have been found to base their evaluations of Congress primarily on performance criteria, such as delivering policy outcomes, while the evaluations of less knowledgeable citizens have been found to rest more on appraisals of presidential and congressional actors (Mondak et al., 2007; see also Bernstein, 2001). In a similar vein, Hibbing and Theiss-Morse (2002: 79–81) have shown that people with high levels of political interest assess government through cognitively demanding factors such as national economic performance and party proximity to personal ideological location. By contrast, people with low levels of political interest assess government against cognitively easier factors such as personal economic situation and perceived effectiveness of the political decision-making process. Longitudinal analyses have shown that as people gain information about a government agency (in this case, water regulatory institutions in the United States), their trust becomes less dependent on generalized evaluations of the government (PytlikZillig et al., 2017). Comparative studies have shown that levels of corruption in a country are more closely tied to trust judgements among highly educated citizens than among less educated citizens (van der Meer, 2010; van der Meer and Hakhverdian, 2017; Noordzij, de Koster, and van der Waal, 2021b).

Other studies, however, have suggested that individual differences in political information have little impact on trust. Thus, in the context of trust in various environmental agencies, it has been shown that these agencies' attributes have little more impact on people's trust among environmentally knowledgeable individuals than among less environmentally knowledgeable individuals (Johnson, 2010: 225–226). Similarly, in a study of popular attitudes towards Dutch state institutions, trust has been shown to be no more shaped by judgements of politicians' competence or responsiveness among well-educated people than among their poorly educated counterparts (van Elsas, 2015; similar findings for Australia are presented by Dassonneville and McAllister, 2021).

To explore how far trust might be shaped by different considerations among people high or low in political information, I ran a similar model to that represented in Figure 6.2, using the post-election wave of the 2005 BES. To measure information, I drew on an eight-item battery of political knowledge questions, summed into a single scale (0 = very low knowledge and 1 = very high knowledge).[15] This measure of political knowledge was then interacted with each variable tapping the assessments already shown to be associated with people's trust in politicians. Some of these assessments might be deemed cognitively 'easy', namely evaluations of one's household economy, feelings about the economy, and evaluations of whether the prime minister is competent. Other assessments might be deemed more cognitively 'difficult', namely evaluations of the national economy, appraisals of government handling of the economy, and assessments of party responsiveness on tax and spending. The regression models also include demographic controls, along with a measure of party support.

The results of these models (which are shown in Appendix 6.2) indicate that individuals' political knowledge has no significant effect on the associations with trust of two of the cognitively 'difficult' assessments, namely evaluations of the national economy and of government economic management. A similar non-effect of knowledge is apparent for one of the cognitively 'easy' assessments, namely household economic evaluations. Yet for the two other 'easy' assessments—economic feelings and evaluations of prime minister competence—the knowledge interaction terms yielded negative and statistically significant coefficients (in the case of economic feelings, the coefficient is only significant at the 10 per cent level). These indicate that the higher the level of knowledge among individuals, the lower the effect of such assessments on trust. These effects can be seen in Figure 6.6. The

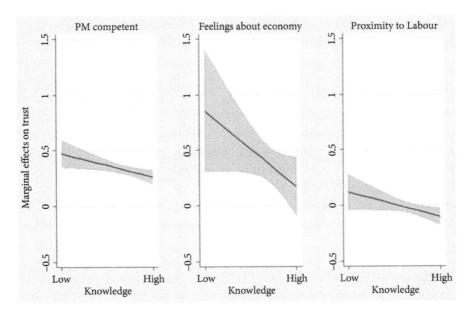

Figure 6.6 Association with trust of evaluations, by knowledge
Source: British Election Study 2005, post-election survey

graphics show how, among low-knowledge individuals, trust is more closely associated with appraisals of prime ministerial competence and generalized feelings about the economy than it is among high-knowledge individuals (for similar results across European countries, see van Erkel and van der Meer, 2016). However, among low-knowledge individuals, trust is also more closely associated with one evaluation deemed cognitively difficult, and thus anticipated to be drawn on more by politically knowledgeable individuals, namely personal ideological proximity to the governing (Labour) party on the issue of taxation and spending.

Hence, the sources of trust among different people are not always consistent, but sometimes vary. When it comes to forming trust judgements, individuals holding high and low stores of political information draw somewhat differently on particular evaluations and appraisals.

The specifics of trust: Institutions

In Chapter 1, I argued that trust is a generalized judgement, in that individuals tend to form broad assessments of trust which they apply across different political actors and institutions. However, in the present chapter,

I have explored how individuals' trust judgements arise from more specific assessments of how political actors are performing, how concerned they are with public needs, and how honest and reliable they are. The role of such specific assessments opens up the possibility of different actors or institutions being evaluated in more particular ways.

The discussion in Chapter 1 noted previous studies that have indeed pointed to variations in the factors underlying people's trust in different political actors and institutions. People appear to trust organizations with an executive function (such as presidents or central banks) largely on grounds of competence or performance, while their trust in agencies with a delivery function (such as a family court) or a representative function (such as a legislature) rests more on assessments of responsiveness to citizens' concerns (Feldman, 1983; Braithwaite, 1998; Richardson. Houston, and Hadjiharalambous, 2001; Kelleher and Wolak, 2007). In the British context, Fisher and colleagues (2010) have argued that people's trust in politicians and political parties reflects different considerations, not similar ones.[16] Across Europe, it has been shown that appraisals of things like national economic performance are more closely tied to people's trust in representative institutions (such as politicians and parliaments) than to their trust in regulatory institutions (such as the courts and the police) (Torcal, 2014; Schnaudt, 2019: 144–156). Even when it comes to different government agencies, people's trust and satisfaction has been shown to rest on somewhat different factors (Morgeson and Petrescu, 2011).[17] Moreover, different factors are also at work in shaping people's trust in different tiers of government. Thus, people's trust in national government has been shown to rest more heavily on evaluations of economic performance than has their trust in local government (Fitzgerald and Wolak, 2016; for similar evidence from the Netherlands about the specificity of judgements on people's trust in different tiers of government, see Proszowska, Jansen, and Denters, 2022).

There is thus some suggestion that people's trust in different institutions might reflect rather different types of evaluations and appraisals. To explore this point in the British context, I again draw on the 2005 BES, but this time construct separate models relating to trust in seven institutions: the government, politicians, parliament, the civil service, local government, the courts, and the police. The variables used to explain trust comprise evaluations of policy outcomes and of national political actors. These evaluations cover assessments of how well the government has handled key policy issues (the national health service, crime, and asylum seekers[18]), expectations of the future path of the country's economy, appraisals of the prime minister (Tony Blair) and the incumbent governing party (Labour), and assessments of procedural fairness (how fairly government treats people). Since these evaluations mainly concern policy delivery and national-level political actors, the assumption is that these factors will be more closely associated with people's trust in government, politicians, and parliament than with their trust in the civil service, local government, the judiciary, and the police. However, feelings of procedural fairness—although referring specifically to the government—represent a more generalized assessment, and so are anticipated to have an impact on people's trust across institutions.

The full results from these seven models—which also control for individuals' demographic characteristics and party support—are shown in Appendix 6.3. They show, first, how the association between party support and trust varies between institutions. For most institutions, levels of trust are higher among Conservative party supporters than among people who did not vote (who serve as the reference category). Yet they are lower when it comes to trust in the (Labour-run) national government. Note also that gender is not consistently associated with trust in different institutions; when it comes to parliament, the civil service, and the courts, males are more trusting than females, but in the case of the police, these trust associations are reversed.[19]

Turning to attitudes and evaluations, we similarly find some variation in the associations with people's trust in different institutions. Evaluations of the governing party are associated with people's trust in a range of institutions but not with trust in the police. Yet evaluations of prime ministerial competence are associated with trust in the police but not with trust in other institutions like the civil service, local government, or the courts. There is also some variation in how people's assessments of government performance on different policy issues shape their trust in particular institutions. Assessments of government performance on health (the single most important issue to the British public in 2005, according to the BES) are significantly associated with people's trust in the government, parliament, and political parties but not with their trust in civil servants, local government, the courts, and the police. Similarly, assessments of performance on asylum seekers are not significantly associated with people's trust in local government or the police, although they are associated with trust in the courts (suggesting people view the issue of asylum claims as having a legal aspect which carries over into their trust in the judiciary). Assessments of the national economy are significantly associated with people's trust in national and local tiers of government but not with their trust in the civil service, the courts, or the police, suggesting that economic considerations are relevant for people's trust only in actors with executive responsibilities.

Finally, how far do particular events shape people's trust across institutions? To test this, I included in the models a term measuring people's disapproval of British involvement in the Iraq war. This decision of the Labour government in 2003 to participate in the invasion of Iraq was immensely controversial, attracting the criticism of almost two-thirds (65 per cent) of the British population, according to the BES. However, while disapproval of the government's decision to commit troops to Iraq is significantly and negatively associated with people's trust in the government and in parliament, it is not significantly associated with their trust in civil servants, local government, the courts, and the police.[20] While the Iraq example is admittedly rather dated, it shows how the spillover from a controversial decision taken by central government may be limited, and may not affect people's trust in other public institutions (reinforcing the argument about the specificity of trust in Chapter 1, Section 1.3).

The specifics of trust: Time

The association between citizens' evaluations and their trust judgements may vary over time depending on shifts in those evaluations' relevance or salience. To see this, we can compare explanatory models of trust among British citizens immediately after two national elections, in 2005 and 2010. In the intervening period, the global economic crash occurred, with significant implications for Britain's economy. In 2005, the post-election wave of the BES found just 6 per cent of people nominating the economy as the most important issue facing Britain. By 2010, that figure had risen to 38 per cent. To gauge the impact of the economic crisis on people's trust judgements, I constructed identical models of trust for 2005 and 2010.[21] Both models included a term that captured how people perceived the economy to be performing, along with terms capturing other factors likely to covary with both economic evaluations and trust, namely appraisals of government performance (on health, crime, and terrorism), whether people liked the incumbent party (Labour) and believed the prime minister to be competent, and perceptions of government fairness. Of particular interest is whether economic evaluations had a stronger association with trust in 2010 than in 2005.

They do. In 2005, evaluations of the future direction of the national economy had no great substantive—and barely statistically significant—association with trust. In 2010, however, the association was substantive and highly statistically significant. The difference in these associations can be seen in Figure 6.7, which shows the close association of economic evaluations and trust in 2010 compared to their meagre effects in 2005.[22] Variations in the association between economic evaluations and trust at different points in time have also been identified in studies of Britain (Whiteley et al., 2013), Germany, the Netherlands, and Sweden (Coromina and Bartolomé Peral, 2016), of countries particularly hit by the economic crash (Torcal, 2017), and indeed across European countries as a whole (Martini and Quaranta, 2020: 126–129).[23]

Hence people appear to form trust judgements based on the 'tools to hand', using criteria that are salient at the time. Moreover, people's trust rests not only on an issue's salience but also on how it is dealt with by public actors. The period after the 2008 financial crash was marked in Britain, as in other countries, by a period of fiscal austerity with substantial cuts to public spending. This raised questions of social equity, particularly when these cuts disproportionately affected poorer individuals and families. It is noteworthy, then, that the models of trust that identified a stronger association with economic evaluations in 2010 than in 2005 also showed a similar effect for evaluations of government fairness. As can be seen from Figure 6.8, trust was associated at both points with people's perceptions of government fairness. Yet the association was rather stronger in 2010—during the period of public austerity after 2008—than in 2005.[24]

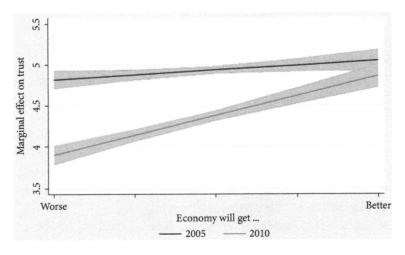

Figure 6.7 Association with trust of economic evaluations, 2005 and 2010
Source: British Election Study, 2005/2010

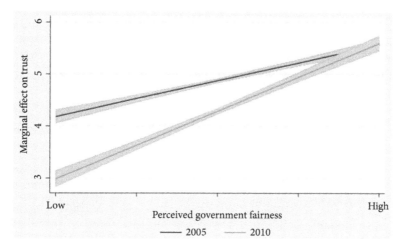

Figure 6.8 Association with trust of fairness evaluations, 2005 and 2010
Source: British Election Study, 2005/2010

6.6 Conclusion

This chapter has addressed the sources of people's trust in political actors and institutions through two core questions: (i) What types of evaluations and perceptions among individuals are associated with trust? (ii) How far do individuals apply these evaluations and perceptions consistently, or more distinctively, in forming trust judgements? Exploring these issues has provided a clearer analytical picture of the sources of trust and of how specific evaluations are applied by individuals in forming trust judgements about particular objects and in particular contexts.

In broad terms, trust arises from evaluations of what governments deliver and the equity of this delivery, along with the competence, benevolence, and integrity of political actors. The voluminous empirical literature highlights the variety of factors associated with trust, ranging from the delivery by government of economic growth through to the behaviour of legislative representatives. These studies suggest that trust is stimulated more strongly by evaluations of political actors' intentions and motivations than by evaluations of their ability or competence. The data from Britain presented here reinforce this conclusion. Yet performance also matters for trust. To 'trust'—whether this involves a known person or a distant political actor—is a broad judgement, involving a variety of considerations.[25]

Yet if trust is a broad judgement, its application is often specific. This is highlighted in the way that the evaluations and perceptions associated with trust often vary across different individuals (trustors), institutions (trustees), and time-points (contexts). Trust might—as suggested in Chapter 1—comprise a generalized judgement. But its application often points to important specificities. There is no 'one size fits all' model of the sources of trust.

These specificities pose challenges to political actors, notably in responding to the numerous evaluations and perceptions that appear to shape individuals' trust, and the variations in the way these appraisals are used to form trust judgements. Expressions of 'trust' represent both wide-ranging yet often specific judgements, and any attempts to respond to these judgements and to stimulate trust will need to be similarly broad yet specific to particular contexts. The importance attached to such responses will largely depend on how serious the consequences of low trust are seen to be. These consequences—the 'so what' question of trust—are explored in the following chapter.

SECTION 3

SO WHAT? THE CONSEQUENCES OF TRUST

7
The effects of trust

Claims that citizens have lost trust in politicians and political institutions often imply that this poses a threat to political systems. In what sense, however, might a lack of trust harm the effective governance of those systems? It is important to ask this question since, as I argued in Chapter 1 and at the end of Chapter 3, surveys pointing to low rates of trust among citizens may, in some case, indicate little more than a dissatisfaction with, or scepticism towards, a set of incumbent political actors. Low recorded rates of trust are not necessarily barometers of deeply negative attitudes towards politicians or, indeed, of active distrust of them. Yet if recorded measures of trust sometimes capture what is little more than public discontent with politicians, the implications of low trust may be limited.

In some cases, we might even anticipate low trust stimulating some positive effects. For example, people who lack trust may be particularly motivated to monitor what their political representatives get up to and to participate in political activities (Levi, 1998; Warren, 2017). Such vigilance and participation strengthen the quality of representative relationships, particularly in contemporary societies where executives and bureaucracies wield extensive power that requires checks via constant monitoring and engagement. Indeed studies have found that citizens who are high in trust are less likely to be interested in politics and to seek out information about government than are citizens who are low in trust. Longitudinal analysis has shown that increasing levels of trust among citizens are associated with declining levels of interest in politics (Peterson et al., 2020). Experimental analysis has shown that citizens manifesting high levels of trust are less keen than citizens manifesting low trust on being exposed to complex information on policy issues such as the economy and environmental problems (Shepherd and Kay, 2012, 2014). We can also see such effects by drawing on data from the International Social Science Program. Asked in 2014 how important it is for citizens to 'keep watch on the actions of government', more low trust British respondents deemed such monitoring to be very important (50 per cent) than did high trust respondents (38 per cent).[1]

Trust may also encourage credulity, which is particularly harmful in cases where public officials provide misleading information (a political counterpart to Autolycus' 'gulling' of the unwary in Shakespeare's *The Winter's Tale*, which was noted in the Introduction). A recent study found that individuals who trusted scientists were more likely than individuals who did not trust scientists to believe and support the dissemination of false information referencing scientific claims over false information referencing no such claims (O'Brien, Palmer, and Albarracin, 2021).[2] Trust thus appears to leave citizens vulnerable to falsehoods propagated by authority figures. Trust can be misplaced and dangerous if it promotes credulity over critical inquiry.

Yet while noting the potential virtues of the vigilance that sometimes appears to accompany low trust, we should also note various dangers that might be associated with this state. If trust equates to the 'loyalty' an individual feels towards an individual or organization, any decline in that loyalty might trigger 'exit' or 'voice' behaviours (Hirschman, 1970). Voice—comprising complaints or expressions of grievance—is generally less disruptive and serious than exit—comprising a withdrawal from a relationship—since it maintains the individual's place within the political system. Yet in the form of protest against incumbent political actors, support for anti-system parties, demands for reform of institutional rules, or rejection of an active role for government in providing goods and services, voice can pose a significant challenge to the political system.[3] Exit, too, presents challenges of varying severity for the political system. A lack of trust can induce people to disengage from the political system, for example, by abstaining at elections and not standing for political office. In turn, lower electoral turnout may weaken politicians' incentives to be responsive, while lower competition for office may reduce the quality of political personnel. Yet even these effects are less serious than other forms of trust-induced exit. These include individuals ignoring government advice and information and refusing to comply with collective obligations. In such guises, citizen exit from collective actions and duties might severely restrict governments' ability to achieve socially optimal outcomes.

This chapter provides a comprehensive review of the effects of low trust on various political, social, and economic outcomes (laid out in Table 7.1). The concluding sections summarize the findings across these behaviours by asking what civic and political life might look like in a low trust society.

7.1 Identifying the effects of trust

Identifying the effects of trust is not a straightforward task, and it is as well to be aware at the outset of the potential difficulties involved in the analysis and how they might be addressed.

Table 7.1 Key outcomes of trust

Outcome	Behaviour	Association with low trust	Section
Voice	Protest activities	Increased likelihood of protest	7.2a
	Support for anti-system parties	Increased likelihood of voting for anti-system candidates and parties	7.2b
	Demands for political reform	Lower support for democratic norms Higher support for democratic reforms Increased likelihood of voting for changes to the political *status quo*	7.2c
	Attitudes towards active government	Lower support for active government	7.2d
Exit	Electoral engagement	Reduced likelihood of voting at elections	7.3a
	Acceptance of official information	Reduced likelihood of accepting official information	7.3b
	Compliance with official rules	Reduced likelihood of observing official rules in areas like health and civic life	7.3c

The first difficulty arises from the measurement of key variables. Both trust and behaviour are usually identified via survey measures of *reported* trust and *reported* behaviour. In the case of reported trust, we have already noted that survey measures tend to capture the absence of trust but not necessarily the presence of distrust. Yet a lack of trust may induce rather different behaviours to distrust. For example, while the former might induce an individual to exercise some caution in their engagement with another actor, the latter might induce the individual to reject engagement with an actor at all. In the case of behaviour, there are well-known problems in using self-reported behaviour to capture individuals' actions. For example, in their study of whether citizens comply with government rules, Esaiasson and Ottervik (2014: 23) found only a modest relationship between people's reports of law-abiding behaviour and more objective measures of legal observance.

The second difficulty arises in identifying the relationship between variables. In many studies, these relationships are established cross-sectionally, where individuals' trust and behaviours are measured at the same point in time. This method makes it difficult to establish whether trust (X) is genuinely a cause of a behaviour (Y), or whether some other factor might be shaping one or both variables, rendering spurious any observed relationship between X and Y. For example, a study sought to identify the association between trust and citizens' compliance with state obligations (such as paying a fare on public transport, not cheating on taxes, and not accepting a bribe). The study tested this by plotting levels of institutional trust against compliance rates across countries. The study found that in some countries, compliance rates significantly exceeded recorded levels of trust (Esaiasson and Ottervik, 2014). In those countries, people appear to comply with official rules for reasons beyond the trust they invest in institutional actors.

Cross-sectional analyses also make it difficult to pinpoint whether any observed relationship between X and Y reflects the impact of the former on the latter ($X \rightarrow Y$) or the opposite ($Y \rightarrow X$). Indeed, empirical studies based on data collected over time—which allows the direction of causal effects to be identified more robustly—have shown that some behaviours shape trust rather more than they are shaped by trust. Hence causal associations have been found to run from political participation to trust and confidence rather than the other way round (Quintelier and Hooghe, 2012; Quintelier and van Deth, 2014; similar effects for social trust are shown by Brehm and Rahn, 1997). Citizenship norms have similarly been found to shape trust rather than reflecting it (Van Deth, 2017). In other cases, there might be reciprocal effects between trust and an outcome. Thus, people's feelings of trust might shape their support for populist parties (see Section 7.2b), yet in claiming and encouraging a distinction between the 'pure' people and a 'corrupt' elite (Mueller, 2016), populism itself encourages and deepens feelings of distrust.

Researchers concerned to identify the effects of trust among national populations thus face a number of obstacles. These make it difficult for researchers to pinpoint the outcomes of trust; given the data to hand, the most that can be done is to identify broad potential outcomes and to bear in mind that these can only be estimated effects.

7.2 The 'voice' consequences of trust

Citizens who lack trust in one set of political actors may press for their replacement by another set of actors. Established democracies accommodate such pressures via elections, which offer voters the opportunity to sanction and replace untrusted incumbents. Yet low trust may present broader and stiffer challenges to democratic governance. It may stimulate individuals to engage in protest activities, to support 'anti-system' parties, to press for reform of the political system, and to reject government adopting an active policy role. Each of these consequences presents a challenge to the smooth operation of the political system.

(a) Political protest

Individuals lacking trust in political actors may be reluctant to register their grievances through traditional routes such as voting at elections (see

Section 7.3a). They may instead prefer to express these grievances outside the confines of formal politics, via protest activities. Previous studies have shown that participation in activities such as demonstrating and petition-signing tends to be higher among people who are negatively oriented towards the political system than among people who are positively oriented towards it (Heath, 2008; Norris, 2011: chapter 11; Hooghe and Marien, 2013; Harrebye and Ejnaes, 2015). Such negative attitudes can occasionally impel people to engage in destructive and violent forms of political protest. Studies have found that one of the key causes of the riots that engulfed some British cities in autumn 2011 was people's lack of trust in the police and a feeling that the police did not treat them with respect (Lewis et al., 2011; Kawalerowicz and Biggs, 2015). Yet in spite of Kinder's (1998: 832) claim that 'If there is an ideology of protest – a configuration of ideas and feelings that sustains activism – then disaffection would seem to be at its center', the empirical relationship between trust and protest is not clear-cut. Some studies have found that feelings of trust and confidence in political institutions do little to shape citizens' tendencies to engage in protest activities (Dalton, 2004: 167–177).

To explore the impact of trust on people's engagement in protest in Britain, I construct a model of protest drawing on data from the British Social Attitudes (BSA) survey from 2011. This survey measured various forms of protest activity, such as reported contacting of a Member of Parliament (MP), a government department, or a media outlet, speaking to an influential person, raising the issue within an organization, signing a petition, and going on a demonstration.[4] Although these comprise different behaviours, their distribution falls onto a single protest scale.[5] The measures of trust derive from survey questions asking how far people trust parliament, politicians, and the government (aggregated into a single trust scale). To ensure that any relationship between participation and trust does not reflect some omitted third variable, the models control for factors that might covary with both participation and trust, namely people's degree of political interest, education level, age, and left–right political ideology.

Once these factors are taken into account, the model suggests that trust has no significant impact on reported engagement in protest (see Appendix 7.1, model 1). Yet this may be too blunt a test. Low trust may shape protest particularly among people who shun electoral forms of engagement. To test this, I constructed a second model which distinguished between people who report engaging in protest activities but not voting at the previous national election and people who report engaging in protest and voting. The results from this model (Appendix 7.1, model 2) show that relative to people who participate across the board, low trust is significantly and positively associated with engaging in protest actions while avoiding the ballot box. Conversely, low trust appears to reduce people's tendencies to participate only at the ballot box, although the term for this effect is not statistically significant. The effects of trust on protest and electoral participation can be seen graphically in Figure 7.1. As people's trust wanes, their tendency to participate only at the ballot box declines, while there is some increase in their tendency to engage in protest but not in voting.

Another way in which trust may shape individuals' engagement in protest activities is via the moderating role of political competence, or 'internal efficacy'. This hypothesis was first put forward by Gamson (1968), who identified the optimal conditions for protest participation as a combination among individuals of high discontent and high levels of internal political efficacy (see also Paige, 1971; Craig, 1980). On this account, people are particularly inclined to engage in protest activities when low in trust yet feeling equipped to register their political demands. Although some analysts have cast doubt on the effects of this combination of factors (e.g. low trust and high political awareness was found by Hooghe and Marien (2013) not to stimulate people's tendency to engage in protest activities), a recent analysis (Christensen, 2016) showed that attendance at protest demonstrations tends to be particularly high among people who are distrustful yet efficacious.

I explore the association between trust and protest activities among people who vary in their feelings of political competence by drawing on the same

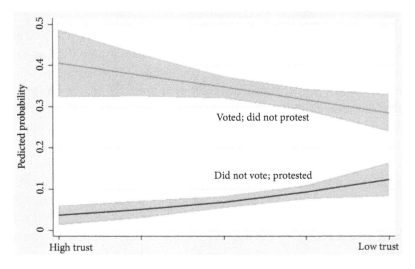

Figure 7.1 Association of trust and protest participation
Source: Model 2 in Appendix 7.1.

BSA survey from 2011. Internal political efficacy is measured through two questions asking respondents whether they feel politics is too complicated for them to understand and whether they feel people like them have no say in politics (disagreement with these statements denotes high internal efficacy). Combining binary measures of trust and efficacy yields four categories. The results are presented in Figure 7.2. These show that compared to people high in trust yet who lack efficacy (the model's reference category), people low in trust but who feel efficacious are significantly more likely to report engaging in protest activities. Feeling efficacious and trusting is also associated with protest participation, although the effect is significant only at the 10 per cent level.[6] In substantive terms, being low in trust yet high in efficacy increases an individual's probability of engaging in protest activity (probability: 0.56) by one-quarter relative to people who are high in trust yet low in efficacy (probability: 0.45).

Overall, trust appears to be associated with individual reports of engaging in protest activities, although this association is specific, not general. People lacking trust in politicians are more likely to engage in protest outside the ballot box but no more likely to engage in protest when combined with voting. A lack of trust is also positively related to engaging in protest but primarily among people who also feel politically competent.

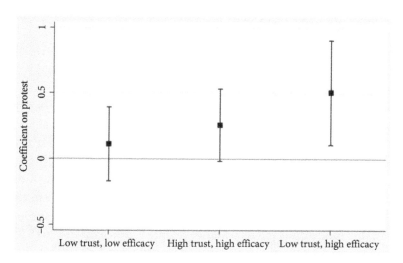

Figure 7.2 Association of trust and efficacy with protest
Source: British Social Attitudes 2011

(b) Support for anti-system parties

At an election, individuals who lack trust in politicians have limited options open to them. They can hold their noses and vote for a party whose representatives they do not trust. They can abstain from participating, on the basis that all politicians are unresponsive or dishonest (a behaviour explored in Section 7.3a). Or they can vote for an 'outsider' or protest party (Bélanger and Nadeau, 2005).

The recent increase across Western Europe in electoral support for populist parties, particularly on the radical right, is often explained by reference to people's growing dissatisfaction with, and distrust of, established political parties and institutions (Lubbers, Gijsberts and Scheepers, 2002; Norris and Inglehart, 2019: 282–287; Kriesi and Schulte-Cloos, 2020). At particular time-points, low trust has been found to be positively associated with electoral support for radical or extreme political parties (Hooghe, Marien and Pauwels, 2011; Dassonneville, Blais, and Dejaeghere, 2015; Ziller and Schübel, 2015; Algan et al., 2017). Longitudinal analyses have identified a similar effect (Bélanger and Aarts, 2006; Rooduijn, van der Brug, and de Lange, 2016), while declines in levels of trust have been found to depress voters' support for incumbent parties and stimulate their support for protest parties of both the radical right and radical left (Hooghe and Dassonneville, 2018a).[7]

Britain does not currently have a credible protest party. At the last general election in 2019, the principal non-mainstream parties—the Brexit party and the UK Independence party (UKIP)—won just 2 per cent of the popular vote. Yet at the 2015 general election, UKIP won 13 per cent of the vote, while at the European Parliament election a year before, UKIP's vote share topped 28 per cent. Analyses of UKIP's electoral fortunes identify public discontent with the political system as a key factor in explaining the party's rise (Ford and Goodwin, 2014: 185–200).

To provide a more systematic test of the link between trust and support for UKIP, I draw on the British Election Study Internet Panel (BESIP) survey. The panel nature of this survey—involving repeated interviews with the same people—enables us to analyse the effects of changes in trust among individuals on UKIP support. Changes in trust are measured by taking data from wave 1 (February–March 2014) and wave 6 (May 2015) of the BESIP survey. The results of this model thus tell us whether people's choices at the 2015 general election (covered by the wave 6 survey) were affected by whether they had become more or less trusting in politicians over the previous year.[8]

The detailed results are shown in Appendix 7.2, with a graphic presentation in Figure 7.3. The latter shows that people whose levels of trust fell between

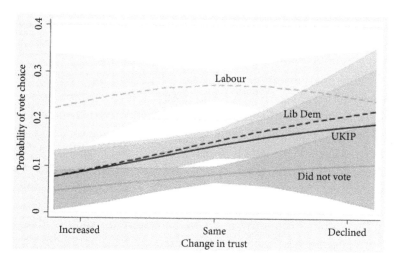

Figure 7.3 Association of change in trust with party vote
Source: Appendix 7.2.

2014 and 2015 were more likely to vote for UKIP in 2015 than people whose trust rose. But the relationship is not that strong; hence the relevant line in Figure 7.3 does not curve upwards that much. People whose trust fell over the period were actually slightly more likely to support the Liberal Democrats than UKIP. (This is somewhat surprising, as the Liberal Democrats held government office until 2015, albeit as the junior coalition partner. This effect suggests that people whose trust fell in the year before the 2015 election blamed the Conservatives and shifted support to the junior coalition partner.) Declining levels of public trust thus appear to stimulate support for some mainstream parties as much as for protest parties. Declining trust also appears to encourage some people to abstain from voting altogether, as can be seen in the modest positive relationship between lower trust and reporting 'did not vote' (for similar results, see Allen, 2017).

What about popular support for candidates who promise to shake up the political establishment; does trust affect people's support for such 'system challenging' politicians? To explore this, we can turn to the United States whose 2016 presidential election saw the triumph of Donald Trump. Trump's victory in the Republican primary race has been shown to reflect voters' lack of trust in the federal government (Dyck, Pearson-Merkowitz, and Coates, 2018), while there is evidence that his election victory over Hillary Clinton owed much to voters' anger with the federal government (Rudolph, 2021).[9] Drawing on American National Election Study data from 2016 enables us to see the clear link between trust and people's choices at that election.

Among people who indicated that they 'never' trust government to do what is right, 78 per cent reported voting for Trump as opposed to 22 per cent who reported voting for Clinton.

Yet was the relationship between voters' trust and their electoral choices particularly pronounced in 2016? And does that relationship stand up when account is taken of other factors that might affect both trust and vote choice? To answer these questions, I run a series of vote choice models for the ten US presidential elections held between 1984 and 2020. Each model includes vote choice (the reference category is always coded as Democrat, so the coefficients indicate the impact on voting for the Republican candidate), trust (coded so that high values equate to low levels of trust), assessments of the state of the national economy, and whether the respondent is ideologically liberal or conservative. To compare the effects of trust in different elections, I estimate the impact of a one standard deviation change in trust on the odds of voting Republican. The results, presented in Figure 7.4, express these odds as a percentage. The bars show a negative value in elections where low trust is associated with voting Democrat (as in 1984, 1988, 2004, and 2020 when the Republicans were already in control of the White House) and a positive value in elections where low trust is associated with voting Republican (as in 1996, when Bill Clinton won a second presidential term for the Democrats). In 2016, Trump's electoral support was higher among people with low trust; but little more so than in 1996 and even less so than in 2012 (when low trust was strongly associated with support for the challenger Republican, Mitt

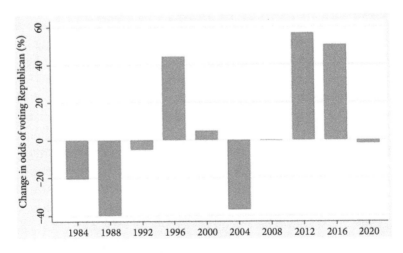

Figure 7.4 Association of trust with vote choice in US presidential elections

Source: American National Election Study

Romney). Thus, a lack of trust may have impelled many American voters to support Trump in 2016; but it equally strongly drove them to support his Republican predecessors in 1996 and 2012.

The evidence from Britain and the United States reinforces the link between feelings of low trust among individuals and support for protest parties and candidates. However, low trust also appears to stimulate support for established parties and candidates (such as the Liberal Democrats in Britain in 2015, and Mitt Romney in the United States in 2012). At elections, then, low trust apparently triggers support for 'pro-system' options as well as for 'anti-system' options.

(c) Demands for political reform

Individuals lacking trust in an existing set of political arrangements are, compared to their more trusting counterparts, more likely to favour changes to those arrangements. Some of these changes may involve granting citizens a greater direct voice in policy decisions (Seyd, Curtice, and Rose, 2018) and thus challenge indirect, or representative, procedures of political decision-making. Yet there is little evidence (as we saw in Chapter 2) that low trust spills over into questioning or even rejecting democratic norms. To explore the evidence from Britain in more detail, I draw on data from the European and World Values Surveys (EVS/WVS) which, in 1999, 2008, 2017, and 2022, asked participants across numerous countries to evaluate various arrangements for governing the state. These options consisted of 'having a strong leader who does not have to bother with parliament and elections', 'having experts, not government, make decisions according to what they think is best for the country', 'having the army rule the country', and 'having a democratic political system'. The EVS/WVS do not measure people's trust but instead their confidence. Although the concept of confidence is not the same as trust, they are sufficiently close that indicators of confidence are likely to provide a fair approximation of the picture for trust.[10]

The distributions of public support for each of the governance options (those responding that each option was a 'very good' or 'fairly good' way of governing the country) broken down by levels of trust are plotted in Figure 7.5. It is immediately apparent that over time, public support in Britain for the three non-democratic options has not increased, although there is considerable support for placing decision-making in the hands of experts.[11] Popular support for democratic governance has increased, from 87 per cent in 1999 to 92 per cent in 2022. The results also provide little evidence that support for democratic norms is closely associated with trust. Granted, by 2022, rather larger proportions of low trusters favoured expert decisions, and thought democracy a bad system, than did high trusters. But the differences between the two groups are modest (for similar evidence from the United States, see Howe, 2017).

There is also little evidence that declining trust among individuals is associated with more democracy-averse attitudes. I explore this using data from the BESIP between 2014 and 2019, comparing respondents at waves 1 (spring 2014) and 17 (November 2019). Over this period—long enough to expect that any declines in trust might have seeped through into reduced support for democracy—I identify individuals whose levels of trust changed, and explore whether these changes are associated with support for a non-democratic arrangement, namely the country being run by 'a strong leader who does not have to bother with parliament or elections' (measured at wave 17).[12] In 2019, six in ten respondents (60 per cent) disagreed with this arrangement, while one quarter (24 per cent) agreed with it. Support for strong leader rule was only modestly higher among people whose trust in MPs fell over the five years up to 2019 (at 29 per cent) than among those whose trust rose over the period (at 20 per cent). Hence, when levels of trust deteriorate, even over a five-year period, there appear to be few knock-on consequences for people's attitudes towards democratic principles and practices.[13] (For further evidence on this point, see the 'Coda: What does a very low trust state look like?' at the end of this chapter.)

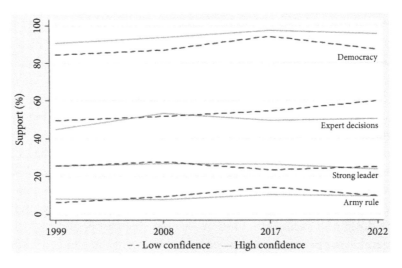

Figure 7.5 Democratic norms, by trust
Source: EVS (1999–2017); WVS (2022)

Undoubtedly the most important change to the British political system in recent times arose from the Brexit referendum in June 2016. This returned a majority of the voting population (52 per cent) in favour of Britain leaving the European Union (EU), an arrangement the country had been a member of for over four decades. For some, the referendum's outcome reflected voters' lack of trust in political and business elites (Evans and Menon, 2017: chapter 2). Given that so many of these elites favoured Britain's position within the EU, a vote for Brexit might well have been a way for people with little trust in those actors to signal their discontent. Indeed, empirical studies (e.g. Curtice, 2017) have shown a strong link between low trust and Leave voting in the EU referendum.[14]

To further test this link, I again draw on the BESIP survey. As before, the main explanatory variable is people's trust in MPs. Among people who said they had no trust in MPs, 62 per cent reported voting Leave, which is substantially higher than the proportion (42 per cent) among people who said they had a great deal of trust in MPs.[15] But was support for Brexit affected by declining rates of trust? We can measure changes in individuals' trust over the period between spring 2014 (Wave 1 of the survey) and summer 2016 (Wave 9).[16] Inspecting reported vote choice in 2016 among people whose levels of trust changed over the previous two years shows *lower* levels of Brexit support among people whose trust fell (at 43 per cent) than among people whose trust increased (at 55 per cent).[17]

There is thus some evidence that low trust among a population is associated with demands for changing the political *status quo*, extending to the type of disruptive break represented by Brexit. Yet popular support for non-democratic forms of governance is not strongly associated with trust, while popular support for fundamental overhaul of the political system does not appear to increase as levels of trust decline (at least over short to moderate periods of time; it is unclear whether people whose trust falls over a longer period are pushed towards more radical demands). People appear to be able to lose some faith in their politicians without demanding wholesale changes to the political system or abandoning democratic norms altogether.

(d) Government activism

Citizens who lack trust in politicians might be particularly unwilling to grant these actors extensive powers and discretion over spending. Why would people accord government sweeping competences and budgets if they do not trust its core personnel to make effective and responsive decisions? This potential problem was clearly in the mind of the former OECD (Organisation for Economic Co-operation and Development) Secretary-General, Angel Gurría, when, in the aftermath of the global economic crisis of 2008, he made this observation about the requisites of government programmes:

> The crisis has highlighted the need to restore confidence in markets, governments and businesses. Crisis-related and urgently needed structural reforms require strong political leadership and a foundation of trust among citizens to be successful.
>
> **(OECD, 2013a: 11)**

Trust might encourage citizens to grant politicians discretionary authority over policy decisions and spending allocations on the grounds that they are likely to use this authority wisely. Conversely, a lack of trust might limit citizens' willingness to extend authority to politicians, and may even induce attempts to wrest back authority, via support for direct democratic mechanisms such as referendums (Seyd, Curtice, and Rose, 2018). In turn, faced with low levels of citizen trust, elected representatives might respond by limiting their decisions to options favoured by citizens rather than selecting unpopular, but potentially socially beneficial, options. Low trust among the population might thus encourage politicians to behave as 'delegates' rather than as 'trustees'. While not intrinsically damaging, this risks introducing short-term considerations and 'pandering' into policymaking, limiting politicians' willingness to take important and necessary decisions if these are seen to run counter to public wishes.

Angel Gurría's claim about the importance of trust for reforming governments is more supposition than demonstrable fact as we lack many studies on the link between individuals' trust and their attitudes to activist government. However, one study of German citizens suggests that government activism gets an easier wind from trusting citizens than from non-trusting citizens. The study found that support for government reforms—in the fields of pensions, healthcare, and family policies—was significantly higher among people who trusted the government than among people who did not trust the government (Gabriel and Trüdiger, 2011). Trust appeared to be associated with a willingness to give policymakers the latitude to undertake changes—often contentious ones—in the provision of economic and social goods. As the study's authors conclude:

> If political institutions and actors are perceived as trustworthy, i.e. honest, fair, reliable and oriented towards the common good, people tend to assume that reforms

of public policies initiated and implemented by those actors are headed in the right direction, while political distrust feeds opposition to those reforms.

(Gabriel and Trüdiger, 2011: 286)

Trust exerts a particular brake on citizens' willingness to accord governments leeway over public service reforms when these reforms extend into the future. People with low levels of trust have been shown to be highly unwilling to support government reforms—where these impose costs on individuals—that stretch decades into the future (Jacobs and Matthews, 2012, 2017).[18]

Even where governments do not wish to reform public services, they may still find that a lack of trust inhibits their ability to provide collective goods and services. The basic logic is the same: the lower individuals' trust in government, the less willing they will be to grant officials the resources and powers to provide extensive public services (Rothstein, 2000).[19] Indeed, empirical studies covering both advanced and developing countries provide evidence of a positive relationship between trust and support for government activism. When it comes to government's role in providing welfare, creating jobs and redistributing income, support has been found to be concentrated among people with high levels of trust and confidence (Edlund, 1999; Habibov, 2014; Goubin and Kumlin, 2022).[20] Examining public attitudes towards various welfare programmes, Hetherington (2005) finds a strong positive relationship between support for government activism and trust (see also Chanley, Rudolph, and Rahn, 2001; Gershtenson and Plane, 2011). Even in conditions where economic inequality is rife and welfare problems are acute, citizens may only favour granting government an extensive welfare role if they trust politicians (Macdonald, 2020). The link between trust and support for government activism extends beyond the provision of welfare services to encompass activities in the field of foreign affairs and defence (Hetherington and Husser, 2012).[21]

However, we should note that trust has not always been found to shape people's support for activist government. Some studies find the relationship between trust and support for government activism to be modest (Edlund, 1999; Habibov, 2014; Peyton, 2020). Others have found that attitudes towards various government welfare functions (such as providing accommodation for the homeless, ensuring access to good education, and providing childcare programmes) are largely unrelated to individuals' trust in government (Gainous, Craig, and Martinez, 2008). A Pew Research Center poll conducted in autumn 2015 found that while levels of trust in government were very low in the United States, most citizens—including supporters of both the Democrat and Republican parties—favoured government involvement in activities such as protecting the environment, ensuring access to quality education, providing a basic income for the elderly, and setting workplace standards (Pew Center, 2015: 45). There is little evidence here of Americans absolving government of responsibility for important social functions; instead, they appear capable of not trusting their government while still looking to it to deliver core public services.

In his analysis of American citizens, Hetherington finds strong relationships over time between aggregate levels of trust and public attitudes towards welfare provision for low-income families (2005: 77) and towards liberal—or active government—law-making (2005: 54). The correlations between trends in trust and public attitudes in these two areas are both strong, exceeding 0.8. In Britain, we can explore similar relationships by examining how far the distribution of trust over time mirrors support for activist government, in the form of support for welfare measures and for government spending. We do so by drawing on the BSA survey, which has measured levels of trust since 1986. Alongside trust, I have selected three survey indicators tapping people's attitudes towards different aspects of government activism, relating to (a) government spending, (b) assistance for the poor, and (c) responsibility for job creation. The wordings of these survey measures are:

(a) Which of these three options do you think the government should choose? Reduce taxes and spend less on health, education and social benefits OR keep taxes and spending on these services at the same level as now OR increase taxes and spend more on health, education and social benefits?
(b) How much do you agree or disagree that ... the government should spend more money on welfare benefits for the poor, even if it leads to higher taxes?
(c) Do you think it should or should not be the government's responsibility to ... provide a job for everyone who wants one?

The trends in trust along with support for increased tax/spending, welfare benefits, and government provision of jobs are shown in Figure 7.6. The correlation between trust and support for more welfare spending over time is moderate (0.64; $p < 0.05$), but the correlations between trust and tax/spending (0.38; $p < 0.08$), and between trust and job provision (0.20; not significant), are weak. There is rather little evidence here that the dynamics of trust align with changes in individuals' support for active government.

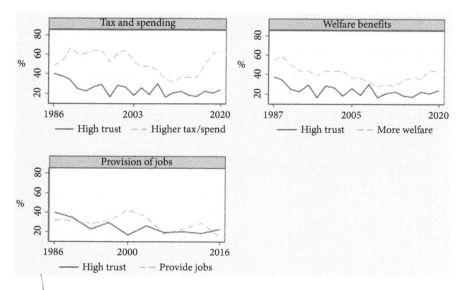

Figure 7.6 Trends in trust and support for active government
Source: British Social Attitudes

If we divide the BSA samples into those 'low' and 'high' in trust and examine support for active government within each group, we again find little evidence of low trust being associated with weaker demands for government activity. Figure 7.7 plots support for higher government tax and spending, government provision of jobs and healthcare, and government help in controlling prices, by levels of trust.[22] As can be seen, there is often very little difference in the demands of government made by low trusters and high trusters. And in many years, those demands appear to be greater, not lesser, among the former group than among the latter group.

To check the robustness of the relationships between trust and support for active government, I constructed models that allow controls to be introduced for a range of factors that might covary with both trust and support for active government. These factors cover ideological beliefs (left–right position), economic status (feelings about household income), and demographic characteristics (age, gender, and education). I constructed eleven models relating to different areas of government activity, covering tax and spending and various services and public policy functions. The data are drawn from the 2016 BSA.

Details of the results from the models are provided in Appendix 7.3. The key finding is that for only two areas of government activism does trust exert any significant impact. And in these areas—providing healthcare and care for

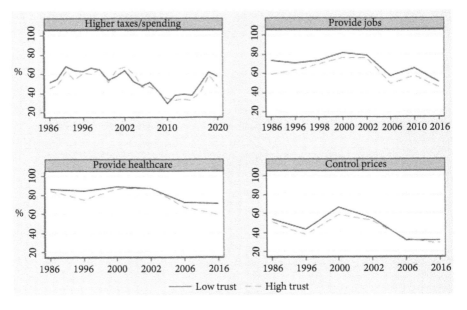

Figure 7.7 Support for active government, by trust
Source: British Social Attitudes

the elderly—the effect suggests that support for active government is actually greater among people low in trust than among people high in trust. Yet as can be seen from the significant coefficients associated with the term measuring left–right position, support for active government in Britain is primarily dependent on individuals' ideological beliefs. Holding right-wing ideological views is associated with significantly lower support for government activism across policy areas than holding left-wing views.

Trust and ideology may not be distinct factors, however, but may be interlinked. In studies of American citizens, Rudolph and Evans (2005) have found trust to be particularly closely associated with support for active government where this support entails some ideological sacrifice, notably among people holding right-wing values. For right-wing individuals, active government is only supportable if those holding elected office can be trusted. To test for such an effect in Britain, I constructed a set of models predicting support for nine policy areas where governments might have an active role. Interaction terms for trust and ideology (i.e. trust x ideology) reveal significant positive coefficients in models predicting support for government responsibility in providing decent housing ($p \leq 0.01$), reducing income differences ($p < 0.05$), keeping prices under control ($p < 0.10$), and providing support for the unemployed ($p < 0.10$). These coefficients suggest that trust is more closely associated with support for active government among right-wing ideologues than among left-wing ideologues. In the other areas of government responsibility (providing jobs, healthcare, care for the elderly, and support for industry, along with imposing environmental laws), the effects of trust are not conditional on ideology. We might surmise that trust is particularly important for right-wing individuals when it comes to government activity involving 'redistributive' welfare provision (where support is targeted on particular social groups, such as non-homeowners and the unemployed) and state involvement in the economy (as with price controls and inequality reduction). When government activity is more 'distributive' (involving support whose effects stretch across the population, such as with healthcare, support for the elderly, and the introduction of environmental laws), trust is less important for right-wing individuals' attitudes towards governments' role.[23]

As a final test, I examined levels of public support for government activism across a broader set of policy fields. At various points, the BSA survey has asked respondents whether they believe the government should play a role in areas such as reducing child poverty, protecting the environment, supporting people in their personal relationships, and dealing with terrorism. While the survey measures vary in the way they are couched, each probes whether respondents favour granting government an active policy role. The results, presented in Table 7.2, show that the association of trust with support for government activism varies between policy areas. When it comes to dealing with terrorists, support for active government is somewhat greater among people low in trust than among people high in trust. Yet when it comes to the areas of personal relationships and environmental protection, support for government activism is greater among people high in trust than among people low in trust. Note, though, that when it comes to protecting the environment, even low trusters are more inclined to favour giving government a role than leaving things to citizens themselves.[24]

We are left to conclude that in Britain at least, and with some exceptions, low levels of trust do not translate into people rejecting an active role for government. At any one point in time, trust is not clearly associated with support for government activism; nor are changes in support for such activism over time clearly paralleled by changes in levels of trust. The weak covariance between trust and support for active government is by no means unusual. As pointed out earlier, some studies in other countries have shown similar results (although analyses conducted in the United States have tended to

Table 7.2 Support for government activism in various fields, by level of trust

	Level of trust	
	Low (%)	High (%)

Child poverty
Who you think should be responsible for reducing child poverty in Britain?

Central government	80	77

Environmental protection
If you had to choose, which one of the following would be closest to your views?

Government should let ordinary people decide for themselves how to protect the environment	48	29
Government should pass laws to make ordinary people protect the environment	52	71

Personal relationships
Please choose the statement that comes closest to your view:

Government should directly provide services to help couples with their relationship; and government should fund services to help couples with their relationship but not be directly involved in providing services	47	55
It is not the role of government to provide or fund services to help couples with their relationship	53	45

Terrorism
Suppose the government suspected that a terrorist act was about to happen.
Do you think the authorities should have the right to:

Detain people for as long as they want without putting them on trial?	71	58
Tap people's telephone conversations?	76	73
Stop and search people in the street at random?	78	73

Trust: For question wording, see note 22 in Chapter 7. Low trust is measured by the response 'almost never'; high trust is measured by the responses 'just about always/most of the time'.
Trust (environmental protection): 'Most of the time we can trust people in government to do what is right'. Low trust: disagree/disagree strongly; High trust: agree/agree strongly.
Sources: British Social Attitudes surveys 2012 (child poverty), 2010 (environmental protection), 2009 (personal relationships), and 2006 (terrorism).

show a stronger role for trust). Part of the reason for the limited association between trust and support for active government could reside in the way trust is measured.[25] More likely, however, is that people's attitudes to active government in Britain are—perhaps unlike attitudes among American citizens (Hetherington, 2005: chapter 3)—shaped primarily by their ideology, not by whether or not they trust government. More specifically, trust assumes a role in shaping attitudes to active government primarily among right-wing individuals, for whom supporting an interventionist state requires a particular investment of trust in political actors.

7.3 The 'exit' consequences of trust

Citizens lacking trust in politicians can register their discontent in a variety of ways, as we have seen. They can vote for anti-system parties, they can engage in protest activities, they can demand changes to the political system and they can reject activist roles for governments. These comprise 'voice' responses of low trust, involving the expression of grievances with political actors and processes. Such grievances can also trigger a different response, involving 'exit', or the withdrawal of individuals from collective political activities. Such exit manifestations of low trust—abstaining at elections, ignoring official information and advice, and not complying with collective obligations—may have significant negative consequences for a country's effective political and civic governance.

(a) Electoral engagement

Low trust might have one of two opposite effects on the likelihood that citizens will participate in elections. The first is a positive effect: people who trust their elected representatives are thereby motivated to participate in contests to select those actors. A positive relationship between trust and turnout is dubbed the 'reward' model by Hibbing and Theiss-Morse (2001). The second is a negative effect: people who do not trust politicians are thereby motivated to participate in elections to sanction and eject incumbent actors. Hibbing and Theiss-Morse dub this the 'repair' model.

Hibbing and Theiss-Morse (2001) claim that the 'repair' model fits the data on turnout better than the 'reward' model, a finding replicated in other cross-sectional (Caillier, 2010) and longitudinal (Ezrow and Xezonakis, 2016) analyses. Other studies find more evidence of the 'reward' model. In his review of the linkages between political support and participation, Dalton (2004: 171–176) reports a consistent positive relationship between trust and electoral turnout (similar results are found by Hooghe and Marien, 2013). Experimental studies also suggest that support for the political system is positively related to ballot participation (Echabe, 2014). Similarly, in Britain, analyses tend to show that people who are positively oriented towards the political system vote at higher rates than people holding negative orientations (Pattie and Johnston, 1998, 2001). However, differences in turnout rates between contented and discontented citizens often appear to be modest (for an example of this in the Canadian case, see Belanger and Nadeau, 2005). Indeed, other studies suggest that trust is substantially unrelated to individual rates of electoral participation (Pew Center, 1998: 49; Cox, 2003; Clarke et al., 2009: chapter 7). In short, there is some doubt over whether people who lack trust are more or less likely to participate in elections than people who trust.[26]

To examine the relationship between trust and electoral turnout in Britain, I begin by identifying historical trends in the distribution of the two factors. Figure 7.8 plots levels of turnout and trust for the 45-year period dating back to 1973. As is visually apparent, there is no close relationship between the two. The slump in electoral turnout in 2001 (an election in which just six in ten of the electorate cast a ballot) was accompanied by a rise, not a decline, in trust, while the slump in trust in 2009 (coinciding with the MPs' expenses scandal) was followed a year later by a modest uptick in turnout. Overall, the pattern of turnout approximates a 'U' shape—declining sharply between 1992 and 2001, followed by a gentle recovery—while levels of trust show more short-term fluctuations. It is thus far from clear that declines in trust coincide with—and might reasonably be thought to trigger—drop-offs in electoral participation.

To further probe the effects of low trust on individuals' electoral participation, I constructed a set of models of (reported) turnout at the 2015, 2017, and 2019 general elections in Britain. Each model estimates the probability of individuals not voting relative to voting. The key explanatory variable is people's trust in MPs. To minimize the risk of omitted variable bias, the models also control for various factors that might covary with both trust and electoral participation, namely an individual's past electoral engagement (their

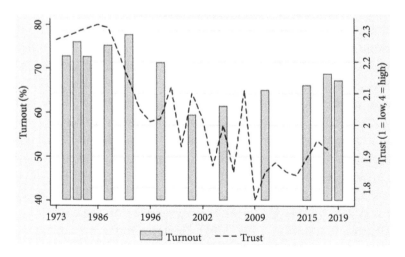

Figure 7.8 Trends in electoral turnout and trust, 1973–2019

Source: Turnout (House of Commons library); Trust (British Social Attitudes)

reported turnout at the previous election), perceptions of ideological differences between the parties, political interest, and various demographic and socio-economic features (education, age, social class, and housing tenure). The results of these models (which are reported in full in Appendix 7.4) indicate that low trust is consistently and significantly associated with individuals not voting at elections. However, these associations are not substantial. Holding the values of all other independent variables constant at their means, and varying trust from its highest to its lowest levels (i.e. going from trust 'a great deal' to 'no' trust), increases the probability of not voting only by around 2 per cent at each election.[27] By contrast, the effect on the probability of not voting of changing levels of political interest from their minimum to maximum values is between 18 per cent and 22 per cent across the three elections.

Overall, the evidence from Britain leans towards the 'reward' model of trust rather than the 'repair' model. Rates of electoral engagement are lower among people who do not trust politicians than among people who trust them. But the differences are not great. Moreover, there is little to suggest that the major dips in electoral participation in Britain in the late 1990s and early 2000s were triggered by low or declining rates of trust.

(b) Acceptance of official information

For citizens to make effective choices and decisions on complex policy issues requires that they have access to accurate information. In today's world, individuals are bombarded with information and in each case have to decide whether its particular source should be trusted or not. Citizens who lack trust in government may, as a result, ignore or discount potentially useful and important official information. Indeed, some commentators have expressed alarm at what they see as citizens' growing resistance to such information arising from their distrust of government and other public actors (D'Ancona, 2017).

Information provided by governments and official agencies is particularly important when it comes to issues and activities involving social risk. Moreover, there is evidence here that trust is positively associated with individual receptiveness to official guidance. The positive effect of trust on accepting important information has been noted in areas such as healthcare (Safran et al., 1998; Hall et al., 2002; Trachtenberg, Dugan, and Hall, 2005; LaVeist, Isaac, and Williams, 2009; Hillen, de Haes, and Smets, 2011), climate change (Pasek, 2018), personal health (Bleich, Blendon, and Adams, 2007), and genetically modified food (Sheldon et al., 2009). Among citizens in the United

States, feeling knowledgeable about global warming has been shown to be associated with greater concern about the phenomenon but only among people who trust scientists; among people who do not trust scientists, knowledge or information is not associated with concern about global warming (Malka, Krosnick, and Langer, 2009). These results suggest that attempts to inform citizens about important matters of personal and public health, social risk and environmental protection are less effective—and thus less likely to contribute to the necessary behavioural changes (which are explored in the following section)—when people do not trust the relevant officials.

We can identify the association between individuals' feelings of trust and their acceptance of official information by drawing on data collected in Britain in 2019. These data were derived from an online survey completed by participants recruited from Prolific Academic (N = 1,180). The survey included measures tapping different forms of negative orientations towards politicians (namely dissatisfaction, scepticism, distrust, and cynicism; see Chapter 2, Section 2.4). It also included four measures of whether citizens are likely to verify official information (a representative survey item is: 'When a politician tells me anything I always double check to make sure it's true') and four measures tapping acceptance of information (a representative survey item is: 'When politicians tell me something I tend to listen'). Details of each of the measures are provided in Appendix 7.5.

To simplify the analysis, I combined the responses to each of the four individual items into single scales, measuring information acceptance (α = 0.63) and verification (α = 0.76). I then correlated each behavioural scale with the different measures of citizens' negative orientations. This exercise showed that verification of political information was particularly associated with scepticism towards politicians (correlation = 0.42) and also, although less strongly, with distrust (= 0.30). Yet accepting information was more closely associated with distrust (correlation = 0.46) than with scepticism (= 0.35), dissatisfaction (= 0.39), or cynicism (= 0.31). Thus, among the various feelings that people have about politicians, trust appears to be particularly closely associated with whether or not they accept official information.

Given this, it is fortunate that people appear to trust at least some of the public actors involved in providing important information around social risk. According to Ipsos' annual 'Veracity Index', people in Britain trust professors more today (80 per cent trust) than they did thirty years ago (70 per cent trust in 1993), while the same is true of scientists, a group that 83 per cent report trusting today as opposed to 60 per cent in 1997.[28] High levels of popular trust in scientists are undoubtedly the reason why, during the Covid-19 pandemic, governments in Britain and many other countries deployed prominent scientific and medical figures to front the official presentation of information to citizens.

(c) Compliance with official rules

Trust may be important not only for individuals' receptiveness to official information but also for whether they comply with that information and any official rules. The next section considers the relationship between trust and citizen compliance in the field of health. The following section considers the relationship between trust and compliance with a broader set of civic behaviours.

Health

One area where it is particularly important that people are receptive to, and accept, official information is the transmission and prevention of disease. In recent years, western countries like Britain have faced a number of public health scares, including bovine spongiform encephalopathy ('mad cow disease') in the late 1980s and 1990s, the H5N1 ('bird flu') and H1N1 ('swine flu') strains of influenza in the 2000s, and the Covid-19 pandemic from 2020. Faced with these public health scares, many governments have encouraged citizens to comply with official rules and to submit to vaccination programmes, in order to reduce the spread of infection.

Empirical studies suggest that low trust often reduces people's willingness to comply with such advice.[29] Analyses of American citizens' reactions to the risk of H1N1 influenza found that acceptance and use of a new vaccination were positively associated with people's trust in government (Quinn et al., 2009; Freimuth et al., 2014). A similar study into people's willingness to vaccinate against H5N1 influenza again found higher reported immunization rates among people who reported high trust in the relevant regulatory agency than among people who reported low trust (Chen, 2015), as was the case for child polio vaccination among Israeli parents (Gesser-Edelsburg, Shir-Raz, and Green, 2016). Trust also appears to shape the adoption of precautionary measures in the face of disease. In Liberia, government-recommended measures to prevent the spread of the Ebola virus were reported to be significantly more prevalent among people who trusted the Liberian government than among people who did not trust it (Blair, Morse, and Tsai, 2017). Most recently, rates of compliance with official rules around Covid-19—for example, over social distancing and mask-wearing—have been found to be higher among people who trust the government and scientists than among people who do not trust these actors (see Seyd and Bu, 2022, and references therein).

Yet in some of these cases, the effects of trust on vaccination are weak (Freimuth et al., 2014). Moreover, longitudinal studies have found that levels of trust measured at one point in time do not predict vaccination take-up at a later date (Gilles et al., 2011). In the context of the Covid-19 pandemic, we can also point to countries—such as Singapore—where high rates of trust among the population did not deliver high rates of communal compliance with coronavirus regulations (Wong and Jensen, 2020) and countries—such as Italy—where low rates of trust were accompanied by high rates of compliance (Guglielmi et al., 2020). A systematic review of public compliance with coronavirus measures found that among the nineteen studies exploring the role of trust in government, just five identified a positive impact on compliance, while three identified a negative impact, and eleven no statistically significant impact (Kooistra and van Rooij, 2020: Table S2).

My own research on the role of trust in shaping people's compliance with official Covid-19 restrictions points to the role of a key conditioning factor, namely individual fear of the virus. In situations where people are concerned about a virus, their compliance with official rules is predominantly shaped by fear and not by whether they trust government. Trust becomes more important, and 'takes up the slack', when individuals are less concerned about the risks posed by a virus (Seyd and Bu, 2022). Thus, trust is an important determinant of whether people engage in pro-social behaviours, but primarily when other determinants of those behaviours—notably fear of infection and of illness—are absent or weak.

Civic behaviour

The coronavirus pandemic has highlighted the importance of individuals following official health guidance and behaving in ways that secure collectively healthy outcomes. Yet effective governance is based on numerous other civic duties that citizens must follow if important collective outcomes are to be realized. Just as low trust may weaken individual observance of officially recommended health-related behaviours like vaccination uptake and social distancing, so it may also undermine their compliance with this wider set of civic obligations. Insights from social psychology suggest that people's willingness to accept collective decisions and to comply with collective obligations is strongly dependent on factors such as the perceived trustworthiness and legitimacy of rule-creating agencies (Tyler and Blader, 2000: chapter 5; Feldman, 2013).

The positive impact of trust in these agencies for individuals' willingness to accept decisions or rules—even if individuals disapprove of their substance—has been shown for a number of political institutions, ranging from the police to local government agencies, the national government, and the US Supreme Court (Tyler and Degoey, 1996; Gibson, Caldeira, and Spence, 2005). On the other hand, low trust has been found to be associated with various behaviours that undermine collective social interests, such as lower rates of tax payment and increased propensity to claim unwarranted government benefits (Bergman, 2002; Slemrod, 2002; Dalton, 2004: 165–169; Richardson, 2008; Steinmo, 2018; Thornton et al., 2019). Analysis of data gathered across European countries shows that the probability of citizens' willingness to dodge such collective obligations more than doubles among people who do not trust government compared to their trusting counterparts (Marien and Hooghe, 2011). Reported compliance with tax obligations in the United States has been found to increase markedly with trust. Even when controlling for feelings of duty to disclose taxable income, the effects of individuals moving from very low to very high levels of trust have been shown to increase tax compliance by a whopping 70 per cent (Scholz and Lubell, 1998).[30] In a study of Australian taxpayers, it was found that resistance to the federal tax office's demands was more strongly shaped by people's trust in that office than by whether its decisions were seen as being personally favourable or not (Murphy, 2004). People's propensity to engage in collectively beneficial actions such as saving water in situations of scarcity has also been found to be greater among people holding a positive view of public agencies than among people whose evaluations are more negative (Capelos et al., 2016).[31]

Studies that measure the way citizens actually behave arrive at similar results. One such analysis examined the impact of trust on citizens' compliance with the law, measured at the country level by rates of criminality (captured by the homicide rate), tax avoidance (captured by the size of the 'shadow' economy), and corruption. Summing these behaviours together to form a 'compliant behaviour index', the researchers found that pro-social forms of behaviour were positively associated with levels of trust, albeit that the relationship existed only for trust in 'output' institutions like the police and civil service rather than for 'input' institutions like government and parliament (Esaiasson and Ottervik, 2014).[32]

To date, there is only a limited body of evidence from Britain on the effects of trust on citizens' observance of collective obligations. Allen and Birch have shown that people's stated willingness to obey the law correlates positively with their degree of trust in government (Birch and Allen, 2012) and their perceptions that politicians are honest (Allen and Birch, 2015: 171–173). Data collected by the polling organization Mori (now Ipsos) suggest that trust also shapes British people's willingness to help the police. Asked whether they would give evidence to a court or help the police if they needed information about a crime, 84 per cent of survey respondents who trusted the police indicated a willingness to engage, compared to 67 per cent figure among people who did not trust the police (Mori, 2003: 23–24).[33] Additional research shows that British citizens are significantly more likely to comply with the law and less likely to report committing offences, if they have some trust in the police (Jackson et al., 2012).

To build on the limited research base on the relationship between trust and compliance with official rules in Britain, I draw on two surveys which contain useful measures of collective behaviour. The first data source is the European Social Survey (ESS). In two of its surveys—in 2004 and 2010—the ESS probed people's attitudes towards complying with such civic obligations as obeying the law, paying taxes, abiding by verdicts reached by courts, and complying with police decisions (details of the measures are provided in Appendix 7.6a). The principal explanatory variable is trust, which comprises an additive scale formed from individual items tapping people's trust in parliament, politicians, political parties, the legal system, and the police.[34] In order to accurately assess the impact of trust on compliant behaviour, the models control for factors that might covary with both compliance and trust, notably demographics (age, gender, level of education, and household income), religious observance, trust in other people, tendency to follow rules, and desire for a strong state (Marien and Hooghe, 2011). Finally, to ensure that attitudes towards compliance with the courts and the police do not simply reflect perceptions of these bodies' operations, controls are introduced to capture how good a job people think both institutions are doing and the fairness of their decisions.

Full results for the seven forms of compliance are shown in Table 7.3. They indicate that reported compliance tends to be higher among religious and older individuals, while gender and education levels have variable effects depending on the type of compliance. Trust also has fairly consistent effects; for almost all collective behaviours, high rates of trust are associated with higher reported compliance. This effect does not extend to trust in other people, since social trust has no significant effect on compliance. The effect of trust on compliance is not that substantial, however. Simulations show that moving from low trust (one standard deviation below the mean) to high trust (one standard deviation above the mean) increases the probability of compliance by at most 3 percentage points (in the case of not avoiding tax).[35]

The results therefore suggest that while trust may shape people's compliance with collective obligations, its effects are not substantial.

The second source of data that allow us to probe the relationship between feelings of trust and observance of collective obligations is the Citizen Audit survey, conducted during 2000–2001. This survey measures a larger variety of collective behaviours than the ESS, ranging across payment of general and sales taxes, obeying the law, informing the Inland Revenue (the UK's central tax office) about tax obligations, not claiming undue government benefits, and willingness to serve on a jury, to donate blood, to contact the police, and to serve as a witness after seeing a robbery take place (details of the measures are provided in Appendix 7.6b). The main explanatory variable comprises an additive scale of trust in various political institutions.[36] Variables are also introduced to control for factors that might covary with both trust and compliance, namely civic duty (measured by perceived duty to vote), moral conservatism (measured by attitudes towards censorship of films), social trust (measured by trust in other people), and religious observance (whether the individual has a religion or not). As with the previous models, terms are also entered to tap respondents' age, gender, education, and income.

The results of the models are shown in Table 7.4. Trust has a consistently positive association with compliant behaviours, although these associations fall short of statistical significance in some cases. As with the effects of trust identified from the ESS data, the substantive impact of trust on compliance is limited. The bottom row in Table 7.4 ('Probability of compliance') presents the predicted effects of shifting from low trust (one standard deviation below the mean level) to high trust (one standard deviation above the mean) on the probability of compliance, holding constant all other variables. The effect of shifting from low to high trust is at most 6 percentage points, in the case of engaging with the Inland Revenue where the effect of trust is to shift the probability of reported compliance from 0.53 to 0.59. Trust therefore contributes, but in a fairly modest way, to individuals' apparent compliance with important collective obligations.

While it would be helpful to assess how far changes in levels of trust over time might have contributed to any shifts in people's feelings of collective obligation, this task is made difficult by the paucity of relevant data in Britain. Yet where such data exist, they provide little sense either that collective obligations among the population have weakened or that any such weakening might be attributed to low trust. Take the obligation to obey the law. Since 1986, the BSA survey has asked people to respond to the question: 'How much do you agree or disagree that ... the law should always be obeyed even if a particular

Table 7.3 Association of trust with collective obligations (European Social Survey)

	Obey law		Not ignore law		Not cheat on tax		Not avoid VAT		Back court		Back police		Call police	
Political trust	0.13	(0.03)**	0.12	(0.03)**	0.15	(0.03)**	0.12	(0.03)**	0.07	(0.03)*	0.16	(0.03)**	-0.05	(0.03)
Social trust	0.02	(0.03)	-0.03	(0.03)	-0.00	(0.03)	-0.03	(0.03)	-0.03	(0.02)	0.03	(0.02)	0.01	(0.03)
Follow rules	0.31	(0.04)**	0.23	(0.04)**	0.14	(0.04)**	0.19	(0.04)**	0.28	(0.04)**	0.26	(0.03)**	-0.05	(0.04)
Strong state	0.12	(0.05)*	0.02	(0.05)	0.11	(0.05)**	0.03	(0.04)	0.13	(0.04)**	0.11	(0.04)**	0.08	(0.05)
Courts good job	–		–		–		–		0.34	(0.06)**	–		–	
Courts fair	–		–		–		–		0.08	(0.03)*	–		–	
Police good job	–		–		–		–		–		0.40	(0.07)**	0.21	(0.08)*
Police fair	–		–		–		–		–		0.45	(0.09)**	0.38	(0.10)**
Religious	0.05	(0.02)*	0.02	(0.02)	0.04	(0.02)	0.05	(0.02)*	0.01	(0.02)	0.06	(0.02)**	-0.00	(0.02)
Income	0.00	(0.02)	0.01	(0.02)	0.00	(0.03)	-0.05	(0.02)*	0.01	(0.02)	0.01	(0.02)	0.08	(0.02)**
Female	0.53	(0.11)**	0.63	(0.11)**	0.35	(0.11)**	0.35	(0.10)**	-0.28	(0.10)**	-0.18	(0.09)*	0.15	(0.11)
Age	0.01	(0.00)**	0.00	(0.00)	0.01	(0.00)**	0.00	(0.00)	-0.00	(0.00)	0.01	(0.00)**	0.01	(0.00)*
Education (ref: ≤age 16)														
≤18	-0.11	(0.14)	-0.01	(0.12)	0.26	(0.14)	0.04	(0.13)	-0.41	(0.15)**	0.20	(0.13)	0.47	(0.16)**
>18	0.13	(0.15)	-0.07	(0.15)	0.43	(0.15)**	-0.01	(0.15)	-0.55	(0.14)**	0.15	(0.13)	0.65	(0.16)**
LRχ^2 (10 df)	200.27		108.13		94.29		91.78		226.86		414.51		78.50	
Prob > F	0.000		0.000		0.00		0.000		0.00		0.000		0.00	
R^2	0.06		0.03		0.03		0.03		0.05		0.05		0.03	
N (unweighted)	1,437		1,439		1,442		1,431		1,736		1,726		1,744	

Coefficients from ordered logit models, and associated standard errors.
Cut-points not shown.
* $p \leq 0.05$; ** $p \leq 0.01$ (two-tailed).
Source: ESS 2 (2004) and 5 (2010), Great Britain samples.

Table 7.4 Association of trust with collective obligations (Citizen Audit)

	Obey law	Pay taxes	Not avoid VAT	Tell Inland Revenue	Claim benefits
Political trust	0.07 (0.03)*	0.11 (0.03)**	0.05 (0.03)	0.13 (0.03)**	0.01 (0.03)
Social trust	0.08 (0.02)**	0.06 (0.02)*	0.00 (0.03)	0.02 (0.02)	0.05 (0.03)*
Sense of duty	0.19 (0.05)**	0.13 (0.05)**	−0.09 (0.05)	0.04 (0.05)	0.12 (0.06)*
Moral conservatism	0.31 (0.05)**	0.18 (0.05)**	0.18 (0.05)**	0.06 (0.05)	0.13 (0.05)*
Belong to religion	0.32 (0.11)**	0.18 (0.10)	−0.04 (0.11)	0.44 (0.11)**	0.26 (0.12)*
Income	−0.05 (0.03)	−0.01 (0.03)	−0.24 (0.03)**	−0.00 (0.03)	0.07 (0.04)
Age	0.02 (0.00)**	0.02 (0.00)**	0.00 (0.00)	0.02 (0.00)**	0.03 (0.00)**
Female	0.36 (0.12)**	0.20 (0.10)*	0.53 (0.10)**	0.31 (0.10)**	0.12 (0.12)
Education (ref: ≤16)					
17–18	0.31 (0.15)*	0.33 (0.14)*	−0.15 (0.14)	0.08 (0.14)	0.32 (0.16)*
≥18	−0.25 (0.14)	0.03 (0.13)	0.02 (0.14)	0.02 (0.14)	0.15 (0.16)
LRχ^2 (10 df)	265.15	182.68	143.69	147.80	135.60
Prob > F	0.000	0.000	0.000	0.000	0.000
R^2	0.10	0.07	0.06	0.06	0.06
N (unweighted)	2,029	1,991	1,954	1,787	2,020
Probability of compliance (−1sd/+1sd)	0.68/0.71	0.58/0.63	0.67/0.69	0.53/0.59	0.80/0.80

Continued

Table 7.4 Continued

	Serve on jury		Donate blood		Contact police		Appear as witness	
Political trust	0.06	(0.03)	0.05	(0.03)	0.11	(0.04)**	0.05	(0.04)
Social trust	0.06	(0.03)*	0.01	(0.03)	0.03	(0.03)	0.01	(0.03)
Sense of duty	0.37	(0.06)**	0.13	(0.05)*	0.24	(0.07)**	0.24	(0.06)**
Moral conservatism	0.05	(0.06)	0.04	(0.05)	0.16	(0.07)*	0.03	(0.06)
Belong to religion	0.07	(0.13)	0.08	(0.11)	0.21	(0.16)	0.11	(0.14)
Income	0.34	(0.05)**	0.17	(0.04)**	0.27	(0.06)**	0.25	(0.05)**
Age	−0.02	(0.00)**	−0.03	(0.00)**	0.00	(0.00)	0.00	(0.00)
Female	−0.28	(0.12)*	−0.33	(0.11)**	0.19	(0.15)	−0.09	(0.13)
Education (ref: ≤ 16)								
17–18	0.23	(0.18)	0.09	(0.16)	0.33	(0.22)	0.20	(0.19)
≥18	0.55	(0.20)**	0.08	(0.16)	0.72	(0.26)**	0.69	(0.22)**
LRχ^2 (10 df)	210.04		136.07		103.82		92.24	
Prob > F	0.000		0.000		0.000		0.000	
R^2	0.10		0.06		0.07		0.05	
N (unweighted)	1,995		1,999		1,987		1,877	
Probability of compliance (−1sd/+1sd)	0.82/0.83		0.73/0.75		0.89/0.91		0.84/0.86	

Coefficients from binomial logit models, and associated standard errors.
Constant not shown.
*$p \leq 0.05$; **$p \leq 0.01$ (two-tailed).
Source: Citizen Audit face to face wave (2000).

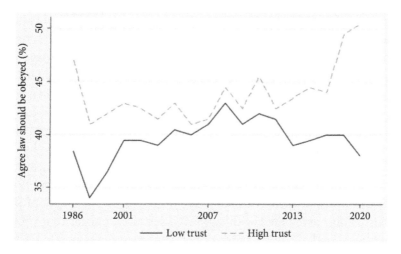

Figure 7.9 Compliance with the law, by trust
Data smoothed using two-year rolling averages.
Source: British Social Attitudes

law is wrong?' In Figure 7.9, I map the distribution of responses over three decades broken down by respondents' levels of trust.[37] The data show that support for obedience to the law sometimes differs little by respondents' level of trust, although by the end of the period, high trusters were significantly more likely to support law abidance (at 51 per cent) than low trusters (at 36 per cent). Over time, however, we have not seen a waning in fidelity to the law in spite of the decline in rates of trust (see Chapter 4, Figure 4.2a).

7.4 Conclusion: What does a low trust society look like?

This chapter has explored the association between people's trust in political actors and a variety of attitudes and behaviours that underpin effective democratic governance. We can try to summarize the results via a thought experiment: what might political and civic life look like in a low trust society? In a context in which levels of trust are consistently low across the population, what might we anticipate the consequences to be? In some areas, of course, there might be some positive consequences; for example, the encouragement of greater vigilance among citizens towards their government. Yet the assumption among most scholars and policymakers is that the consequences of low trust will be largely negative and detrimental to the health of the political system.

To explore these consequences, we distinguished two forms of behaviour (see the summary in Table 7.5). The first is 'voice', which suggests that discontented citizens will engage in various actions to express their grievances, such as participating in protest activities, voting for an anti-system party, demanding reform of the political system, and rejecting an active role for government. These behaviours represent a challenge to the governing process and, in the case of demands for political reform, potential upheaval of the democratic system. Yet the evidence presented here suggests that in the main and in Britain at least, low trust does not provide a strong stimulant to these outcomes. Low trust is associated with engaging in protest activities but primarily in certain situations and among certain types of people. Low trust is also associated with support for protest parties like UKIP, but also for established candidates and parties. While trust is associated with support for political reform, there is little evidence that low or declining levels of trust encourage citizens to query the value of democratic norms. Nor does low trust appear to induce citizens to reject an active role for government in providing support and services. Overall, and contrary to the claim made sixty years ago (Almond and Verba, 1963), there is little sense in which low trust imperils the existence of a 'civic culture'.

The second type of behaviour is 'exit', which suggests that discontent may lead citizens to disengage from the electoral process, to reject official advice and information, and to reduce their compliance with important collective obligations. Such behaviours would, if realized, constitute a real impediment to effective government. The evidence presented here suggests that low trust may be partially corrosive of good governance. In particular, people lacking trust in governments appear less likely to accept official information and guidance on issues like vaccination. This was highlighted during the coronavirus pandemic, when governments and officials commanding high public trust often found it easier to convince people to comply with official restrictions than did actors who were not trusted. This points to the important social costs flowing from low rates of trust among national populations.

Yet these costs are perhaps not as great as sometimes supposed. As the coronavirus pandemic progressed, we learned that trust may be important for people's compliance with official restrictions; but other factors like fear of the virus are also important and can motivate compliant behaviours in the absence of trust. Low trust does not necessarily doom governments' efforts to encourage citizens to behave in socially optimal ways. Similarly, while low trust may make citizens less likely to comply with the law and to pay their taxes, it does not appear to make them much less likely to do so.

Table 7.5 Key outcomes of trust

Outcome	Behaviour	Measure	Finding
Voice	Protest activities	Increased likelihood of protest	Low trust is particularly associated with protest among people who do not vote and also feel politically competent
	Support for anti-system parties	Increased likelihood of voting for anti-system candidates and parties	Low trust is associated with voting for protest parties, but also with voting for non-incumbent mainstream parties
	Demands for political reform	Lower support for democratic norms. Higher support for democratic reforms. Increased likelihood of voting for changes to the political *status quo*, such as Brexit	Low and declining trust are not associated with increases in anti-democratic beliefs. Low trust was associated with Leave voting in the Brexit referendum; but declining trust did not stimulate higher levels of Leave voting
	Attitudes towards active government	Lower support for government role in areas like welfare provision	Low trust is generally not associated with reduced support for active government in key policy areas
Exit	Electoral engagement	Reduced likelihood of voting at elections	Low trust is associated with lower electoral participation. But the effects of trust on turnout are minor, while changes in turnout do not coincide with changes in trust
	Acceptance of official information	Reduced likelihood of accepting official information	Low trust is associated with a lower reported likelihood of accepting information from official sources
	Compliance with official rules	Reduced likelihood of observing official rules in health (e.g. vaccination uptake) and civic life (e.g. payment of taxes)	Low trust is associated with lower compliance with official guidance (e.g. around health), particularly where other motivating factors—such as fear or risk—are absent. Low trust is associated with lower observance of civic behaviours, although the effects are not substantial

Over the past forty years, Britain has become a less trusting country. As we saw in Chapter 4, this distinguishes Britain from many other Western European countries where levels of trust are higher and have maintained over time. This makes Britain a useful case through which to examine the effects of low trust. Yet even in the British case, people's declining trust in their political rulers does not appear to have been matched by a fall-off in their attachment to collective obligations like observing the law. Moreover, low trust does not appear to have stimulated greater opposition to active government. Overall, low trust might pose a challenge to effective governance. But it does not undermine it altogether.

7.5 Coda: What does a very low trust society look like?

Levels of trust in Britain have declined over the past few decades and have now reached a low ebb. Yet as shown in Chapter 4, this decline has taken place over a long period of time, and rates of trust have not quite hit basement levels. To understand what might follow in contexts where trust suddenly plummets to extremely low levels, we have to look beyond Britain, and to those countries hardest hit by the global financial crash of 2007–2008, namely Greece, Ireland, Italy, Portugal, and Spain. In each of these countries, the economic fall-out of the crash was accompanied by precipitous declines in public trust. In Ireland, the proportion of people trusting the national government fell from 41 per cent in 2007 to 16 per cent in 2010; in Portugal, the fall was from 40 per cent in 2007 to 13 per cent in 2013, in Italy from 34 per cent in 2007 to 12 per cent in 2013, in Spain from 55 per cent in 2007 to 9 per cent in 2013, and in Greece from 45 per cent in 2007 to just 7 per cent in 2012 (Figure 7.10). If trust has knock-on effects on people's behaviour, it is surely in these kinds of conditions that we might expect to see clear evidence of such outcomes.

Yet evidence collected before and after the financial crash suggests the decline in trust in these countries did not trigger markedly lower rates of civic compliance among citizens. Take the two cases witnessing the sharpest declines in trust: Spain and Greece. In Spain, when asked in 2007 whether 'cheating on taxes' could be justified or not, 64 per cent of respondents said this behaviour was 'never justified'; by 2011, that proportion had increased to 68 per cent.[38] Among Greeks, 37 per cent of the population responded to the same question in 1999 by indicating that cheating on taxes was never justified, a proportion that rose to 55 per cent in 2008, before falling back slightly to 47 per cent in 2018/2019.[39] Among Spaniards, the proportion who said it was 'very important' to obey the law increased from 58 per cent in 2004 to 61 per cent in 2014.[40]

Nor did the decline in levels of trust appear to weaken people's support for state activities. Asked about a situation in which the government suspected a terrorist attack, plenty of Spaniards in 2006 said they thought government

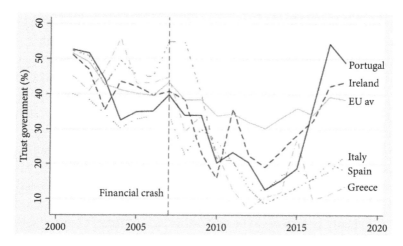

Figure 7.10 Levels of trust in countries hit by financial crash
Source: Eurobarometer

should 'definitely' or 'probably' have the right to detain people indefinitely without trial (50 per cent), to tap people's telephone conversations (49 per cent) and to conduct random stop and searches in the street (31 per cent). Yet in 2016, these proportions had either stayed stable or even increased.[41] Among Greeks, 17 per cent believed in 1999 that greater respect for authority would be a good thing; by 2008 and 2018, this figure had inched up slightly (to 22 per cent and 20 per cent, respectively). And even though the financial crash wreaked particular havoc on Greece's economic and political system, its citizens' commitment to democratic norms did not waver. Asked whether a democratic political system is a good or bad way to govern the country, 83 per cent thought it 'very good' in 1999. This proportion slipped to 75 per cent in 2008 but increased again by 2018 to 78 per cent.

Hence, in spite of the fact that by 2012 and 2013 just 7 per cent of the Greek population and 9 per cent of the Spanish population said they trusted their national governments, there appear to have been few knock-on consequences for people's reported compliance with collective obligations, their support for state activity, their respect for authority, or their commitment to democratic practices.

Are these results any different if we measure people's actual behaviour rather than their attitudes or reported behaviour? As outlined earlier, people lacking trust in their government to take effective decisions and make wise use of public funds may seek to limit how much tax they pay to the state. If many people behave in this way, a 'tax gap' emerges, representing the difference between the tax income owed to the state for a given amount of economic activity and the amount collected by the state. A high tax gap indicates that individuals are seeking to minimize the tax they contribute to the state. Given the lack of data on tax gaps across countries and over time (Murphy and Guter-Sandu, 2018), I use as a measure of tax compliance the 'VAT gap'; the amount of value-added tax (VAT) owed to the state against the amount of VAT collected (Poniatowski et al., 2019), which represents a general measure of tax avoidance. Higher scores indicate a greater gap between tax owed and tax collected.

I take the example of Greece which, as we have just seen, experienced a very sharp decline of trust between 2007 and 2012 (Ervasti, Kouvo, and Venetoklis, 2019). There is some evidence that this lack of trust led many Greeks to boycott paying for some collective services, such as public transport (Exadaktylos and Zahariadis, 2014). Yet at the same time, the VAT gap fluctuated but showed no systematic increase. The main rise in the tax gap occurred in the early 2000s, prior to the financial crash; thereafter, while trust fell, the VAT gap dipped up and down rather than increasing (Figure 7.11).[42] Thus, while the financial crisis triggered a sharp decline in Greeks' trust of their government, it triggered little clear decline in contributions to the state in the form of tax payments on goods and services.

Another form of compliance with civic obligations that was earlier shown to be affected by trust is medical vaccination. If trust is an important

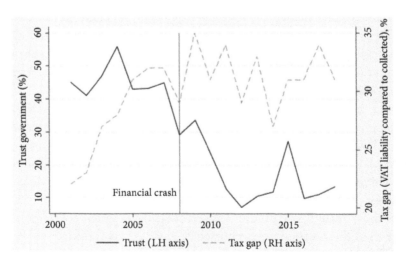

Figure 7.11 Levels of trust and tax evasion in Greece, 2001–2018
Source: Trust data: Eurobarometer; Tax gap: OECD

contributor to people's acceptance of official guidance to vaccinate themselves and their children, we should find vaccination rates declining as levels of trust fall. Using data from the World Health Organization and UNICEF, it is clear that vaccination rates of young children in Greece, Portugal, and Spain did not decline after the financial crash.[43] Here, again, there is no evidence that declining public trust in political actors seeps through into public resistance to official guidance on such collectively beneficial behaviours as infant inoculation.

Countries like Greece and Spain were particularly severely affected by the financial crash of 2007–2008, and, as governments struggled to deliver economic goods and services, levels of public trust plummeted. These countries thus provide useful 'natural laboratories' in which to identify the potential effects of declining public regard for political actors. Some effects often associated with low trust are clearly detectable, notably the electoral shift away from incumbent governing parties and the rise in support for anti-system protest parties such as Golden Dawn in Greece (Teperoglou and Tsatsanis, 2014). Yet when it comes to a broader set of civic behaviours and attitudes—payment of taxes to the state, heeding of official advice over vaccinations, and commitment to democratic norms—there is less evidence of malign effects arising from low trust. Apparently, people's trust in political actors can fall to very low levels without citizens rejecting democratic arrangements or seeking to remove themselves from important social obligations.

Conclusion
The problem of trust

Trust is now a central concern for policymakers, business leaders, and public organizations. The annual gathering of financial and political elites at the World Economic Forum selected as the theme for its 2022 meeting 'working together to regain trust'. There is a widespread concern that trust—the vertical ties connecting individuals with actors and organizations—has weakened in recent years. As recently as 2017, Edelman's annual review of global attitudes was titled 'Trust in crisis' (Edelman, 2017b). The perceived decline of trust is seen to bring in its wake a medley of negative consequences. This decline and the perceived negative effects flowing in its wake are driving initiatives designed to shore up trust. This concluding chapter reflects on what the evidence and data presented in the previous chapters tell us about the 'problem' of trust, and what can—and should—be done in response.

Is there a problem of trust?

In some countries, and for some organizations, there is little hesitation in diagnosing a 'problem' of trust. In countries like Britain and the United States, significantly fewer people trust political actors today than was the case fifty or more years ago. According to the latest figures (from 2020) in the British Social Attitudes survey, just 24 per cent of the British population trusts government 'most of the time' or 'almost always', down from 40 per cent in 1986. The Pew Center reports that Americans' trust is now down to 20 per cent. During the Kennedy and Johnson era in the mid-1960s, trust reached 77 per cent, and as recently as 2001 the figure was as high as 49 per cent.[1]

Concerns about this decline in trust are not limited to government officials and policymakers. Ordinary citizens themselves appear to recognize the problem and are worried by it. In 2018, 75 per cent of Americans said they thought that their fellow citizens' trust in the federal government had shrunk. Not far short of this figure, 64 per cent, said they thought low trust in the federal government made it harder to solve problems (Pew Center, 2019b).

Yet even among British and American citizens, low trust is not endemic. Americans still express positive views about important public and civic office-holders like police officers and religious leaders (Pew Center, 2022). Moreover, levels of trust in groups like business, the media, and non-governmental organizations (NGOs) have, on at least some measures, increased over time rather than declined. Data from the Edelman Trust Barometer show that among Americans, trust in business increased from 41 per cent in 2002 to 49 per cent in 2022, with trust increasing also in the media (30 per cent to 39 per cent) and in NGOs (38 per cent to 45 per cent). Among Britons, 80 per cent currently profess to trust judges, while well over one-half professes trust in the police (63 per cent) and in civil servants (56 per cent) (Ipsos, 2022). Other important actors like business leaders and local government councillors are trusted rather less (by 32 per cent and 38 per cent of the population, according to the same survey). Yet even these figures are significantly higher than the measly 16 per cent who profess trust in government ministers and 12 per cent who profess trust in politicians. Citizens are perfectly willing to trust some actors performing important state roles, and even more willing to trust other actors who do not have a state role (such as doctors, who are trusted by 85 per cent of British people). Very low trust is reserved for state actors performing representative or partisan roles.

The 'problem' of trust is specific not only to objects (actors and institutions) but also to contexts (countries). As noted in Chapter 4, trust in the national government is widespread among individuals in Scandinavian countries. Outside these countries, more people currently trust the national government than do not trust it in countries like Germany, Luxembourg, and Switzerland.[2] Across Western Europe, it is mistaken to diagnose a general crisis of trust; instead, there are three trust groupings: 'high trust' populations in countries like Denmark and Sweden; 'medium trust' populations in countries like Ireland and Germany; and 'low trust' populations in countries like Britain, France, and Italy.

Levels of trust are therefore specific to particular objects and to particular contexts. Yet trust is often not specific to individuals. In Chapter 4, we examined the distribution of trust within the British population and concluded that trust does not vary greatly between different demographic groups. Nor, as we identified in Chapter 5, do changes in trust over time reflect the distinct experiences and preferences of particular generations. Rather, levels of trust change over time more or less consistently across different generations, in the form of 'period effects'. This suggests that the distribution of trust is general, a judgement about political rulers that is broadly consistent across the population.

Yet as we also found in Chapter 5, over-time changes in trust reflect different dynamics among groups within the population. In particular, we identified distinct dynamics of trust over the past four or so decades among individuals we broadly termed the social and economic 'haves' and 'have nots'. Over this period, levels of trust among poorly educated and less affluent individuals have fallen significantly faster relative to levels among well-educated and affluent individuals. We observed such dynamics not only in Britain (see Chapter 5, Figures 5.1 and 5.3) but also in other European countries (Figure 5.2), although not in the United States. There is thus evidence that trust judgements are becoming more varied between different social groups, albeit that these distinctions are less pronounced than those between national populations.

Each of these findings suggests that there is no general crisis of trust facing western democracies. Within countries, there are actors and institutions that citizens still appear to trust, to set alongside the (partisan) actors in whom low trust is more evident. Between countries, there are significant variations in levels of trust, with some national populations manifesting high and consistent rates of trust to set alongside countries—like Britain—in which trust is lower and has fallen over time. Within populations, there are variations in the dynamics of trust between different socio-economic groups, with certain types of individual losing trust more rapidly than others. Collectively, these results suggest that any 'problem' of trust is specific and not generalized across objects, countries, or even individuals.

Analysing how trust is distributed within and across national populations represents one way of approaching the 'problem' of trust. Another involves identifying its effects or outcomes. Is low trust among individuals associated with beliefs and behaviours that, aggregated across the population, present serious impediments to effective democratic governance? As already noted, there is widespread concern about the potential negative consequences of low and declining rates of public trust. In the Introduction, I quoted Edelman's Chief Executive, who claimed that 'We have moved beyond the point of trust being simply a key factor in product purchase or selection of employment opportunity; it is now the deciding factor in whether a society can function' (Edelman, 2017a). What should we make of such an apocalyptic statement?

The analysis in Chapter 7 provided a framework for thinking about the potential effects of trust, based on Albert O. Hirschman's (1970) well-known distinction between 'voice' and 'exit' strategies among individuals. Voice entails the expression of individuals' grievances, in this case through demands for political reform and denying state actors key areas of authority.

Exit entails disengaging from a relationship, in this case by ceasing to participate in elections and by ignoring collective information and civic obligations.

While voice behaviours are generally easier to accommodate, and less politically disruptive, than exit behaviours, they still present a major challenge to the political system. In recent years, we have seen large and disruptive public protests directed against various western governments, including the *gilets jaunes* movement in France and the Covid-19 gatherings by Canadian truckers in 2022. Populist candidates and parties seeking to upend established political norms and practices have been elected to office in numerous countries in Europe and beyond. Many individuals have lent their support to calls for more direct citizen input into decision-making, in the form of referendums, for example (Hernández, 2016). Occasionally, such direct citizen input breaks through into the mainstream political process and disrupts its political arrangements, as with the Dutch and French 'No' votes in the 2005 European Union (EU) constitution referendums or, most notably and recently, the 'Leave' vote in the 2016 referendum on British membership of the EU.

Each of these examples of voice shares some roots in citizens' lack of trust in political elites. Yet a detailed analysis of the data from Britain—where, it should be remembered, levels of trust have declined to levels below those in most other Western European countries—suggests that the effects of trust on such voice behaviours are less strong than is sometimes supposed. When it comes to engagement in political protest, the evidence presented in Chapter 7 points to higher activity rates only among certain people, not among all low-trusting individuals. In the case of support for system-challenging parties, the evidence suggests that declining trust among individuals is associated not only with increased support for populist outlets like the UK Independence Party but also with increased support for some mainstream parties. Similarly in the United States, the evidence suggests that low trust shaped support for mainstream Republican presidential candidates like Mitt Romney in 2012 just as much as it did for the more populist candidate, Donald Trump, in 2016. While 'Leave' voting in Britain's Brexit referendum was more common among low trusters than high trusters, there is little evidence that declining trust pushed people into supporting Britain's departure from the EU. Nor is there evidence that low trust impels people to question the basic practices and norms of the democratic system or to deny governments a role in providing and funding an extensive range of public services.

Low levels of trust thus do not appear to translate straightforwardly into widespread, serious, and disruptive forms of voice behaviour among citizens.

Rather, the effects of trust are more conditional and often rather weak. As such, low trust cannot be said to clearly undermine the political order.

The same is true when it comes to 'exit' forms of behaviour. Granted, there are examples where low trust does appear to be associated with exit behaviours, such as abstaining from voting. Low levels of trust also appear to be associated with a lower inclination among individuals to comply with civic obligations such as obeying the law and paying taxes. Most obviously of all, following the outbreak of the coronavirus pandemic in early 2020, trust has been widely argued to have been a central element in authorities' efforts to ensure that their populations comply with important health-related rules and restrictions. Given this, it is hardly surprising that the commentary of the Organisation for Economic Co-operation and Development (OECD) on the pandemic concluded that 'governments need to give priority to addressing issues of trust' (2021: 3).

Yet the analysis presented in Chapter 7 highlighted various qualifications to the association between low trust and such potentially damaging behaviours. In some cases, these qualifications concerned the modest magnitude of the relationships identified between trust and exit activities. Thus, while levels of electoral engagement are lower among people who lack trust than among their more trusting counterparts, the difference is not that large. Similarly, while low trust citizens manifest less inclination to abide by such civic obligations as obeying the law and paying taxes than their high trust counterparts, the gap between the two groups is not great. Trust does not serve as a substantial demarcator between individuals who comply with civic duties and those who do not.

In other cases, the qualification concerns the conditional nature of the effects of trust. When it comes to people's compliance with official coronavirus rules, for example, trust is important, but primarily when other factors that also motivate compliance—such as fear of infection and illness—are low or absent. In other cases, the qualification concerns the differential effects of trust, which arise on some issues but not on others. Take the example of public support for activist government. Here, we found that trust appears to shape public attitudes on governments' role in the area of environmental protection but not in the areas of state taxation and spending and appropriate levels of welfare support (although this conclusion may be particular to Britain; there is evidence that trust is more closely associated with such attitudes in the United States).

The importance of trust for the effective operation of the political system should not be ignored. But neither should it be exaggerated. The evidence from Britain suggests that low levels of trust among citizens can coexist with a widespread popular commitment to, and engagement in, the practices and norms of political life. Even in countries where levels of trust plummeted to rock-bottom levels—like Greece and Spain in the aftermath of the 2007–2008 financial crash—there is little evidence of a major hit to important civic and political behaviours such as paying taxes, heeding advice on vaccination, and favouring democratic rule over non-democratic alternatives. An absence of trust might pose some stiff challenges to political rulers and systems, but it does not undermine their status and capacities altogether.

What, then, is the 'problem' of trust? For a phenomenon to be at crisis-point, there must be evidence either that it exists at a very low level and/or that it is closely associated with a set of socially damaging outcomes. For now, neither is clearly the case with trust. The overall *level* or *amount* of trust is not consistently low across different actors or contexts. Low trust in some actors and countries coexists with high trust in other actors and in other countries. Nor do the *consequences* of trust present a clear existential challenge to civic and political life. Low trust may encourage certain 'voice' and 'exit' behaviours among citizens, but not sufficiently consistently or strongly to undermine existing democratic practices and norms. In this context, the problem of trust is specific and conditional, rather than general and absolute. The problem of trust is just that: a problem. It is not—at least yet—a crisis.

The nature of trust

A key element in understanding the 'problem' of trust is clarity about the concept's nature and meaning. Existing studies tend to adopt a deductive, or top-down, approach to this task, identifying the key features of trust by reference to its broad qualities and principles. While this approach may be conceptually useful or satisfying, it tells us little about how individuals apply trust judgements, and therefore about what trust means and entails for people in practice. The coverage presented here (notably in Chapter 1) has sought to rebalance the dominant top-down, or conceptual, perspective on trust by applying a more bottom-up, or observational, perspective.

One way of approaching a more individual-centred analysis of trust is to consider how this relates to an idealized perspective of the subject. Trust is often seen to arise from deliberative and cognitive evaluations of an actor, resting on perceptions of how the actor behaves and what they deliver. Offe (1999: 55) argues that 'Trust is a thoroughly cognitive phenomenon. It depends upon knowledge and belief'. Faced with a choice over whether or not to trust an object, an individual engages in a cognitive review of the object and of their performance on a particular task or function. This is the implication—or ideal—of the conceptual or top-down picture of trust.

Our more individual-focused or bottom-up perspective suggests that this ideal captures some important elements of the way individuals form trust judgements. For example, we noted in Chapter 1 that people's trust in some institutions is distinct from their trust in other institutions. Critical incidents or crises arising in relation to one institution or set of actors—for example, the 2008 global financial crash and the 2009 scandal over MPs' expenses in Britain—often do not 'spill over' into critical trust judgements of other institutions and actors. Associated with this, we also saw in Chapter 6 how people's trust in particular institutions reflects a somewhat different balance of factors to their trust in other institutions. An issue or appraisal that shapes people's trust in central government, say, may play less of a role in shaping their trust in institutions like local government, the courts, or the police. Similarly, as we also found in Chapter 6, people's trust judgements may rest more heavily on specific factors at particular moments in time; trust judgements reflect considerations that are particularly 'live' or salient to individuals. Finally, and in the same chapter, we also saw how the trust judgements of particular individuals—those commanding high or low levels of political information, say—draw to different degrees on specific beliefs or perceptions.

Individual expressions of trust are thus frequently 'specific' to the particular object being evaluated, the particular context or time-point at which evaluations take place, and the particular characteristics of the individual making the evaluation. Each of these features broadly aligns with a deliberative or evaluative model of trust.

However, people's expressions of trust also suggest a more generalized, and less evaluative, side to trust. Thus, when we capture individuals' expressions of trust in a range of actors and institutions, these often manifest a singular, rather than a distinctive, structure. An individual's trust in government ministers, say, thus overlaps with their trust in senior judges. In addition, while conceptual studies emphasize the importance of the function or domain of trust—*A* trusts *B* in relation to *X* but not necessarily in relation to *Y*—the evidence presented in Chapter 1 pointed to limited variation in trust between domains. '*A* trusts *B* in relation to *X*' is sometimes less evident in people's attitudes than simply '*A* trusts *B*'. Moreover, as noted in Chapter 1, trust is a largely stable judgement. Outside major disruptive political events or crises, individuals' trust is broadly consistent across time. People do not seem to reappraise actors each time they are asked to form a trust judgement. Instead, they either appear to carry around pre-formed evaluations which can be applied when required, or they form trust judgements on the spot based on a well-worn and habitual set of considerations.

People's expressions of trust therefore arise from both specific appraisals and evaluative processes and more generalized perceptions and stimuli. The balance between the two is likely to reflect various factors, such as the nature of the trustor (notably how much information they possess) and the context in which trust is being evaluated (notably how personally important or salient particular issues or concerns are to individual trustors).

A wider point is that the nature of people's trust judgements is likely to shape both the outcomes of these judgements and how receptive they are to changing conditions and new information. Expressions of trust arising primarily from impressionistic and affect-driven stimuli may not be associated with significant behavioural outcomes among individuals. Where those expressions lack deliberative and evaluative foundations, there may be insufficient cognitive triggers to generate discernible alterations in individuals' attitudes and behaviours. The net effect is that individuals may express a lack of trust for routine or shallow reasons without this having a knock-on effect on their wider beliefs and actions.

Moreover, generalized and non-deliberative expressions of trust may also be resistant to change. We have noted that individuals' trust judgements tend to be fairly consistent over time. These judgements can change, as when a critical event makes individuals re-evaluate their views of an actor; hence, for example, the changes in trust in particular actors after crises (see Figure 1.1). Yet aside from such shocks that might trigger more deliberative evaluations, trust—for many people and in relation to many objects—often reflects generalized impressions and feelings that are not continually updated in response to new information. For this reason, studies reported in Chapter 1 find that providing people with new information about an object does little to shift their trust in the object. Instead, trust is often 'sticky' and resistant to new information. The implications of this for any attempts to boost levels of trust among national populations are examined in the next section.

An individual-centred, or bottom-up, analytical approach also yields important conclusions about the 'states of trust' among citizens. We pointed in Chapters 1 and 3 to the unfortunate tendency of existing (often survey-based) measures of trust to pigeon-hole individuals as either 'trusting' or 'distrusting'. In fact, many people hold both positive and negative attitudes about political actors and are thus 'ambivalent'. Studies reported in Chapter 1 show that more than one-half of Americans are ambivalent in their orientations to core political actors and institutions, while data presented in the same chapter show that almost two-thirds of British citizens are similarly conflicted. Rather than evaluating an actor in a blanket fashion ('politicians are bad'), many people take a more discriminatory approach, being critical of some aspects of politicians' work while more positive about others.

Nor are people scoring low on measures of trust necessarily distrustful. Trust equates to a condition in which an individual believes an actor is likely to act in a way consistent with their interests. Distrust equates to a condition in which an individual believes an actor is likely to act in a way detrimental to their interests. Withholding trust ('I do not believe an object will act in my interests; they are therefore not trustworthy') comprises a different belief to active distrust ('I believe an object will act against my interests; they are therefore untrustworthy'). The questions and response options in most opinion surveys lend themselves to identifying conditions of high or low trust but not of distrust. In fact, where surveys have explicitly measured low trust and distrust, they have typically found rather little overlap between the two (Cook and Gronke, 2005).

These points highlight two important aspects of trust that have gained insufficient recognition among academics and policymakers. First, individuals are often more conflicted or equivocal in their appraisals of political actors than implied by the stark labels 'trust' or 'distrust'. Second, individuals identified by opinion surveys as lacking trust are not thereby also distrustful. These points have significant implications—which were explored in Chapter 3—for the way analysts gauge trust. These implications point to the desirability of measuring trust through multiple items, and of allowing individuals to report different (positive or negative) evaluations on particular aspects of an actor's performance and behaviour. They also point to the desirability of survey question response scales being specifically calibrated to capture distrusting evaluations, not just non-trusting evaluations.

If we accept the relevance of accurately measuring citizens' orientations towards political actors and of discriminating between different orientations (trusting, non-trusting, and distrusting), these points are important. A failure to recognize them may lead to misdiagnosing levels of trust and therefore the magnitude of the trust 'problem'. Survey measures that force people into a position on a singular 'trust–no trust' scale fail to do justice to more specific attitudes—some highly positive, others highly negative—that people have towards different aspects of politicians and their work. Potential error is exacerbated by the knee-jerk responses some people almost certainly provide to questions that explicitly reference 'trust' and 'politicians' in the same sentence. As we saw in Chapter 3, when trust is captured in a different way—through implicit measures, for example—recorded levels of trust turn out to be significantly higher.

Beyond misdiagnosis of the 'condition', coarse measurement of trust may also hinder accurate identification of its consequences. While low trust is often seen to be closely associated with a range of negative civic and political outcomes, its wider implications are—as we saw in Chapter 7—sometimes milder and less serious than scholars and policymakers often assume. One explanation might be that existing measures of trust are capturing, and lumping together, a broad strata of the population, ranging from people who are mildly discontent with their political rulers to people who are more seriously disaffected. This point was made cogently by Citrin (1974) almost fifty years ago but still plagues our measurement—and thus understanding—of trust. Until analysts take more seriously the need to distinguish between different forms of political discontent, the effects of any decline in assessed trust on outcomes underpinning the effective operation of the political system will remain unclear.

What can be done to improve trust?

The existing scholarly literature on trust has not provided a great service to policymakers in helping them understand whether low trust is a problem that should be addressed, and if so, what kinds of strategies and approaches might provide effective responses. Analyses of the effects of trust have not kept pace with the voluminous range of studies on the levels and causes of trust. As a result, we know less than we should about the outcomes of low and declining levels of trust. A major concern of this book has been to rebalance this focus and to address these effects more systematically. The conclusion outlined above and in Chapter 7 was that the effects of trust are often more specific, more modest, and more conditional than is often made out. Faced with this, policymakers might be inclined to dismiss the 'problem' of trust and to ignore strategies for improving trust.

That would be a mistake. Although the analysis in Chapter 7 challenged apocalyptic claims about the effects of declining public trust, it also pointed to examples where low public regard for political rulers carries significant negative consequences. We only have to look at the role played by trust in encouraging public compliance with collective health rules during the coronavirus pandemic to see an example where trust contributes to important collective goods. Moreover, if individual trust judgements rest (at least in part) on evaluations of government trustworthiness, it would seem odd for politicians to ignore any deterioration in these judgements. One would hope that politicians concerned about their electorates would not ignore their judgements and would take steps to make themselves more worthy of citizens' trust.

Assuming policymakers are motivated to respond in this way, what kind of approaches should they adopt? This section identifies some general principles to guide policymakers in this task. It does not explore the role of specific initiatives, since reviewing these would take too long, and in any case I am sceptical about the role that specific, stand-alone initiatives might play in triggering major shifts in citizens' judgements. I have in mind here injunctions running along the lines of 'Trust would be solved if only politicians would …', followed by a variety of loosely connected initiatives, such as transparent budgeting processes, participatory policymaking, more representative electoral systems, and the like.

The limitation of such specific initiatives was made clear in Chapter 6, one of whose key findings was the breadth of factors associated with citizens' trust judgements. Trust does not rest on one or two factors—which might be addressed by specific or piecemeal initiatives—but, rather, on a variety of judgements relating to an actor's competence, benevolence, and integrity. Moreover, even where an actor is evaluated highly on one of these factors, this does not appear to obviate the need for the actor to perform well on others (see Chapter 6, note 11). Even in cases where trust-building initiatives might be targeted at specific groups within the population, the necessary measures are far from simple. Take the evidence from Chapter 5, which highlighted the decline of trust primarily among socio-economically disadvantaged individuals. A recent study has shown that trust among individuals with lower levels of education is particularly receptive to improvements in national-level economic performance, more so than is trust among highly educated individuals (Martini and Quaranta, 2020: 196–202). Yet if this is correct, it implies that a narrowing of the trust gap between the socio-economic 'haves' and 'have nots' rests on securing continued national economic growth, and presumably also in a way that produces significant material improvements for those at the lower end of the socio-economic scale. Neither of these conditions is an easy ask of governments in today's pinched and competitive economic climate.

For policymakers concerned to improve levels of public trust, two additional hindrances—touched on in Chapter 1—should be noted. The first is the role of good and bad government performance, or rather government performance that citizens appraise in either positive or negative terms. We have already raised the concern that if individual trust judgements rely more on general impressions and feelings than on deliberative and evaluative processes, any improvements in government performance may not necessarily stimulate more positive attitudes among citizens. Yet even if individuals do access and evaluate information on government performance, the effects on trust may still be limited.

To understand why, we must begin by acknowledging that positive information about politicians' behaviour can stimulate citizens' trust (Hetherington and Rudolph, 2015: 189–192; Martin et al., 2020) just as negative information or examples of negative behaviour can depress it (Faulkner, Martin, and Peyton, 2015). In principle, then, appropriate behaviour and effective performance among politicians can increase the stock of public trust. This 'performance-based' focus to improving trust has also been validated in two recent studies that look at very different aspects of government administration. The first study explores the 2008 financial crisis, in the aftermath of which trust in national governments fell among citizens across Western Europe, before rebounding. Yet the impact of changes in economic performance (both in negative and positive directions) on trust was found to be no greater in countries and in years where economic performance was very poor than in countries and years where economic performance was very good (Hooghe and Okolikj, 2020). The implication is that improvements in economic conditions might have just as great an effect in boosting trust as deteriorations in these conditions have on lowering trust.

The second study is of the Swedish Election Authority, an agency of the Swedish government which mishandled ballot counting in a regional election in 2010, resulting in the result being declared void. At the time of the bungled election, 55 per cent of the region's inhabitants rated the performance of the Election Authority as good, a figure that fell to 42 per cent a year later when the election was rerun. Yet by 2012, the proportion saying the Authority was doing a good job had more than rebounded to 66 per cent of the population (Lundmark, Oscarsson, and Weissenbilder, 2020). Apparently, any hits to an institution's perceived trustworthiness may be offset by subsequent improvements in performance.

There are good reasons, however, to be somewhat sceptical about the capacity of performance improvements by governments and public agencies to reinvigorate lost trust. For a start, there is evidence that individuals' trust judgements draw on evaluations of economic performance primarily when the state of the economy is important or salient to them. Yet the salience of the economy tends to increase when economic times are bad, which has the effect of lowering levels of trust (Chapter 6, note 22). Economic good times would, in theory, be accompanied by more positive trust judgements. Yet in these circumstances, individuals tend to discount the importance of the economy. The net effect is that economic slumps tend to have a greater (negative) effect on trust than the (positive) effect on trust induced by economic booms (Hetherington and Rudolph, 2008, 2015: 66–69).

Moreover—and the second hindrance to policymakers seeking to boost levels of trust—any performance improvements by governments or agencies are unlikely to be evaluated by citizens on a blank slate but rather against the backdrop of their existing feelings and beliefs. Numerous studies in psychology tell us that individuals receive and interpret information in light of their existing predispositions and values and are more likely to accept (or reject) information where this accords with (or goes against) these predispositions (Kunda, 1990). Hence individuals already harbouring negative impressions of public actors and institutions may be less receptive to any performance improvements by these bodies. Experiments conducted in the United States, for example, have provided individuals who are positively disposed either to the private sector or to the public sector with information about good and bad service provision on the part of an organization whose public or private nature is concealed. Among individuals holding more pro-private sector views, a noticeably larger proportion interpreted information about positive performance as suggesting the organization in question was in the private sector, while individuals holding more pro-public sector views were more likely to interpret positive performance information as suggesting the organization was in the public sector. In a reworking of the same experiment, other participants were told about the public or private status of the service provider but were not told about how well the provider was performing. This time, people holding pro-private sector views were more likely to interpret the performance of the public provider in negative terms than they were to similarly interpret the performance of the private provider (Lerman, 2019: 73–88; see also Marvel, 2016; Hvidman, 2019; van den Bekerom, van der Voet, and Christensen, 2021). Thus, even though participants did not know the identity of the service provider (in the first experiment) or the quality of the service provision (in the second experiment), they drew—consciously or unconsciously—on existing predispositions about public and private sector organizations to reach conclusions.

Such confirmation biases are likely to shape how citizens respond to information about government performance, particularly among citizens who already hold low levels of trust in political actors. A separate experimental analysis conducted in the United States showed that citizens' evaluations of information about the performance of government agencies are shaped not solely by the source of the information (i.e. whether this was a government agency or an independent body) but specifically by the provision of positive information on the part of a government agency. It appears that when citizens do not trust the government, they react against information provided by governing agencies that presents their performance in a positive light (James and Van Ryzin, 2017; see also van den Bekerom, van der Voet, and Christensen, 2021). This finding has been reinforced by a study of government transparency during the coronavirus pandemic. Among a sample of Irish citizens, those provided with extensive information about Covid-19 contagion rates and hospital admissions became more trusting of government but only if their initial level of trust was high. By contrast, among participants whose trust was low, the provision of information further depressed their negative judgements (Crepaz and Arikan, 2021).

If people's existing predispositions about public agencies exert such a strong effect, and if those predispositions are often negatively valenced (as suggested by the low levels of trust currently witnessed among populations in countries like Britain and the United States), it is unlikely that simply presenting citizens with information about good government performance will suffice to convince swathes of the public to increase their feelings of trust. Too many citizens already hold negative predispositions towards government and are likely to discount information that presents government actors and institutions in a positive light.

This may help explain the case just noted, concerning the rebound in trust in the Swedish Election Authority after its mishaps in 2010. This rebound was possible because Swedish citizens generally trust their state institutions, and the Election Authority's performance ratings were generally high. State institutions that are trusted might find it easier to regain trust after a crisis than institutions that are not trusted. We saw in Chapter 1 that negative information is particularly corrosive of trust in the case of bodies that are already distrusted (Cvetkovich et al., 2002). Similarly, more positive information might have greater restorative effects on bodies that are already trusted. In this sense, existing levels of trust among individuals may create dynamics or 'spirals' that are enduring and difficult to surmount.

We saw at the beginning of this chapter that ordinary people are well aware of the problem of trust. Polling among American citizens shows that most people perceive levels of trust in government among the population to have declined, while a majority also believes this decline makes it more difficult to resolve collective problems. Yet citizens are also optimistic that the problem of trust can be resolved. Asked in 2018 whether levels of trust could be improved or not, fully 84 per cent of the American population believed they could be improved, while only 15 per cent believed they could not (Pew Center, 2019b). Given the low regard with which most Americans regard their political rulers, this optimism is (pleasantly) surprising. Yet given the points just made about the role of positive and negative information and about the effects of individual predispositions, the task of restoring trust looks trickier than many people perhaps appreciate.

Political science and the study of trust

Trust is a vital issue in today's world. It is a useful barometer of citizens' relations with their political rulers and has some important implications for the health of civic and political life in contemporary states. Little wonder trust is a focus for policymakers around the world. Academics have also been busily attentive to the issue, with a recent slew of books, review studies, and journal articles dedicated to the study of trust. Research on trust has been particularly active in academic disciplines like business and management studies, risk analysis, criminology, and health studies. Trust has also received extensive coverage among political scientists, whose work has been summarized in two recent review volumes (Zmerli and van der Meer, 2017; Uslaner, 2018). Yet the concern of policymakers and media commentators with trust has not, to date, been adequately reciprocated by political scientists in their research. Public debates and commentaries about trust have run ahead of academic studies on the topic. As a result, our understanding of the nature and significance of trust rests on rather shaky research foundations. In this final section, I consider what the discipline of political science has already contributed to our understanding of trust, and which areas might require new lines of research to buttress that understanding.[3]

To date, the bulk of political scientists' work on trust has focused on issues of conceptualization, distribution, and determinants. Political scientists have predominantly asked questions about the broad nature of trust, its distribution among the population, and its causes. In each of these areas, academic research has contributed significant new knowledge and understanding (for summaries, see Zmerli and van der Meer, 2017 and Uslaner, 2018). Yet political scientists have paid rather less attention to other important issues around trust.

One such issue is the way that individual citizens express trust judgements. As I argued in Chapter 1, the concern among political scientists to identify the nature of trust has largely consisted of top-down or deductive exercises. The focus on broad conceptualizations of trust has not been matched by a similar analysis of the way in which trust is understood and deployed by individual citizens. The restricted reach of academic analysis impoverishes our understanding of trust, a limitation that is particularly significant given the widespread concern with trust *as manifested among citizens*. One of the main concerns of this book has been to devote more attention to the way trust judgements are formed and expressed by individuals, and thus to provide new and complementary evidence about the nature of trust. There is scope for much more work here, though, particularly for studies using qualitative methods capable of providing more detailed and richer data on how individuals think about trust and how they form and deploy trust judgements.[4]

A second issue that would benefit from greater attention among political scientists is the status of trust. While some studies have explored where trust sits within a broader set of orientations falling under the label of 'political support' (discussed in Chapter 2, in particular Section 2.4), little sustained attention has been paid to the relationship of trust with other evaluations of the political system, and to whether judgements of trust are distinctive to these other evaluations. As a result, it is almost by default that contemporary academic and policy discourse focuses on trust as opposed to any one of the other evaluatory judgements that citizens may form of the political system. Yet if trust is so important and commands a central place in these discussions and analyses, we need to be clear about why: what does trust entail, and how does it relate to alternative evaluations that citizens may form of their country's political institutions and personnel? While this book has sought to provide some answers to these questions, additional research that maps and explores the continuum of citizens' orientations to the political system would be welcome.

Clarifying the position or status of trust also requires that additional attention to be paid to a third issue, namely how trust is measured. At present, much of our empirically derived understanding of trust draws on a rather coarse set of survey indicators—single-item questions of the form 'how much do you trust X?'—that arguably fail to accurately and fully capture the concept's meaning. Our understanding of trust would benefit from a more extensive and refined battery of measurement instruments, enabling analysts to more accurately tap the concept, to gauge ambivalence among citizens and to distinguish more clearly minor expressions of discontent from more serious political doubts and grievances. Such instruments would enable analysts to distinguish between states of high trust, low trust, and distrust among individuals, an important distinction that is often obscured by the blunt nature of our present measures.

More sophisticated and refined measures would also help analysts to extend our understanding on a fourth issue, namely the consequences or outcomes of trust. Trust might be studied and fretted over simply because the ties of trust between citizens and state officials are central to understanding the quality of representative relations in modern democracies. Yet trust is primarily studied for more instrumental reasons, due to the outcomes it is seen to produce. Our understanding of these effects remains, however, in its infancy. No doubt partly due to the complexity of identifying causal relationships between individual-level beliefs and aggregate-level behaviours, the study of trust's effects has lagged behind analyses of other aspects of the concept and also behind the (rising) concern of policymakers with the issue. As stressed at various points in the previous chapters, we would be better placed to identify the effects of trust if we could more discerningly measure—and thereby distinguish more clearly between—different forms and degrees of popular discontent. If the observable effects of trust are sometimes fairly modest (as we concluded in Chapter 7), this might partly reflect our current inability to distinguish between mildly discontented citizens and their more stringently negative counterparts. In addition, analysts might also draw on the framework laid out in Chapter 7 to provide more systematic appraisals of the effects of trust in contexts beyond the British setting explored here.

Trust is too important an issue for us to lack robust answers to questions about its nature, causes, and effects. This book has tried to provide some of these answers, and to construct a more solid foundation for our understanding of trust. It is only proper to conclude, however, that more foundational filling will be needed to underpin our understanding of the trust relations between citizens and their political rulers.

Appendix

Appendix 2.1 Measures used to assess dimensionality of political support

Democracy may have problems, but it is better than any other form of government
(Response options: 1–4 'disagree–agree' scale)

How important to democracy is it that every adult living in Britain has the right to protest against government decisions they disagree with?
(Response options: 1–7 'not important–very important' scale)

The present system of governing Britain ...
(Response options: 1 = needs a great deal of improvement, 2 = could be improved quite a lot, 3 = could be improved in small ways but mainly works well, 4 = works extremely well and could not be improved)

On the whole, how satisfied are you with the way democracy works in Britain?
(Response options: 1–4 'not at all' to 'very' satisfied)

How much do you trust British governments of any party to place the needs of the nation above the interests of their own political party?
How much do you trust politicians of any party in Britain to tell the truth when they are in a tight corner?
(Response options: 1–4 'almost never' to 'just about always')

Generally speaking, those we elect as MPs lose touch with people pretty quickly
Parties are only interested in people's votes, not in their opinions
(Response options: 1–5 'agree–disagree' scale)

How good or bad a job do you think the UK government in Westminster has done over the past four years?
(Response options: 1–4 'very bad' to 'very good' job)

Source: British Social Attitudes survey 2005 (post-election and self-completion elements)

Appendix 2.2 Measures used to assess different forms of political discontent

Dissatisfaction (summed scale α = 0.68)

I am not very happy with most of the things politicians in this country do (pol1_1)
Sometimes politicians get things wrong (pol1_2)
Politicians quite often make mistakes (pol1_3)

Scepticism (α = 0.89)

Politicians do not always give us the full picture (pol2_1)
Occasionally, politicians hide information they do not want you to hear (pol2_2)
Politicians sometimes ignore evidence to make their decisions look good (pol2_3)
Politicians sometimes distort facts in their favour (pol2_4)

Distrust (α = 0.93)

Most politicians do not know much about the issues they have to deal with (pol3_1)
Most politicians do not do a capable job (pol3_2)
Politicians tend to waste a lot of public money (pol3_3)
Politicians rarely show good judgement when making decisions (pol3_4)
Politicians do not care much about ordinary people (pol4_1)
Politicians rarely listen to what their constituents tell them (pol4_2)
Politicians are motivated by their own interests, not the needs of other people (pol4_3)
Politicians tend not to tell the truth (pol5_1)
Politicians will usually mislead you about things (pol5_2)
Politicians do not keep the promises they have made (pol5_3)

Cynicism (α = 0.79)

Politicians are only interested in getting and maintaining power (pol6_1)
No person can hope to stay honest when they become a politician (pol6_2)
All politicians are bad—some are just worse than others (pol6_3)
People only get to become politicians because of who they know, not because of their abilities (pol6_4).

Appendix 4.1 Survey questions used to measure trust (in Figure 4.7)

Australia

'In general, do you feel that the people in government are too often interested in looking after themselves, or do you feel that they can be trusted to do the right thing nearly all the time?' (Australian Election Study)

European Union

'Do you tend to trust it or tend not to trust it ... the national government / ... the national legal system?' (Eurobarometer)

United States

'Trust in government index', built from ANES variables VCF0604, VCF0605, VCF0606, and VCF0608.

Country	Period	Trust: government	Time points	Trust: justice	Time points	Source
Australia	1969–2022	−1.12*	13	–	–	AES
Austria	1997–2022	−0.03	35	−0.05	35	Eurobarometer
Belgium	1997–2022	0.00	35	0.76**	35	Eurobarometer
Denmark	1997–2022	0.14	35	0.32**	35	Eurobarometer
Finland	1997–2022	0.02	35	0.55**	35	Eurobarometer
France	1997–2022	−0.26*	35	0.32**	35	Eurobarometer
Germany (W)	1997–2022	0.83**	35	0.48**	35	Eurobarometer
Greece	1997–2022	−1.01**	35	−0.40**	35	Eurobarometer
Ireland	1997–2022	0.20	35	0.32**	35	Eurobarometer
Italy	1997–2022	−0.24*	35	−0.06	35	Eurobarometer
Netherlands	1997–2022	0.09	35	0.74**	35	Eurobarometer
Portugal	1997–2022	0.10	35	0.17*	35	Eurobarometer
Spain	1997–2022	−1.13**	35	−0.17	35	Eurobarometer
Sweden	1997–2022	0.54**	35	0.61**	35	Eurobarometer
UK	1997–2022	−0.26*	35	0.56**	35	Eurobarometer
US	1958–2020	−0.90**	26	–	–	ANES

Coefficients represent regressions of trust on time.
*$p ≤ 0.10$; **$p ≤ 0.01$ (two-tailed test).
Sources: Eurobarometer; AES: Australian Election Study (Cameron and McAllister, 2022); ANES: American National Election Study (https://electionstudies.org/data-tools/anes-guide/).

Appendix 5.1 Media effects on trust

It is widely believed that negative coverage of current affairs in the media (visual, aural, print, and, more recently, online and digital) serves to reduce levels of trust among citizens. Media effects are difficult to identify with precision, and studies examining the relationship between individuals' media usage and trust have produced a range of findings (a good review of these studies is provided by Schuck, 2017). The following represents a summary of these results. They point to a lack of clear evidence that media exposure is systematically associated with low and declining rates of trust.

Negative media effects

Some analyses have found that exposure to critical commentary on political actors and institutions is associated with lower rates of trust (Miller et al., 1979). Other studies identify an association between changes in trust (or other indicators of political support, such as government satisfaction) and the negative or positive tone of newspaper coverage of politicians in some countries, but not in others. Thus, Norris' (2011: 181–186) analysis of the early-mid-2000s showed that negative newspaper coverage was associated with lower levels of government satisfaction in Britain, but not in the United States. A similar association between negative newspaper coverage and low trust has also been found in the Netherlands (Kleinnijenhuis et al., 2006). When newspapers focus their coverage on the actions and manoeuvrings of politicians (as in the Netherlands), the effect has been found to lower rates of trust, while when newspapers focus on policy issues (as in Denmark), the effect has been found to increase trust (de Vreese, 2005). There is also evidence that use of online news sources (such as Twitter) is associated with lower levels of trust (Ceron, 2015).

Critical newspaper coverage may reinforce existing attitudes among individuals rather than stimulating negative or positive regard where this does not already exist. Studies have shown that critical newspaper reporting serves to reduce rates of trust, particularly among individuals who are ideologically distant from government compared with individuals who are ideologically closer to government (Ceron and Memoli, 2015). In the United States, exposure to newspaper reporting has been found to increase rates of trust, while exposure to television has been found to reduce trust. Yet in both cases, these effects arise only for people who are already trusting; exposure to the media has no effect on people who are already low in trust (Avery, 2009).

Positive media effects

Some studies exploring the relationship between media exposure and trust have identified a positive association (Marcinkowski and Starke, 2018), such that exposure to newspapers and television is associated with higher rates of trust.

Minimal media effects

In Britain, readership of down-market, or 'tabloid', newspapers has been found to have no significant effect on people's trust, although readership of up-market or 'broadsheet' newspapers is associated with higher trust (Newton, 1999b). Other studies have found minimal associations between media exposure and trust, whether relationships are explored within countries (e.g. Moy and Scheufele, 2000; Aarts and Semetko, 2003; Adriaansen et al., 2012) or across countries (e.g. Aarts, Fladmoe, and Strömbäck, 2012).

Appendix 5.2 Pooled models of trust, 1986–2016

	Model 1 Year/time only		Model 2 Plus age cohort		Model 3 Plus socio- economic status		Model 4 Interaction: socio- economic status		Model 5 Interaction: attitudes, engagement, and media	
Year										
1996	−0.81	(0.08)**	−0.81	(0.08)**	–		–		–	
2000	−1.02	(0.06)**	−1.02	(0.07)**	−1.14	(0.08)**	–		–	
2006	−1.27	(0.08)**	−1.25	(0.08)**	−1.44	(0.08)**	–		–	
2010	−1.28	(0.08)**	−1.27	(0.08)**	−1.41	(0.09)**	–		–	
2016	−0.98	(0.08)**	−0.96	(0.09)**	−1.21	(0.09)**	–		–	
Time	–		–		–		−0.09	(0.04)*	0.02	(0.09)
Age cohort										
1930s	–		−0.09	(0.08)	−0.05	(0.10)	−0.08	(0.10)	0.03	(0.12)
1940s	–		−0.25	(0.08)**	−0.29	(0.10)**	−0.25	(0.10)*	−0.12	(0.12)
1950s	–		−0.31	(0.08)**	−0.39	(0.10)**	−0.36	(0.10)**	−0.07	(0.12)
1960s	–		−0.31	(0.08)**	−0.33	(0.10)**	−0.33	(0.10)**	−0.03	(0.13)
1970s	–		−0.10	(0.09)	−0.21	(0.11)	−0.27	(0.11)*	0.07	(0.14)
1980s	–		−0.15	(0.11)	−0.26	(0.13)*	−0.28	(0.13)*	0.01	(0.16)
1990s	–		−0.07	(0.21)	−0.09	(0.21)	0.20	(0.21)	0.31	(0.27)
Education										
School qualifications	–		–		−0.42	(0.07)**	0.07	(0.20)	0.32	(0.24)
No qualifications	–		–		−0.65	(0.09)**	−0.08	(0.21)	0.34	(0.27)
Time*school qualification	–		–		–		−0.12	(0.04)**	−0.11	(0.06)*
Time*no qualifications	–		–		–		−0.15	(0.05)**	−0.13	(0.06)*
Economic feelings										
Coping on household income	–		–		−0.46	(0.06)**	−0.08	(0.13)	0.05	(0.16)
Struggling on household income	–		–		−0.68	(0.08)**	−0.07	(0.16)	−0.00	(0.20)
Time*coping	–		–		–		−0.09	(0.03)**	−0.12	(0.04)**
Time*struggling	–		–		–		−0.15	(0.04)**	−0.18	(0.05)**

Policy position				
Extremist views	–	–	–	0.41 (0.18)*
Time*extremism	–	–	–	-0.07 (0.05)
Political engagement				
Low interest in politics	–	–	–	-0.15 (0.07)*
Time*low interest	–	–	–	-0.03 (0.02)
Expectations of government				
Government to provide jobs	–	–	–	-0.20 (0.07)**
Time*expectations	–	–	–	0.02 (0.02)
Newspaper reader				
Broadsheet	–	–	–	0.56 (0.24)*
Middle market	–	–	–	0.46 (0.20)*
Tabloid	–	–	–	0.20 (0.17)
Time*middle	–	–	–	-0.11 (0.05)*
Time*tabloid	–	–	–	-0.09 (0.05)
LR χ^2(df)	409.29 (5)	435.87 (12)	566.83 (15)	457.40 (16)	486.33 (28)
$p > \chi^2$	0.00	0.00	0.00	0.00	0.00
R^2	0.02	0.03	0.05	0.04	0.05
N	7,979	7,956	5,559	5,559	4,123

Ordinal logistic regression model; standard errors in brackets.
For categorical variables, the reference categories are: *Year*: 1986; *Age cohort*: born in 1900s–1920s; *Education*: degree-level qualification; *Economic feelings*: currently living very comfortably/comfortably on household income; *Policy position*: moderate policy views; *Newspaper reader*: does not read a newspaper.
Cut-points not shown.
* $p \leq 0.05$; ** $p \leq 0.01$. Two-tailed test.
Source: British Social Attitudes surveys, 1986, 1996, 2000, 2006, 2010, and 2016.
The 'economic feeling' question appeared in a different section of the survey to the trust question, meaning associations between the two cannot be identified. The 1996 data are thus omitted from models 3 onwards.

Appendix 6.1 Details of model summarized in Figure 6.5

	Trust Coef	(se)
Competence		
Government handled policy issues well	0.58	(0.10)**
National economic situation will get better	0.24	(0.07)**
Parties capable of strong government	0.68	(0.18)**
Benevolence		
Governing party is responsive on tax-spending	−0.04	(0.03)
Parties are in touch	1.04	(0.20)**
Integrity		
Parties keep promises	0.97	(0.19)**
Fairness		
Government is fair	0.41	(0.08)**
Controls		
Male (ref: female)	0.28	(0.12)*
Age (ref: 18–29)		
30s	0.24	(0.23)
40s	0.21	(0.22)
50s	0.19	(0.22)
60s	0.76	(0.24)**
70s +	0.76	(0.23)**
Social class (ref: unskilled)		
Skilled manual	−0.00	(0.18)
Skilled non-manual	−0.12	(0.18)
Managerial/technical	0.01	(0.17)
Professional	0.23	(0.22)
Education (to <15 years)		
To 16	0.11	(0.15)
To 18	0.35	(0.17)*
19 and above	0.34	(0.16)*
Party vote (ref: did not vote)		
Labour	0.45	(0.17)**
Conservative	0.54	(0.18)**
Liberal Democrat	0.61	(0.20)**
Other parties	0.15	(0.22)
Constant	−3.96	(0.45)**
F	30.46	
Model significance (prob > F)	0.00	
Adjusted R^2	0.41	
N (weighted)	1,423	

*$p \leq 0.05$; **$p \leq 0.01$ (two-tailed test).
Source: 2005 British Election Study, self-completion wave.

Appendix 6.2 Details of model summarized in Figure 6.6

	Trust Coef	(se)
Political knowledge	0.69	(1.00)
Cognitively 'easy' evaluations		
Household financial situation will get better	−0.18	(0.17)
Prime minister competent	0.47	(0.06)**
Positive feelings about economy	0.85	(0.28)**
Household financial situation will get better × knowledge	0.32	(0.23)
Prime minister competent × knowledge	−0.21	(0.09)*
Positive feelings about economy × knowledge	−0.68	(0.38)
Cognitively 'difficult' evaluations		
National economic situation will get better	0.23	(0.15)
Government handled economy well	0.02	(0.15)
Governing party is responsive on tax-spending	0.12	(0.08)
National economic situation will get better × knowledge	−0.11	(0.21)
Government handled economy well × knowledge	0.22	(0.20)
Governing party is responsive on tax-spending × knowledge	−0.22	(0.11)*
Controls		
Male (ref: female)	0.10	(0.07)
Age (ref: 18–29)		
30s	−0.17	(0.12)
40s	0.05	(0.13)
50s	−0.05	(0.13)
60s	0.26	(0.14)
70s +	0.41	(0.15)**
Social class (ref: unskilled)		
Skilled manual	−0.08	(0.13)
Skilled non-manual	0.01	(0.11)
Managerial/technical	−0.16	(0.11)
Professional	0.11	(0.16)
Education (to <15 years)		
To 16	0.19	(0.10)*
To 18	0.31	(0.11)**
19 and above	0.47	(0.10)**
Party vote (ref: did not vote)		
Labour	0.27	(0.10)**
Conservative	0.37	(0.11)**
Liberal Democrat	0.18	(0.12)
Other parties	−0.27	(0.15)
Constant	0.80	(0.75)
F	36.85	
Model significance (prob > F)	0.00	
R^2	0.36	
N (weighted)	3,442	

*$p \leq 0.05$; **$p \leq 0.01$ (two-tailed test).
Source: 2005 British Election Study, post-election wave.

Appendix 6.3 Impact of evaluations on trust in different institutions

	Government	Politicians	Parliament	Civil service
Policy performance				
Government handling well:				
Health	0.16 (0.03)**	0.08 (0.03)*	0.11 (0.03)**	0.05 (0.04)
Crime	0.14 (0.03)**	0.12 (0.04)*	0.12 (0.04)**	0.15 (0.04)**
Asylum seekers	0.09 (0.03)**	0.14 (0.04)**	0.08 (0.04)*	0.12 (0.04)**
Positive evaluation of national economy	0.20 (0.03)**	0.06 (0.04)	0.05 (0.04)	0.01 (0.05)
Prime minister is competent	0.20 (0.02)**	0.09 (0.02)**	0.16 (0.02)**	0.03 (0.02)
Governing party capable of strong government	0.24 (0.07)**	0.15 (0.08)	0.31 (0.08)**	0.39 (0.10)**
Intentions				
Prime minister is responsive	0.37 (0.02)**	0.20 (0.02)**	0.18 (0.02)**	0.14 (0.03)**
Governing party in touch	0.40 (0.07)**	0.23 (0.08)**	0.26 (0.08)**	0.40 (0.10)**
Procedural evaluations				
Government treats people fairly	0.35 (0.03)**	0.38 (0.04)**	0.37 (0.04)**	0.24 (0.05)**
Policy issues				
Disapproval of decision over Iraq	−0.16 (0.03)**	−0.05 (0.04)	−0.11 (0.04)**	−0.05 (0.05)
Party vote (ref: did not vote)				
Labour	0.39 (0.08)**	0.22 (0.10)*	0.31 (0.10)**	0.06 (0.12)
Conservative	−0.20 (0.08)*	0.83 (0.10)**	0.83 (0.10)**	0.77 (0.12)**
Liberal Democrat	0.03 (0.09)	0.27 (0.11)*	0.41 (0.11)**	0.37 (0.13)**
Other parties	0.05 (0.11)	0.15 (0.13)	−0.00 (0.13)	0.14 (0.16)
Male (ref: female)	−0.00 (0.06)	0.06 (0.07)	0.20 (0.07)**	0.19 (0.08)*
Age (ref: 18–29)				
30s	0.03 (0.11)	−0.09 (0.14)	−0.07 (0.14)	−0.22 (0.16)
40s	0.08 (0.11)	0.03 (0.13)	0.07 (0.14)	−0.26 (0.16)
50s	0.00 (0.11)	−0.00 (0.14)	0.01 (0.14)	−0.26 (0.16)
60s	0.21 (0.12)	0.36 (0.14)*	0.34 (0.15)*	0.07 (0.17)
70s +	0.19 (0.12)	0.42 (0.14)**	0.35 (0.15)*	0.41 (0.17)*
Social class (ref: unskilled)				
Skilled manual	−0.03 (0.09)	0.08 (0.11)	0.07 (0.11)	0.11 (0.12)
Skilled non-manual	−0.08 (0.08)	0.14 (0.10)	0.08 (0.10)	0.13 (0.12)
Managerial/technical	−0.14 (0.08)	0.04 (0.10)	0.02 (0.10)	0.12 (0.12)
Professional	−0.24 (0.13)	0.10 (0.16)	0.26 (0.16)	0.37 (0.19)*
Education (to <15 years)				
To 16	−0.05 (0.07)	0.09 (0.09)	0.06 (0.09)	0.17 (0.11)
To 18	−0.02 (0.08)	0.14 (0.10)	0.22 (0.10)*	0.37 (0.12)**
19 and above	−0.04 (0.09)	0.24 (0.11)*	0.37 (0.11)**	0.59 (0.12)**

	Government		Politicians		Parliament		Civil service	
Constant	−0.84	(0.22)**	−0.08	(0.27)	0.33	(0.28)	1.14	(0.32)**
F	273.17		55.44		70.46		26.78	
Model significance (prob > F)	0.00		0.00		0.00		0.00	
Adjusted R^2	0.74		0.36		0.42		0.22	
N (unweighted[1])	2,562		2,564		2,546		2,533	

	Local government		Courts		Police	
Policy performance						
Government handling well:						
Health	0.02	(0.04)	0.08	(0.05)	0.00	(0.04)
Crime	0.20	(0.05)**	0.21	(0.05)**	0.28	(0.05)**
Asylum seekers	0.03	(0.05)	0.20	(0.05)**	0.07	(0.05)
Positive evaluation of national economy	0.15	(0.05)**	−0.06	(0.05)	0.08	(0.05)
Prime minister is competent	−0.01	(0.03)	0.05	(0.03)	0.06	(0.03)*
Governing party capable of strong government	0.41	(0.10)**	0.50	(0.11)**	0.14	(0.10)
Intentions						
Prime minister is responsive	0.14	(0.03)**	0.09	(0.03)**	0.12	(0.03)**
Governing party in touch	0.54	(0.10)**	0.36	(0.11)**	−0.03	(0.10)
Procedural evaluations						
Government treats people fairly	0.30	(0.05)**	0.23	(0.06)**	0.22	(0.05)**
Policy issues						
Disapproval of decision over Iraq	−0.03	(0.05)	−0.04	(0.06)	−0.09	(0.05)
Party vote (ref: did not vote)						
Labour	0.12	(0.12)	−0.19	(0.13)	0.11	(0.12)
Conservative	0.85	(0.13)**	0.73	(0.14)**	0.78	(0.13)**
Liberal Democrat	0.30	(0.13)*	0.53	(0.15)**	0.32	(0.13)*
Other parties	0.17	(0.16)	0.25	(0.18)	0.11	(0.16)
Male (ref: female)	−0.03	(0.08)	0.33	(0.09)**	−0.19	(0.09)*
Age (ref: 18–29)						
30s	−0.02	(0.17)	0.12	(0.18)	0.18	(0.17)
40s	0.15	(0.17)	0.25	(0.18)	0.25	(0.16)
50s	0.02	(0.17)	0.35	(0.18)	0.11	(0.17)
60s	0.24	(0.18)	0.39	(0.20)*	0.37	(0.18)*
70s +	0.49	(0.18)**	0.44	(0.20)*	0.64	(0.18)**
Social class (ref: unskilled)						
Skilled manual	0.04	(0.13)	0.13	(0.14)	0.03	(0.13)
Skilled non-manual	0.09	(0.13)	0.19	(0.14)	0.06	(0.13)
Managerial/technical	0.09	(0.12)	0.40	(0.13)**	0.10	(0.12)
Professional	0.10	(0.20)	0.31	(0.22)	0.01	(0.20)

(Continued)

Continued

	Local government	Courts	Police
Education (to <15 years)			
To 16	0.14 (0.11)	0.27 (0.12)*	−0.01 (0.11)
To 18	0.10 (0.12)	0.54 (0.14)**	0.19 (0.12)
19 and above	0.31 (0.13)*	0.84 (0.14)**	0.14 (0.13)
Constant	0.70 (0.34)*	0.48 (0.37)	2.93 (0.34)**
F	24.06	22.25	16.72
Model significance (prob > F)	0.00	0.00	0.00
Adjusted R^2	0.20	0.18	0.14
N (unweighted[1])	2,539	2,530	2,560

Figures represent coefficients (standard errors).
*$p \leq 0.05$; **$p \leq 0.01$ (two-tailed test).
[1] Since the data derive from more than one survey, and since the surveys had differently designed weighting schemes, the data reported here are unweighted.
Source: British Election Study 2005; post-election and self-completion waves.

Appendix 7.1 The relationship between trust and protest participation

	Model 1 Protested		Model 2 Did not vote; protested		Voted; did not protest	
(Estimation)	*Binary logit*		*Multinomial logit*			
Low trust	0.08	(0.07)	0.33	(0.14)*	−0.07	(0.08)
Interested in politics	0.53	(0.05)**	−0.45	(0.09)**	−0.41	(0.06)**
Right-wing ideology	−0.19	(0.08)*	−0.11	(0.14)	0.26	(0.09)**
Age (ref: 18–24)						
25–34	−0.08	(0.25)	−0.29	(0.40)	0.41	(0.35)
35–44	0.28	(0.24)	−0.86	(0.40)*	0.05	(0.34)
45–54	0.27	(0.25)	−1.18	(0.41)**	0.09	(0.34)
55–64	0.63	(0.26)*	−1.52	(0.44)**	−0.24	(0.35)
65+	0.57	(0.25)*	−1.87	(0.46)**	−0.17	(0.34)
Education (ref: no qualifications)						
School-level qualifications	0.93	(0.16)**	−0.53	(0.32)	−0.99	(0.18)**
University degree	1.60	(0.20)**	−0.49	(0.37)	−1.79	(0.23)**
Constant	−2.67	(0.47)**	0.45	(0.87)	1.68	(0.56)**
LR χ^2 (df)	274.23(10)		553.91 (30)			
Prob > χ^2	0.00		0.00			
Pseudo R^2	0.12		0.13			
N (unweighted)	1,689		1,681			

Figures are parameter estimates and associated standard errors.
Model 1 derives from a binary logistic regression; Model 2 derives from a multinomial logistic regression. For Model 2, the reference category is 'Voted and protested'. A final category ('Did not vote and did not protest') was included in the model, but the figures are not shown here.
*$p \leq 0.05$; **$p \leq 0.01$ (two-tailed tests).
Source: British Social Attitudes 2011.

Appendix 7.2 Impact of change in trust on vote choice, 2015

	Voted UKIP	Voted Labour	Voted Lib Dem	Did not vote
Trust				
Increase in low trust	0.21 (0.06)**	0.14 (0.06)*	0.22 (0.07)**	0.20 (0.09)*
Attitudes				
National economy has got worse	1.13 (0.09)**	1.24 (0.10)**	0.61 (0.12)**	0.88 (0.13)**
Right-wing ideology	−0.19 (0.04)**	−1.08 (0.05)**	−0.65 (0.05)**	−0.47 (0.06)**
Immigration numbers should fall	0.77 (0.12)**	−0.31 (0.08)**	−0.53 (0.09)**	−0.21 (0.11)
Demographics				
Gender				
Female	−0.51 (0.16)**	−0.12 (0.16)	−0.10 (0.18)	0.15 (0.22)
Age (ref: under 24)				
25–34	−0.76 (0.58)	−0.50 (0.53)	0.84 (0.82)	−0.97 (0.58)
35–44	−0.94 (0.54)	−0.53 (0.51)	0.97 (0.82)	−0.89 (0.54)
45–54	−0.56 (0.51)	−0.23 (0.50)	0.79 (0.82)	−1.20 (0.53)*
55–64	−0.61 (0.49)	−0.63 (0.48)	1.07 (0.80)	−1.77 (0.52)**
65+	−0.95 (0.50)	−0.81 (0.49)	1.16 (0.81)	−1.81 (0.53)**
Education (ref: no qualifications)				
School-level qualifications	−0.25 (0.26)	−0.18 (0.32)	0.31 (0.47)	0.18 (0.46)
Beyond school qualifications	0.07 (0.37)	0.08 (0.41)	1.14 (0.53)*	0.88 (0.54)
University-level qualifications	−0.66 (0.28)*	0.02 (0.32)	1.10 (0.46)*	−0.26 (0.48)
Annual household income (>£50,000)				
£20,000–£49,999	0.08 (0.20)	0.38 (0.20)	0.17 (0.21)	0.62 (0.31)*
< £20,000	0.35 (0.23)	0.16 (0.24)	−0.25 (0.27)	0.81 (0.35)*
Constant	−4.22 (0.86)**	3.96 (0.77)**	1.60 (1.07)	0.31 (1.00)
LR χ^2 (90 df)		2,233.56		
Prob > χ^2		0.000		
Pseudo R^2		0.31		
N (unweighted)		2,308		

*$p \leq 0.05$; **$p \leq 0.01$ (two-tailed test).
Results derive from a multinomial logistic regression model. Reference category for vote choice is the Conservative Party. The sample is limited to voters in England.
Source: British Election Study internet panel, waves 1 and 6.

Appendix 7.3 Trust and support for government activism

	Increase tax and spending		Increase welfare spending		Provide jobs		Government's responsibility to: Provide healthcare		Control prices		Provide for the old	
Low trust	0.14	(0.12)	−0.01	(0.10)	−0.07	(0.10)	0.39	(0.12)**	0.04	(0.11)	0.26	(0.11)*
Right-wing ideology	−0.51	(0.11)**	−0.89	(0.10)**	−0.68	(0.10)**	−0.58	(0.11)**	−0.61	(0.10)**	−0.47	(0.10)**
Feelings about present income (Ref: comfortable)												
Neither comfortable/struggling	−0.36	(0.18)*	0.01	(0.16)	−0.12	(0.16)	−0.61	(0.19)*	0.21	(0.17)	0.02	(0.18)
Struggling	−0.36	(0.24)	0.95	(0.22)**	0.63	(0.22)**	−0.52	(0.27)**	1.12	(0.24)**	0.47	(0.25)
Female	0.30	(0.16)	0.36	(0.14)**	0.55	(0.14)**	0.17	(0.17)	0.39	(0.15)**	0.49	(0.15)**
Age (ref: 18–24 years old)												
25–34	0.12	(0.40)	−0.76	(0.35)*	−0.40	(0.36)	0.17	(0.41)	0.21	(0.37)	−0.33	(0.40)
35–44	0.11	(0.37)	−0.79	(0.32)*	−1.08	(0.34)**	0.04	(0.38)	−0.29	(0.34)	−0.45	(0.38)
45–54	0.49	(0.38)	−0.60	(0.33)*	−0.73	(0.34)*	0.30	(0.39)	−0.13	(0.35)	−0.24	(0.38)
55–64	0.35	(0.38)	−0.41	(0.33)	−0.99	(0.34)**	0.50	(0.39)	−0.31	(0.35)	−0.27	(0.38)
65+	0.79	(0.37)*	−0.14	(0.32)	−1.03	(0.33)**	0.17	(0.38)	−0.24	(0.34)	−0.41	(0.37)
Education (ref: university degree)												
School qualifications	−0.36	(0.19)	−0.19	(0.16)	0.64	(0.17)**	−0.59	(0.21)**	0.49	(0.18)**	0.15	(0.18)
No qualifications	−0.56	(0.26)*	0.18	(0.24)	1.30	(0.24)**	−0.59	(0.30)*	0.96	(0.25)**	0.45	(0.27)
LR χ^2 (12 df)	46.60		148.07		135.35		58.31		116.10		61.61	
Prob > χ^2	0.00		0.00		0.00		0.00		0.00		0.00	
Pseudo R^2	0.05		0.07		0.07		0.06		0.07		0.05	
N (unweighted)	731		749		709		744		737		737	

(Continued)

Appendix 7.3 Continued

<table>
<thead>
<tr><th></th><th colspan="2">Help industry</th><th colspan="2">Help the unemployed</th><th colspan="2">Reduce income differences</th><th colspan="2">Provide housing</th><th colspan="2">Impose environmental laws</th></tr>
</thead>
<tbody>
<tr><td>Low trust</td><td>0.09</td><td>(0.11)</td><td>-0.04</td><td>(0.11)</td><td>0.07</td><td>(0.11)</td><td>0.14</td><td>(0.11)</td><td>0.01</td><td>(0.11)</td></tr>
<tr><td>Right-wing ideology</td><td>-0.38</td><td>(0.10)**</td><td>-0.58</td><td>(0.10)**</td><td>-1.58</td><td>(0.11)**</td><td>-0.90</td><td>(0.10)**</td><td>-0.54</td><td>(0.10)**</td></tr>
<tr><td colspan="11">Feelings about present income (Ref: comfortable)</td></tr>
<tr><td>Neither comfortable/struggling</td><td>-0.31</td><td>(0.17)</td><td>-0.26</td><td>(0.17)</td><td>0.31</td><td>(0.17)</td><td>-0.12</td><td>(0.17)</td><td>-0.11</td><td>(0.17)</td></tr>
<tr><td>Struggling</td><td>-0.10</td><td>(0.23)</td><td>0.69</td><td>(0.23)**</td><td>0.52</td><td>(0.24)*</td><td>0.64</td><td>(0.24)**</td><td>-0.45</td><td>(0.24)</td></tr>
<tr><td>Female</td><td>0.12</td><td>(0.15)</td><td>0.60</td><td>(0.15)**</td><td>0.24</td><td>(0.15)</td><td>0.28</td><td>(0.15)</td><td>0.30</td><td>(0.15)*</td></tr>
<tr><td colspan="11">Age (ref: 18–24 years old)</td></tr>
<tr><td>25–34</td><td>-0.08</td><td>(0.38)</td><td>-0.73</td><td>(0.37)*</td><td>0.23</td><td>(0.38)</td><td>0.43</td><td>(0.38)</td><td>-0.30</td><td>(0.39)</td></tr>
<tr><td>35–44</td><td>-0.13</td><td>(0.36)</td><td>-0.87</td><td>(0.35)*</td><td>-0.21</td><td>(0.35)</td><td>0.18</td><td>(0.35)</td><td>0.24</td><td>(0.36)</td></tr>
<tr><td>45–54</td><td>0.01</td><td>(0.36)</td><td>-0.72</td><td>(0.35)*</td><td>0.31</td><td>(0.36)</td><td>0.56</td><td>(0.36)</td><td>0.36</td><td>(0.37)</td></tr>
<tr><td>55–64</td><td>-0.09</td><td>(0.36)</td><td>-0.47</td><td>(0.35)</td><td>0.01</td><td>(0.36)</td><td>0.44</td><td>(0.35)</td><td>0.14</td><td>(0.36)</td></tr>
<tr><td>65+</td><td>-0.04</td><td>(0.35)</td><td>-0.21</td><td>(0.34)</td><td>0.07</td><td>(0.35)</td><td>0.38</td><td>(0.35)</td><td>0.30</td><td>(0.36)</td></tr>
<tr><td colspan="11">Education (ref: university degree)</td></tr>
<tr><td>School qualifications</td><td>0.24</td><td>(0.18)</td><td>-0.40</td><td>(0.17)*</td><td>-0.44</td><td>(0.17)*</td><td>-0.14</td><td>(0.17)</td><td>-0.44</td><td>(0.17)*</td></tr>
<tr><td>No qualifications</td><td>0.24</td><td>(0.25)</td><td>-0.20</td><td>(0.25)</td><td>0.24</td><td>(0.26)</td><td>0.42</td><td>(0.25)</td><td>-0.88</td><td>(0.25)**</td></tr>
<tr><td>LR χ^2 (11 df)</td><td colspan="2">23.14</td><td colspan="2">90.02</td><td colspan="2">294.06</td><td colspan="2">138.54</td><td colspan="2">53.32</td></tr>
<tr><td>Prob > χ^2</td><td colspan="2">0.00</td><td colspan="2">0.00</td><td colspan="2">0.00</td><td colspan="2">0.00</td><td colspan="2">0.00</td></tr>
<tr><td>Pseudo R^2</td><td colspan="2">0.02</td><td colspan="2">0.05</td><td colspan="2">0.16</td><td colspan="2">0.09</td><td colspan="2">0.04</td></tr>
<tr><td>N (unweighted)</td><td colspan="2">723</td><td colspan="2">708</td><td colspan="2">711</td><td colspan="2">733</td><td colspan="2">727</td></tr>
</tbody>
</table>

Question wording for the outcome measures is provided on the following page.
Models are binary logit (increase tax/spending) and ordinal logit (increase welfare spending; government responsibility).
Figures are parameter estimates and associated standard errors. Constants and cut-points are not shown.
* $p \leq 0.05$; ** $p \leq 0.01$ (two-tailed tests).
Source: British Social Attitudes 2016.

Question wording of outcome measures for Appendix 7.3

Tax and spending

Suppose the government had to choose between the three options on this card. Which do you think it should choose?
Reduce taxes and spend less on health, education, and social benefits; keep taxes and spending on these services at the same level as now; increase taxes and spend more on health, education, and social benefits.

Welfare spending

The government should spend more money on welfare benefits for the poor, even if it leads to higher taxes.

Government responsibility

On the whole, do you think it should or should not be the government's responsibility to:
Provide a job for everyone who wants one.
Provide healthcare for the sick.
Keep prices under control.
Provide a decent standard of living for the old.
Provide industry with the help it needs to grow.
Provide a decent standard of living for the unemployed.
Reduce income differences between the rich and the poor.
Provide decent housing for those who can't afford it.
Impose strict laws to make industry do less damage to the environment.

Appendix 7.4 Trust and electoral abstention, 2015–2019 elections

	2015		2017		2019	
Low trust	0.12	(0.02)**	0.12	(0.05)**	0.13	(0.02)**
Party differences	−0.24	(0.04)**	−0.24	(0.10)*	−0.19	(0.05)**
Political interest	−0.95	(0.03)**	−0.85	(0.08)**	−0.83	(0.03)**
Education (ref: university)						
Other	−0.18	(0.19)	0.34	(0.34)	0.16	(0.19)
A level	0.03	(0.08)	0.17	(0.17)	−0.01	(0.09)
GCSE	−0.26	(0.09)**	−0.00	(0.21)	−0.30	(0.11)**
No qualifications	−0.12	(0.13)	0.03	(0.27)	0.10	(0.13)
Age	−0.01	(0.00)**	−0.00	(0.01)	0.00	(0.00)
Social class (ref: group A)						
B	−0.10	(0.12)	−0.30	(0.26)	0.14	(0.14)
C1	−0.26	(0.11)	−0.33	(0.23)	0.07	(0.13)
C2	−0.16	(0.12)	−0.34	(0.26)	0.43	(0.14)**
D	−0.16	(0.13)	−0.05	(0.28)	0.60	(0.15)**
E	−0.24	(0.13)	−0.16	(0.27)	0.48	(0.15)**
Housing tenure (ref: owner occupier)						
Renter	0.26	(0.12)*	0.24	(0.17)	0.57	(0.08)**
Did not vote at previous election	2.14	(0.07)**	2.68	(0.15)**	2.30	(0.07)**
Constant	0.02	(0.26)	−0.38	(0.55)	−1.61	(0.28)**
LR χ^2(17)	3,096.16		724.68		3,239.19	
Prob > χ^2	0.000		0.000		0.000	
Pseudo R^2	0.28		0.30		0.34	
N (unweighted)	25,590		4,775		16,460	

Logistic regression models predicting reported turnout at the general election (0 = yes; 1 = no).

Independent variables: *Trust*: trust in MPs (from 1 = great deal to 7 = no trust); *Party difference*: considering everything the Conservative and Labour parties stand for, would you say that: 1 = There is not much difference between them, 2 = some difference, or 3 = a great difference? *Interest*: how interested are you in the general election? 1 = not at all, 2 = not very, 3 = somewhat, or 4 = very interested; *Education*: highest educational qualifications; *Age*: age in years; *Social class*: social groups A, B, C1, C2, D, E; *Housing tenure*: 0 = owner occupier, 1 = rented; *Did not vote at previous election*: recalled vote at previous general election (0 = voted, 1 = did not vote).

*$p \leq 0.05$; **$p \leq 0.01$ (two-tailed tests).

Source: British Election Study internet panel, 2014–2019.

Appendix 7.5 Items used to measure acceptance/verification of official information

Verification of information

When a politician tells me anything, I always double-check to make sure it is true.
It is fine to accept what politicians tell us without checking whether they are right.
It is too risky to automatically accept the advice of politicians; people should always check this advice for themselves.
When politicians tell me something important, I typically try to get a second opinion.

Acceptance of information

When politicians tell me something, I tend to listen.
I tend not to accept information provided by politicians, even when that information is supposedly factual.
I usually accept what politicians tell me on important issues.
People should always follow the advice given to them by politicians.

Appendix 7.6A Acceptance of collective obligations—items from the European Social Survey.

All measures are from the 2004 (Round 2) survey, except measures marked * which are from the 2010 (Round 5) survey.

Dependent variables

How much do you agree or disagree that:

You should always strictly obey the law even if it means missing good opportunities?
Citizens should not cheat on their taxes?
Everyone has a duty to back the final verdict of the courts?*
Scale running from 1 (=strongly disagree) to 5 (=strongly agree)

Occasionally, it is alright to ignore the law and do what you want to?
Scale running from 1 (=strongly agree) to 5 (=strongly disagree)

How wrong, if at all, do you consider the following ways of behaving to be:
Someone paying cash with no receipt so as to avoid paying VAT or other taxes?
Scale running from 1 (=not wrong) to 4 (=seriously wrong)

To what extent is it your duty to back the decisions made by the police even when you disagree with them?*
Scale running from 1 (=not at all my duty) to 10 (=completely my duty)

Imagine that you were out and saw someone push a man to the ground and steal his wallet. How likely would you be to call the police?*
Scale running from 1 (=not at all likely) to 4 (=very likely)

Independent variable

Trust: Summed scale of trust in parliament, politicians, political parties, the legal system, and the police), running from 0 (no trust) to 10 (high trust).

Control variables: attitudes/values

Social trust: 'Would you say that most people can be trusted, or that you can't be too careful in dealing with people?'
Scale running from 0 (=can't be too careful) to 10 (=most people can be trusted)

Is this person like or not like you?
She/he believes that people should do what they're told. She/he thinks people should follow rules at all times, even when no one is watching
It is important to her/him that the government ensures his safety against all threats. She/he wants the state to be strong so it can defend its citizens
(Scale running from 1 = not like me at all to 6 = very much like me)

Taking into account all the things the courts in Britain are expected to do, would you say they are doing a good job or a bad job?*

Taking into account all the things the police are expected to do, would you say they are doing a good job or a bad job?*
(Scale running from 1 = very bad job to 5 = very good job)

How often do you think the courts make fair, impartial decisions based on the evidence made available to them?*
(Scale running from 1 = never to 10 = always)

How often do you think the police make fair, impartial decisions in the cases they have to deal with?*
(Scale running from 1 = not often to 4 = very often)

Control variables: demographics

Religion: 'How religious would you say you are?'
Scale running from 0 (=not at all religious) to 10 (=very religious)
Income: total household income in groups (Twelve bands; poorest to richest)
Gender (male = 0; female = 1)
Age (continuous in years, 15–98)
Education: highest educational qualification achieved

Appendix 7.6B Acceptance of collective obligations—items from the Citizen Audit

Dependent variables

All responses are recorded (or, where measured on an ordinal scale, recoded) on a 0 (=non-compliant) and/to 1 (=compliant) format.

How important do you think it is to: (a) never evade paying taxes; (b) always obey the law?

Some service providers accept cash as a means of avoiding VAT. Have you ever paid cash in order to avoid VAT?

Suppose the Inland Revenue makes a mistake in your favour. Would you tell them about it?

What would you do if you saw a person being robbed in the street? Would you: (a) call the police and give your name; (b) make yourself available as a potential trial witness?

Can they be justified or not? Claiming government benefits which you are not entitled to.

Would you be willing: (a) to serve on a jury; (b) to donate blood?

Independent variable

Scale of trust (in government, House of Commons, the courts, civil service, politicians, and local government), running from 0 (no trust at all) to 10 (trust completely).

Control variables: attitudes/values

Social trust: 'Can people with whom you have contact be trusted?'
Scale running from 0 (=most people cannot be trusted) to 10 (=most people can be trusted)

Civic duty: It is every citizen's duty to vote in elections
Scale running from 1 (=strongly disagree) to 5 (=strongly agree)

Moral conservatism: Censorship of films and magazines is necessary to uphold moral standards
Scale running from 1 (=strongly disagree) to 5 (=strongly agree)

Control variables: demographics

Religion: 'Do you regard yourself as belonging to any particular religion? (0 = no; 1 = yes)
Income: total household income (eight bands; poorest to richest)
Gender (male = 0; female = 1)
Age (continuous in years, 18–99)
Education: age finished FT education; aged 16 or less = 1, aged 17–18 = 2, aged above 18 = 3)

Notes

Introduction

1. Citizens themselves appear to recognize this vertical conflict. Asked in 2021 whether they felt that political differences between ordinary people and elites are larger than the differences between citizens themselves, 54 per cent of Dutch citizens agreed, while only 15 per cent disagreed (source: Dutch Parliamentary Election Study 2021).
2. The data come from the 2019 British Social Attitudes survey.
3. The data come from the American National Election Study and the Pew Center.
4. The vertical form of trust between citizens and rulers (i.e. political or institutional trust) is distinguished from the horizontal form of trust between citizens themselves (i.e. interpersonal or social trust).
5. Citizens may sometimes compensate for a lack of trust by introducing arrangements (such as formal monitoring of politicians' actions and sanctioning devices like elections) to ensure that politicians stick to their promises. Yet monitoring and sanctioning arrangements do not cover all politicians' activities, and in areas they do not cover, politicians must be trusted to act appropriately. Ultimately, a complete absence of trust would prevent any significant delegation of power from citizens to politicians. In this sense, trust is foundational for representative democracy (Warren and Gastil, 2015).

Chapter 1

1. Bianco's (1994) description of constituents' trust in their elected representatives—where trust consists of voters granting representatives some leeway to take decisions based on a judgement about their mutual compatibility of interests—also fits this approach to trust.
2. The survey was conducted as part of a broader project into political discontent. The total number of valid responses to the question was 744. Note that the sample is not representative of the wider UK population, and no weights have been applied to the results reported here.
3. The prevalence of ambivalent attitudes among US and British citizens highlights a problem in the way trust is often measured, which is further explored in Chapter 3. Single-item survey indicators of trust ('How much do you trust the government?') shoehorn a potential variety of negatively and positively valenced evaluations into a single judgement. Behind such summative measures of trust may lie a more complex range of opinions.
4. Some analysts have labelled an absence of trust short of active distrust as *mistrust*. Mistrust is held to represent a doubt about, or suspicion of, an actor or agency (Lenard, 2008; Citrin and Stokes, 2018). To my mind, this state is better characterized as 'scepticism' than as mistrust.

5. In Saunders, Dietz, and Thornhill's (2014) analysis of organizations, for example, there is some overlap in the considerations that lead to trust (Table 5) and distrust (Table 6). Qualitative studies based on interviews with individual citizens have sometimes found that negative views of political elites reflect different rationales to more positive views (van Wessel, 2017). Yet quantitative analyses have largely failed to support this insight, while other qualitative exercises suggest that political distrust rests on similar considerations to political trust, albeit in negative form (Bertsou, 2019b). Studies that have measured trust as an implicit (or automatic) attitude rather than as an explicit (or considered) attitude have found that individuals manifest trust and distrust in the same object (Burns, Mearns, and McGeorge, 2006). This has been taken to indicate that trust and distrust are separate concepts. However, the presence of simultaneous positive and negative evaluations might also plausibly be taken as evidence of ambivalence, reviewed earlier. It should also be noted that studies have pointed to the origins of trust and distrust judgements in different parts of the brain. Trust judgements trigger activity in the area of the brain associated with cognitive processes, while distrust judgements trigger activity in the area of the brain associated with emotional activity (Dimoka, 2010).
6. Jennings and colleagues' (2021) study of attitudes across four countries (Australia, Italy, the United Kingdom, and the United States) argues for the presence of separate states of trust and distrust. The results of the authors' factor analysis indeed point to distinctive states of trust and distrust. The items used to measure these states tap both similar considerations (measured in positively or negatively directed forms) and different considerations. Hence, it is difficult to know whether the identified distinctiveness of trust and distrust reflects differently valenced judgements (i.e. trust and distrust reflect similar considerations but in either positive or negative form) or different types of judgements (i.e. trust and distrust reflect different considerations).
7. A survey conducted by the RAND Corporation found that people expressing distrust in the United States Congress were particularly likely to say that integrity was the key factor in their judgement, while people expressing trust in Congress were particularly likely to say that the key factor was competence. However, the authors of the study note that differences in the considerations affecting trust and distrust in Congress are 'somewhat limited' (Kavanagh et al., 2020: 73).
8. One suggestion is that people who distinguish their trust in different institutions ('critical trusters') are somehow more informed about politics and thus better equipped to identify variations in trustworthiness between institutions than are people who apply the same trust rating to different institutions (Wu and Wilkes, 2018). I tested this finding on the sample of respondents to the 2018 British Social Attitudes survey. To mirror Wu and Wilkes' analysis, I measured variations in trust judgements by computing standard deviations across individual trust scores in different institutions. Using this method suggests that few people (8 per cent of the sample) assigned exactly the same trust score across these institutions (standard deviation of 0). But 28 per cent of the sample exhibited a standard deviation of less than 0.5 and could thus be counted as giving very similar trust scores across the seven institutions. Their counterparts, the roughly 28 per cent exhibiting a standard deviation above 0.8, were counted as being more discriminating in their trust. We can then model being a 'critical truster' (SD ≥ 0.8) against being a 'consistent truster' (SD ≤ 0.5). I included as measures of political information either educational attainment (those reporting a degree or at least school-level qualifications against those reporting

no formal qualifications) or interest in politics. Entering these two information measures separately into a logit regression model (consistent trustor = 0 and critical trustor = 1) yielded no significant effect. Contrary to Wu and Wilkes (2018), then, I do not find discriminating trust to be explicable by variations in the political information held by individuals.

9. The survey question asked respondents whether they generally trusted each actor to tell the truth or not.
10. The fieldwork for the 2008 survey was conducted in November, after the nationalization of the British bank Northern Rock, the collapse of the American bank Lehmann Brothers, and the British economy's move into recession. Note that the financial crash had a greater effect on people's trust in countries like Greece, Ireland, Italy, Portugal, and Spain (see Chapter 7, Section 7.5).
11. The fieldwork for the 2009 survey was conducted in September, well after the start of the MPs' expenses scandal in the spring of that year.
12. In the same vein, studies highlighting the effect that changes in unemployment rates in European countries have on people's trust in politicians and parliaments also show that these changes do not have a similar effect on people's trust in the police, although they are associated with trust in the legal system (Algan et al., 2017: 32–33). Natural disasters—like the Tohoku earthquake in Japan in 2011, which led to the Fukushima nuclear plant meltdown—have also been shown to trigger a decline in people's trust in risk managers closely linked to the disaster but not their trust in risk managers in other fields (Nakayachi, 2015). Finally, political scandals that relate closely to one institution (the European Commission, say) have been found to damage people's trust in that institution but not in other institutions (such as the European Parliament and national government) (van Elsas et al., 2020).
13. We find very similar levels of stability in trust judgements if we take the 456 individuals who answered every BESIP survey between 2014 and 2022 and thus focus on the same individuals across a long period of time. Indeed, fully 35 per cent of these individuals gave exactly the same trust rating to MPs in spring 2022 as they had done in spring 2014.
14. Stability in levels of political trust is mirrored by stability in levels of social or interpersonal trust (Uslaner, 2016: 78).
15. The measures are based on the Ten-Item Personality Inventory. The survey used is wave 15 of the BESIP.
16. Political attentiveness is measured by a question, 'How much attention do you generally pay to politics?' Personal efficacy is measured using an additive scale (α = 0.65) of three survey items: 'I have a pretty good understanding of the important political issues facing our country', 'It takes too much time and effort to be active in politics and public affairs', and 'It is often difficult for me to understand what is going on in government and politics'. Items 2 and 3 are reverse coded; the scale runs from 1 (low efficacy) to 5 (high efficacy).
17. Experimental studies also suggest that people's trust in politicians is sometimes triggered by immediate or gut-level reactions to political conduct rather than by considered judgements (for an example drawing from peoples' reactions to incivility in political debate, see Mutz and Reeves, 2005).
18. Although other studies find less evidence that negative and positive information have an asymmetrical effect on trust and confidence (in the field of public administration, see

James, 2011; in the field of police studies, see van Damme, 2015 and Oliveira et al., 2021; in the field of risk analysis, see White and Eiser, 2005).

19. As the authors note, this asymmetric effect may be due to people placing more weight on economic factors in their trust judgements when the economy is weak than when it is strong. In other words, the economy only becomes a salient issue (and therefore integral to people's trust in government) when economic times are bad; when economic times are good, the issue becomes less salient (and thus less consequential for trust).
20. The data are from waves 10 (November–December 2016) and 16 (May–June 2019) of the BES internet panel.
21. This mill is already well supplied by the British media, which has been found to produce more negative stories than its counterparts in other countries. A 2019 analysis found that 50 per cent of the content of newspaper, television, and radio output in the UK was negative in tone—the joint highest of any of the six countries studied—against just 14 per cent of content that was positive ('UK tops the charts for negative news stories', 25 June 2019, https://www.prmoment.com/pr-research/uk-tops-the-charts-for-negative-news-stories).
22. Critical attitudes towards public figures and agencies may not only colour people's judgements of these actors but may also encourage people to share negative information about them. A recent study has shown that information about self-interested politicians is more widely transmitted between individuals than is neutral information (Bøggild, Aaarøe, and Petersen, 2021). This suggests that citizens' negative dispositions towards politicians encourage them to share negative information about politicians more than they share positive information.

Chapter 2

1. For a similar typology, extending from specific judgements ('democratic reality') to generalized judgements ('constitutional ideal'), see Peffley and Rohrschneider (2014).
2. Other authors have pointed to the methodological problems of empirically distinguishing between specific and diffuse forms of support (e.g. Loewenberg, 1971: 184; Craig, 1993: 8–9).
3. 'Governing party supporters' are those identifying with the Conservative party between 1986 and 1996 and 2011 and 2020 (in which years 'opposition party supporters' are those identifying with the Labour party) and the Labour party between 1997 and 2010 (in which years 'opposition party supporters' are those identifying with the Conservative party).
4. The association often identified between people's evaluations of incumbent actors and their expressions of trust may partly reflect the way that trust is measured. David Easton observed that trust is frequently measured by reference to named political actors ('politicians', 'government', etc.), which might encourage survey respondents to focus on incumbent actors rather than on the political system as a whole (Easton, 1975: 450). I explore this argument in more detail in Chapter 3.
5. Thus, for example, some of the survey items used to measure political cynicism in the early studies by Agger, Goldstein, and Pearl, (1960) and Baloyra (1979) could also be deemed suitable for use in measuring political (dis)trust.

6. (Dis)satisfaction with a government or politician is different from—and based on a set of more specific evaluations than—(dis)satisfaction with democracy which, as identified shortly, is a more general measure of political support.
7. However, note that the distinction between trust and assessments of the political system is not strong and disappears altogether in an analysis that extends across eight Latin American countries (Booth and Seligson, 2009: 55).
8. The analysis employed factor analysis rather than an Item Response Theory model such as Mokken scaling as there was limited evidence of non-normality in the distribution of the data (for the individual items, maximum skewness = −1.17; maximum kurtosis = 4.30).
9. However, there are overlaps between the different forms of political support. Thus, for example, the latent variable measuring 'distrust' correlates 0.53 with the latent variable measuring 'cynicism', 0.42 with 'dissatisfaction', and 0.29 with 'scepticism'.
10. The data used here are drawn from the face-to-face element of the Audit. Details of the Citizen Audit can be found on the website of the UK Data Archive (study number 5099).
11. The Citizen Audit survey asks respondents for their trust in a number of different institutions. Yet since satisfaction with democracy and appraisals of government management of public services are each measured by a single item, I also measure trust through a single item.
12. Many scholars assume that trust depends on holding information about another actor's motivations. Thus, Cook, Hardin, and Levi, (2005: 6–7) suggest that trust can only be forthcoming if a person believes that an agent is genuinely concerned with their interests. And in Chapter 1, I quoted (see Section 1.1) a well-cited definition of trust from the management studies field: 'the willingness of a party to be vulnerable to the actions of another party based on the expectation that the other will perform a particular action important to the trustor, irrespective of the ability to monitor or control that other party' (Mayer, Davis, and Schoorman, 1995: 712). Section 1.1 omitted the final part of the sentence, which suggests that trust depends on appropriate motivations on the part of the trustee. In interpersonal contexts (for example, in the workplace where one worker is deciding whether to trust a co-worker or manager), it might make sense to think about trust as arising only if the trustee's motivations can be observed and verified. Yet this is not possible where trust relations occur with a distant actor or organization. In these contexts, citizens cannot assume that actors are motivated to serve their interests. Instead, trust rests on the existence and operation of appropriate monitoring and constraining devices over decision-makers rather than on assumptions about their motivations. Cook, Hardin, and Levi (2005) acknowledge this since they go on to say that judgements of trustworthiness can be based either on direct knowledge of an agent or a knowledge of the 'structures' in which their relationship with an agent is embedded (Cook, Hardin, and Levi, 2005: 7). Thus, the structures—the incentives and constraints—built into the relationship between a citizen and a decision-maker may provide robust grounds on which an individual can appraise trustworthiness.

Chapter 3

1. A fifth question was initially used to measure trust, this time gauging whether respondents thought that 'the people running the government are smart people who usually know

what they are doing ... or that quite a few of them don't seem to know what they are doing'. This question was fielded on the NES only until 1980. See http://www.electionstudies.org/.

2. Hetherington (2005: 51) suggests that 'trust in government is a simple concept, about which almost all people will express true attitudes'. However, he provides no evidence to justify this claim.

3. A single-item indicator may be justified if this is held to provide a summary, or 'global', measure of a concept. In this situation, although a concept may be held to comprise various elements or components, a single indicator would be capable of capturing the essence of the concept that underlies each of these elements (Fuchs and Diamantopolous, 2009: 200; Petrescu, 2013). Yet among the numerous studies that rely on the conventional single-item indicator of trust, little evidence—or even argument—is produced to justify the choice of measurement instrument on these grounds.

4. When it comes to using trust as an independent variable to explain outcomes, multi-item indicators of concepts such as social trust have been found to yield stronger relationships than single-item indicators (Zmerli et al., 2007: 46–50), presumably because the former better measure the concept than the latter. Not only is the concept of trust itself best conceptualized and measured in multidimensional terms, but its effects are sometimes specific to particular components. Thus, for example, a study of people's willingness to pay environmental taxes found that this outcome is affected less by people's general trust, as measured by traditional survey indicators, than by a particular component of trust, namely the credibility of government promises (Fairbrother, 2019). Similarly, people's support for reform of the United States' social security system has been shown to be more strongly shaped by judgements about whether public officials waste resources than about whether public officials are responsive and not corrupt (Jacobs and Matthews, 2012). Similar evidence in the context of people's willingness to defer to scientists is provided by Besley, Lee, and Pressgrove (2021). In other words, just as the concept of trust may contain various important dimensions, so its effects may also depend on particular components or dimensions of the concept.

5. To illustrate the danger of this, consider an example from an adjacent field within political science. Studies of electoral behaviour have shown that measurement error arising from the use of single-item indicators of public attitudes on complex policy issues significantly biases the conclusions reached about the role of issue voting (Ansolabahere, Rodden and Snyder, 2008).

6. A study that compared a multi-item measure of evaluations of democratic performance against the widely used single-item 'satisfaction with democracy' (SwD) measure showed the latter to only partially overlap with the former. The analysis counselled 'that caution should be taken when using it [i.e. SwD] as a measure of democratic performance at the individual level, as it is not clear what it gauges as it does not overlap substantially with a measure based on multiple indicators accounting for several aspects of democracy' (Quaranta, 2018: 21).

7. The fit indices for the multidimensional trust model are: CFI = 0.970, RMSEA = 0.042. Those for the unidimensional trust model are CFI = 0.919, RMSEA = 0.069.

8. These variations are also shown in the different ratings the Prolific Academic respondents gave to politicians on each dimension of trust (measured by computing additive scales for each from the relevant items on the list of measures). On a scale in which 1 = low trust

and 6 = high trust, ratings were significantly higher ($p < 0.000$) in the case of politicians' competence (mean score = 2.89) than in the case of their benevolence (mean score = 2.63) and integrity (mean score = 2.50).
9. This is not a new argument. Almost five decades ago, Jack Citrin suggested that conventional measures of trust may not only capture evaluations of incumbent politicians rather than appraisals of the political system's health but also that expressions of a lack of trust may reflect little more than knee-jerk reactions to survey interviewers. Citrin (1974: 975) suggested that 'the current *zeitgeist*, which legitimizes, even encourages, the expression of anti-political rhetoric, makes it fashionable to denigrate politicians and to criticize established institutions. As a result, the burgeoning ranks of the politically cynical may include many who are verbalizing a casual and ritualistic negativism rather than an enduring sense of estrangement that influences their beliefs and actions'.
10. Intawan and Nicholson (2018: 611–612) explain the higher scores on the implicit measure of trust by reference to individuals' lack of self-awareness rather than by reference to self-suppression arising from social desirability considerations. However, it is not clear that the measures the authors use to tap social desirability effects (various 'self-monitoring' items) really enable them to distinguish between an individual who expresses low trust in government out of social desirability considerations and an individual whose low trust does not reflect such considerations. This leaves open the potential for reported levels of trust in government to reflect social desirability effects.
11. For details, see note 10, Chapter 2.
12. Trust in the police was measured on a scale from 0 (no trust) to 10 (high trust). People scoring 8–10 on the scale were treated as 'high trusters', while those scoring 0–2 were treated as 'low trusters'.

Chapter 4

1. London's Metropolitan police was in the public eye over the 'Plebgate' affair in 2014, in which a police officer was jailed for public misconduct, and more recently over its mishandling of sexual crime incidents and relations with ethnic minority Londoners. Various healthcare workers and hospitals have been the subject of recent public outcries over the preventable deaths of adult patients and newborn babies. There have been numerous examples of poor practice on the part of UK banks, contributing to the financial crisis in 2008 and the mis-selling of insurance to individuals. The charity Oxfam was accused in 2018 of having covered up a scandal involving the hiring of sex workers by some of its overseas staff. Various national newspapers in Britain were revealed in 2011 to have hacked into the mobile phones of private individuals, including celebrities. The resulting furore resulted in the jailing of a newspaper editor and the closure of the paper he edited (the *News of the World*), which had been in print for 168 years.
2. For similar results, see Heath et al., (2013: chapter 10).
3. For wider evidence on the impact on trust of education and cognitive ability, see Schoon and Cheng (2011) (for the UK), Hooghe, Marien, and de Vroome (2012) (for the Netherlands), and Mayne and Hakhverdian (2017) (for a cross-national picture).
4. Against such negative expressions must be set the high levels of trust recorded by the ANES in the late 1950s and early 1960s, when over three-quarters of Americans indicated

they trusted the federal government 'all' or 'most' of the time (Alford, 2001: 31 and https://electionstudies.org/data-tools/anes-guide/index.html).

5. When the same survey question (whether people think politicians are out for themselves, for their party, or for their country) was repeated in 2021, the proportion believing politicians to be out for themselves had jumped to 63 per cent (Quilter-Pinner et al., 2021: 10).
6. 'Cash for Peerages' involved allegations that financial donors to the governing Labour party were being rewarded with seats in the upper legislative chamber, the House of Lords. The MPs' expenses scandal arose from MPs' misuse of parliamentary expense schemes for personal financial gain. Note that in Chapter 1, trust was found to comprise a largely stable judgement, with individuals' trust being broadly consistent over time. However, trust often shifts significantly in response to particular events which encourage citizens to revise their assessments of politicians either upwards or downwards.
7. While trust in the police in general has maintained (see also YouGov, 2022), trust in specific police forces—such as London's Metropolitan police—has declined. Data from the London Mayor's Public Attitudes Survey show that among Londoners, levels of agreement with the statements 'The police are dealing with the things that matter to this community' and 'The police can be relied upon to be there when needed' fell from around three-quarters in December 2014 to just over half in autumn 2022.
8. The Ipsos data also suggest that trust in government ministers and politicians has not declined as sharply as suggested by the British Social Attitudes survey data reported in Figure 4.2. The most plausible explanation is that levels of trust in ministers and politicians recorded by Ipsos were already very low in 1983, with 'floor effects' reducing the scope for significant further decline. By contrast, the British Social Attitudes recorded higher levels of trust in government in 1986, providing greater scope for subsequent decline.
9. Trust in the civil service (2016) is measured by responses to the statement 'Most civil servants can be trusted to do what is best for the country'. Trust in government (2014) is measured by responses to the statement 'Most of the time we can trust people in government to do what is right'. Both statements were accompanied by a five-point agree–disagree response scale. Those responding 'strongly agree' or 'agree' are treated as trusting. The surveys were conducted by the International Social Science Programme.

Chapter 5

1. For details, see note 6 to Chapter 4.
2. Some have argued that people in disadvantaged social groups are more affected by government decisions, in both malign and benign ways. Given this vulnerability, low trust among members of such groups may be both more likely and more rational (Zeineddine and Pratto, 2014).
3. Analysis is conducted over the past forty years for those variables (notably education and generation) that were included in the Protest, Dissatisfaction and Change survey in 1973. Analysis is limited to the past thirty years for variables (notably economic status) only measured in the BSA surveys from the 1980s.

4. The results for those with intermediate-level qualifications are omitted. The measures derive from the self-reported highest educational qualification achieved by respondents to the BSA survey.
5. The gap between the two would have been even more stark if the data had not extended to 2019 and 2020, years that were heavily clouded by the aftermath of the Brexit referendum. People's trust in the government has been found to have been associated with their views on Brexit (Whiteley et al., 2023: 296–297), while those views have also been shown to have been closely associated with individuals' educational status (Clarke, Goodwin, and Whiteley, 2017: 149–170). As can be seen from Figure 5.1, the trust gap between low and high educated citizens narrowed in 2019 and 2020, plausibly due to the Brexit effect.
6. The relevant educational categories here are: 'low' (for European countries, those educated to age 15; for the United States, those educated to below college level) and 'high' (for European countries, those educated to more than age 20; for the United States, those educated to college level). For other accounts of an increasing trust gap by education, see van der Brug and van Praag (2007) (on the Netherlands) and Aarts, van Ham, and Thomassen (2017), Dotti Sani and Magistro (2016), and Martini and Quaranta (2020: 171–173, 191–193) (on various European countries). However, a cross-national review by Aarts, Thomassen, and van Ham (2014) suggests the impact of education on changes in people's regard for the political system may be slight.
7. Social class is measured by reference to survey respondents' occupations. Economic feelings are measured via a question asking 'Which of these comes closest to your feelings about your household's income these days?'.
8. By contrast, trends in social or interpersonal forms of trust have been found to manifest a stronger generational component (see Clark, Clark, and Monzin, 2013).
9. The source for this is the Protest, Dissatisfaction and Change survey.
10. The source for these data is the BSA survey.
11. Although when it comes to government performance on elderly care, people's evaluations were not more strongly related to their trust evaluations in 2006 than in 1973.
12. Other studies have similarly shown little evidence of higher expectations of government among citizens in countries such as the United States; see Oldendick and Bennett (2019).
13. Using the 'jobs' question means we can track relationships back to 1973, drawing on the Protest, Dissatisfaction and Change survey. The relevant response categories for the job question in this survey were: providing jobs is 'essential for the government to do' (high expectations) or a task for which government has 'some' or 'no responsibility' (low expectations).
14. The specific BSA survey items used to measure ideology are: 'Government should redistribute income from the better-off to those who are less well off'; 'Big business benefits owners at the expense of workers'; 'Ordinary working people do not get their fair share of the nation's wealth'; 'There is one law for the rich and one for the poor'; and 'Management will always try to get the better of employees if it gets the chance'. Policy attitudes are measured by agreement or disagreement with each of these statements, with the responses being summed into a single ideology scale.
15. I produce a single figure for the representation gap, which covers the summed distance from individuals to both the Conservatives and Labour. The point here is that trust should be particularly low among people who feel unrepresented by both the major

parties, as opposed to people who feel represented by at least one party. No question on trust was fielded on the 2001 BES, so the association between policy representation and trust cannot be computed for that year.
16. Another long-term study in Sweden showed that levels of policy representation have largely maintained, or fallen only slightly, since the 1980s (Holmberg, 2014: Figure 8.1).
17. See https://www.prmoment.com/pr-research/uk-tops-the-charts-for-negative-news-stories (further details in Chapter 1, note 21).
18. Studies on the media's impact on levels of trust have returned a variety of results. There is no space here to detail these variations, although a summary is provided in Appendix 5.1.
19. Broadsheet newspapers comprise the *Daily Telegraph*, *Financial Times*, *Guardian*, *The Independent or 'The i'*, and *The Times*. Tabloid newspapers comprise the *Daily Mirror*, *Daily Star*, *The Sun*, and the *Daily Record*.
20. For each year, the figure is calculated as the difference in trust between broadsheet/tabloid readers and non-readers relative to trust among non-readers:

$$\frac{\text{mean trust broadsheet/tabloid reader - mean trust non-newspaper reader}}{\text{mean trust non-newspaper reader}} \times 100.$$

21. Measured on a scale from 1 (none at all) to 5 (great deal), mean levels of political interest rose from 2.84 in 1986 to 3.45 in 2020.
22. The model cannot be extended beyond 2016 as later BSA surveys did not carry measures of indicators such as economic feelings and newspaper readership.
23. We find similar results if we use social class and income level as measures of economic status. In each case, the low economic status group (the working class or bottom income tercile) are significantly less trusting than the high economic status group (professionals or the top income tercile).
24. To aid visual representation, the results in Figure 5.10 were obtained from a linear regression model, not the ordinal logistic regression model used in Appendix 5.2 (the substantive results of the linear and ordinal models are similar).
25. Over the period, the association with trust of reading a tabloid newspaper relative to reading no paper at all falls just short of statistical significance at the 5 per cent level. A similar exercise conducted in Sweden found that readership of tabloid newspapers had no significant impact on changes in trust over time (Strömbäck, Djerf-Pierre, and Shehata, 2016).
26. These findings are similar to those applying to citizens' participation in politics. Dalton (2017b: 172–185) has identified a growing gap across countries in rates of electoral turnout and other forms of political participation between high and low educated citizens, and between individuals in high and low socio-economic groups. The highly educated in particular are becoming more participatory relative to the less educated, just as I have shown here that they are becoming more trusting.
27. That levels of trust among even well-educated citizens have fallen over time helps to explain why the increase in educational attainment in countries like Britain over the past four decades or so has not led to increased levels of trust. The implication of the results presented here is that if aggregate levels of education had not increased, then, all other things being equal, levels of trust across the population might have declined even more than they already have.

Chapter 6

1. The distinction between outcomes and processes as drivers of attitudes towards political actors mirrors other analyses; for example, Scharpf's (1999: 6–13) model of 'output-based' and 'input-based' legitimacy.
2. The distinction drawn here between an actor's competence, intentions, and integrity is similar to that drawn between politicians' performance, process, and probity (see Hetherington and Rudolph, 2008, 2015: 34–35, 48–50).
3. This identification and classification of factors associated with trust have primarily arisen from researcher-driven exercises. Happily, studies that have adopted a more bottom-up approach—in which research participants themselves identify the factors associated with trust—tend to arrive at similar conclusions. Thus, studies of citizen attitudes towards public office-holders in Britain have found trust to rest most heavily on perceptions of honesty, consistency, and public-regardedness (Graham et al., 2002). A similar set of attributes emerged from an analysis of the elements of trust employed by African Americans (Meredith, 2007). In the context of social risk, other studies have shown trust to be associated most strongly with impartiality and a lack of bias (Frewer et al., 1996). Among citizens in two Latin American countries, trust has been found to reflect the qualities of integrity, competence, and responsiveness (Carlin, 2014). Hence analysts' efforts to identify the determinants of individuals' trust judgements are largely corroborated by the criteria used by ordinary people in assessing whether a decision-maker is worthy or not of their trust.
4. Studies have suggested that judgements about the state of the national economy ('sociotropic' evaluations) are more closely associated with feelings of trust than judgements about individuals' personal economic circumstances ('egocentric' evaluations) (Torcal, 2014).
5. Correlations between trust and policy proximity inevitably raise questions about causal ordering. However, studies which measure responsiveness in objective terms (with the policy 'gap' between citizens and politicians derived from separate measures of citizens' and politicians' policy positions rather than from citizens' appraisals alone) find that this gap is significantly—and negatively—associated with citizen satisfaction (André and Depauw, 2017; Noordzij, de Koster, and van der Waal, 2021b). In the field of risk studies, the 'value similarity' model locates trust in an individual's belief that an actor or agency shares their values or goals (Siegrist, Earle, and Gutscher, 2003).
6. The depressive effects of corruption or misconduct on trust can be long-lasting. Some studies find the effects of events like major financial scandals to have largely worn off within a matter of months (Ares and Hernández, 2017). Yet other studies suggest the effects of scandals last longer than this, for many months (van Elsas et al., 2020) or even years. Keele (2007) estimates the negative effect of the Watergate scandal on American's trust in government to have endured for eight years after the resignation of President Nixon in 1974.
7. Although some studies (e.g. Gibson, Caldeira, and Spence, 2005) find that when bodies such as the Supreme Court and Congress take decisions marked by partisan division, this generates no lower levels of legitimacy among the public than when their decisions are marked by consensus. The same appears to be true when it comes to public evaluations of legislation passed by Congress (Harbridge, Malhotra, and Harrison, 2014).

8. People's evaluations of government delivery on these issues were strongly interrelated, as suggested by a Mokken scale analysis which showed a moderately strong ($H_S = 0.34$) unidimensional scale. Testing the association with trust of assessments on each policy area separately showed statistically significant positive effects for all issues bar the level of taxation (suggesting that individuals' assessments of delivery on 'technocratic' issues may be less important for their trust than assessments of delivery on more substantive issues).
9. Negative feelings are measured by survey respondents describing themselves, on each policy issue, as one or more of 'angry', 'disgusted', 'uneasy', and 'afraid'. Positive feelings are measured by respondents describing themselves as one or more of 'happy', 'hopeful', 'confident', and 'proud'. On the economy, more positive feelings were expressed (53 per cent) than negative ones (47 per cent). On the health service, more negative feelings were expressed (63 per cent) than positive ones (37 per cent).
10. Party vote is measured as the party the respondent indicated they would be likely to support in the forthcoming national election.
11. Previous studies have suggested that there might be trade-offs between these different sources of trust. Thus, the more closely trust is associated with evaluations of an actor's competence, the less closely it will be associated with evaluations of the actor's benevolence, and vice versa (Brockner and Wiesenfeld, 1996; for a recent study across European countries which also points to this effect, see Magalhães (2016)). The implication is that people's trust rests on judgements either about an actor's competence or their benevolence but not on both. I tested for a similar effect by including in the model an interaction between evaluations of the prime minister's competence and responsiveness and, separately, between evaluations of government policy delivery and perceptions of government fairness. None of the resulting coefficients was statistically significant. This suggests that there is no direct trade-off for trust of people's appraisals of political actors' competence/policy performance and their evaluations of those actors' motivations/fairness. Perhaps unfortunately for Britain's politicians, citizens' trust appears dependent on them being perceived both as competent/delivering policy outcomes and as responsive/fair.
12. The necessity of recording attitudes at wave 1, prior to any changes in trust, explains why the results reported in Table 6.1, Model 1, and in Figure 6.3 draw on the pre-election wave of the 2005 BES.
13. Although the survey measures ask about people's perceptions of parties, I take this to tap evaluations of politicians within these parties.
14. The questions on parties keeping/breaking promises and being capable/incapable of strong government elicited high numbers of 'don't know' responses for the third main party, the Liberal Democrats; I therefore omitted evaluations of this party from the measures.
15. Examples of such knowledge questions were 'Polling stations shut at 10 pm' and 'The minimum voting age is 16'. Respondents were asked to indicate whether each statement was true or false.
16. In particular, Fisher, van Heerde, and Tucker (2010) argue that 'moral' factors (i.e. how far an actor is likely to share my interests) are likely to drive trust in politicians, while 'deliberative' factors (i.e. whether policy issues are subject to full and open public debate) are likely to drive trust in political parties. However, it is difficult to assess the relative

effects of these two sets of factors, since the models of trust in each institution use different measures of each factor. For example, when it comes to trust in politicians, the moral factor is gauged by a survey item that asks for responses to the statement 'Politicians share the same goals and values as me'. When it comes to trust in political parties, however, the moral factor is gauged by a survey item that asks for responses to the statement 'People involved in political parties are people just like me'. Where factors are measured in such different ways, it becomes difficult to compare their effects on trust (for a similar argument, see Hooghe, 2011).
17. Studies in the field of risk analysis have similarly shown variations in the criteria people draw on to evaluate trust in different organizations involved in, for example, land management (Johnson and White, 2010).
18. These issues were selected as, at the time, they were deemed by the public to be the most important issues facing Britain, as measured by a question fielded elsewhere on the BES survey.
19. Females now trust the police less than do males, unsurprisingly given the numerous incidents of police misconduct against women that have recently attracted public attention. Yet according to Ipsos' Veracity Index, as late as 2021, levels of trust in the police were higher among females than among males.
20. However, the negative Iraq coefficient on trust in the police is significant at $p < 0.10$.
21. I measure people's trust in parliament and politicians combined in a single scale from 0 (no trust) to 10 (great deal of trust).
22. The assumption is that economic evaluations were closely associated with trust in 2010 because the economic crash in 2008 primed people to think about the state of the economy. Studies in the United States have shown that people place more emphasis on economic judgements when economic times are bad than when they are good (Hetherington and Rudolph, 2008). Hence the effects of economic judgements on trust tend to be greater when the economy is contracting than when it is expanding.
23. However, somewhat surprisingly, in Greece, evaluations of economic performance apparently did not shape levels of trust more strongly after the 2008 crisis than beforehand (Ellinas and Lamprianou, 2014).
24. The coefficients for government fairness in 2005 and 2010 are significantly different from one another ($p < 0.001$). For similar results using different data, see Whiteley et al. (2016).
25. Other studies that similarly find levels of political support to rest on a broad range of factors—including assessments of government performance, political representation, and corruption—include Dahlberg, Linde, and Holmberg (2015) and OECD (2022: Table 1.1).

Chapter 7

1. The importance of monitoring government is gauged by respondents who rated this function as 7 on a 1–7 scale, where 1 = not at all important and 7 = very important. The measure of trust derives from responses to the statement 'Most of the time we can trust people in government to do what is right'; high trusters are deemed those agreeing with the statement, while low trusters are deemed those disagreeing with it.

2. Low trust individuals have also been found more likely than their high trust counterparts to base their assessments of the reality of global warming on data on global temperatures (MacInnis and Krosnick, 2016: 500–501). Hence, low trust appears to push individuals to monitor the data themselves rather than accepting the line of experts. However, in this case, annual climate data—which fluctuate quite extensively—arguably provide a less accurate platform for citizens' judgements than scientific consensus—which tally climate trends over a number of years. Thus, effective individual judgements can in some instances be helped, but in other instances be hindered, by relying on—or trusting in—official or scientific information.
3. The examples I give of 'voice' and 'exit' behaviours do not necessarily tally with those provided by Hirschman (1970), from whom the terms derive.
4. The survey asked respondents whether they had ever undertaken these behaviours in response to a government action they deemed unjust and harmful.
5. A Mokken scale analysis shows that each of the reported behaviours falls onto a single scale, with coefficients of homogeneity for individual items (H_I) all above 0.35 and for the scale as a whole (H_S) at 0.44. I coded the resulting scale so that 0 equates to no protest actions and 1 to at least one protest action.
6. The number of people falling into each category is: high trust/low efficacy = 651, low trust/low efficacy = 674, high trust/high efficacy = 636, and low trust/high efficacy = 203.
7. Hooghe and Dassonneville's analysis shows that declining trust is also associated with avoiding casting a valid vote, the equivalent to abstaining from the electoral process altogether. See Section 7.3a.
8. Trust is measured by a question, 'How much trust do you have in Members of Parliament in general?' Responses are recorded on a 7-point scale, ranging from 1 ('No trust') to 7 ('A great deal of trust'). Levels of trust increased from wave 1 (mean trust = 3.09) to wave 6 (mean = 3.38).
9. Note, however, that Hooghe and Dassonneville (2018b) find that low trust among individuals was not a significant predictor of voting for Donald Trump in 2016, net of other contributory factors. Nor was a belief that the US political system lacks legitimacy (Weinschenk and Dawes, 2019).
10. I use the EVS/WVS question on how much confidence respondents have in parliament since this was the sole institution asked about in 1999. Those answering 'a great deal' and 'quite a lot' of confidence are treated as high in confidence, while those answering 'not very much' or 'none at all' (in 1999) or 'none at all' (all other years) are treated as low in confidence.
11. In his analysis of democratic deconsolidation, Mounk (2018: 111) suggests that support among British citizens for strong leader governance of the country has doubled from 25 per cent in 1999 to 50 per cent. The end-date and origin of Mounk's figure go unreferenced and are thus unclear. In fact, data from the EVS/WVS show that across the British population, support for strong leader governance has remained constant, at 26 per cent in 1999 and 25 per cent in 2022.
12. For the measurement of trust, see note 8.
13. A similar study conducted in the Netherlands that captured changes in people's trust over time (in this case, over a three-year period) also found that falling levels of trust had no significant effects on people's support for authoritarian (i.e. strong leader) forms of decision-making (Ouattara and van der Meer, 2023).

14. Studies of people's choices at EU referendums in other countries have similarly shown a substantial effect of trust on *status quo*-disrupting choices (Hobolt, 2009: chapter 3). However, in the Dutch 2016 referendum, held to ratify the agreement between the EU and Ukraine, vote choice was found to be essentially unaffected by citizens' trust in their national government (Jacobs, Akkerman, and Zaslove, 2018). Some analyses of the Brexit referendum have similarly found little effect of trust on voters' choices (Dennison, Davidov, and Seddig, 2020).
15. For the measurement of trust, see note 8. The 'No trust' category consisted of people selecting value 1 on the trust scale, while the 'Great deal' of trust category consisted of people selecting values 6 and 7 on the scale. The distribution of referendum vote choices—which were measured immediately after the referendum in June/July 2016—almost exactly match those recorded by that year's BSA survey (Curtice, 2017).
16. Over the period, levels of trust dropped by two or more points on the 1–7 trust scale for 1,628 respondents to the two surveys and rose by two or more points for 1,696 respondents; for the remaining 11,130 respondents, levels of trust remained more or less constant.
17. If we model the effect of trust while controlling for people's attitudes towards the EU (measured through a survey item that asked people whether they favoured Britain uniting fully with the EU or retaining its independence from the EU), the parameter for declining trust remains negatively associated with voting Leave but short of statistical significance.
18. Although other studies have found that trust does not have a significant effect on individuals' preferences for either long-term or short-term policies (Christensen and Rapeli, 2021).
19. The relationship between trust and government activism may also work in the opposite direction. Governments that deliver a range of supportive programmes—for example, an effective welfare state—may be trusted more than governments that provide fewer public goods (for evidence of the impact of welfare programmes on trust, see Kumlin, 2011).
20. Goubin and Kumlin (2022) also provide evidence that trust is positively associated with support for welfare provision not only at single points in time but also over time. They show that as individuals become more trusting over time, their support for state welfare provision increases.
21. The other side of a reluctance among low trust individuals to grant extensive policy competences to government is an enthusiasm for private (i.e. individual) provision over public provision. Recent studies have found that individuals holding negative views of government are, relative to their more positive counterparts, more likely to support and use private security firms to police their area and to live in gated communities (Lerman, 2019: 232–237) and more likely to drink bottled water rather than consuming the publicly provided tap variant (Teodoro, Zuhlke, and Switzer, 2022).
22. Support for increased government tax and spending is measured by question (a) in the text above. Support for government activism in the other three areas is measured by questions about whether it 'should be the government's responsibility to provide a job for everyone who wants one/provide health care for the sick/keep prices under control'. Supporters of active government are deemed those responding 'definitely/probably should be' (on jobs) and 'definitely should be' (on healthcare and prices). Trust is measured by the question 'How much do you trust British governments of any party to place the needs of the nation above the interests of their own political party?' Low trusters are measured

by those responding that they trust 'only some of the time' or 'almost never', while high trusters are measured by those responding that they trust 'most of the time' or 'almost always'.
23. The 'redistributive' and 'distributive' terms derive from the work of Hetherington (2005). Hetherington postulates and demonstrates empirically among a sample of US citizens that trust is particularly closely associated with support for active government where state programmes entail individual sacrifice. Thus, where governments pursue 'redistributive' programmes designed to help particular sections of the population (such as poorer individuals), the association of trust with activist support is stronger than where governments pursue 'distributive' programmes that benefit all citizens. The logic is that citizens asked to make sacrifices for government programmes are only likely to do so if they trust government to spend (their) money wisely and efficiently. Yet there is no evidence of this effect in Britain. I tested for its presence by rerunning the models predicting support for active government presented in Appendix 7.3, using the 2016 BSA survey data. The models included interaction terms of trust and (a) household income (in terciles) and (b) feelings about household income. In no case did the interaction terms yield a statistically significant effect on support for active government. Thus, trust is no more important for public support for active government among citizens asked to make material sacrifices. But as we have just seen, there is evidence that trust does play a greater role among citizens making ideological sacrifices.
24. The relationship between trust and support for government intervention on environmental protection is robust to the introduction of relevant control variables, such as people's level of concern with the environment. A positive association between trust and support for government activism on environmental policy issues has been identified in other studies (e.g. Konisky, Milyo, and Richardson, 2008; Fairbrother, 2016). It is unclear whether the positive effect of trust on government activism is specific to environmental issues, and if so why.
25. The point was made in Chapter 3 about the shortcomings of many survey measures of trust. For evidence that alternative survey measures of trust show different relationships with attitudes, including individuals' support for active government, see Gershtenson and Plane (2011).
26. These doubts are reflected in Kinder's (1998: 831) observation that 'the connection between conventional forms of participation [such as electoral turnout] and distrust has proven elusive, to put it mildly'.
27. I also replicated the models in Appendix 7.4, replacing *levels* of trust with *changes* in trust (by comparing levels of trust in the election wave of the BES survey with levels of trust in waves roughly one year before the election). The results showed a significant effect of declining trust on turnout in 2015 and 2017, although a non-significant effect in 2019. However, the effects of declining trust on turnout were not that substantial: the greatest effect was in 2017, when the effect of declining trust increased the probability of abstention by 6 per cent. For the effect of changes in trust on turnout in the 2015 election, see also Figure 7.3 and the results in Appendix 7.2.
28. Source: Ipsos 'Veracity Index 2022'.
29. Overview studies are provided by Siegrist and Zingg (2014), Yaqub et al. (2014), and Larson et al. (2018).

30. The authors find that social trust (i.e. trust between individuals) also increases tax compliance but to a lesser degree than political trust. Note, however, that a recent study of US citizens found that individuals' trust in the government played no significant role in shaping rates of tax compliance (Robbins and Kiser, 2020).
31. In certain circumstances, studies have found that the impact of trust on decision acceptance is more conditional. Thus, in an experimental study of compliance with the decisions of a water regulator under conditions of aquatic scarcity, it was found that trust in the regulator only affected compliance when the regulator's decision was consistent with evidence about water quantities and was seen as likely to increase water supply. When decisions did not manifest these positive qualities, trust had no effect on compliance (Hamm et al., 2013b). Other studies have suggested that trust has little impact on people's compliance with government guidance. For example, Ulbig (2002) finds that US citizens' feelings of trust in government are substantially unrelated to their inclination to obey or disobey the law.
32. Other studies of citizen behaviour find little impact of people's trust in political actors. Thus, for example, Sears et al. (1978) find that during the energy crisis of 1974, citizens in Los Angeles who did not trust government were no less compliant with official guidance to reduce car and electricity usage than were citizens who did trust government.
33. However, the same Mori study found that people's trust in their local council and health providers had no effect on their willingness to get involved with these bodies in planning public services.
34. A Mokken scale analysis shows trust in each of these institutions to fall onto a single scale ($H_S = 0.59$ in 2004 and $H_S = 0.63$ in 2010).
35. These probabilities are estimated using the SPost suite of commands (Long and Freese, 2006).
36. Trust is measured in relation to the government, House of Commons, the courts, civil service, politicians, and local government A Mokken scale analysis shows people's trust in these institutions to fall onto a single scale ($H_S = 0.55$).
37. For the measurement of trust and the classification of low/high trusters, see note 22.
38. Source: World Values Survey. Asked by the International Social Science Program about the importance of not evading tax payments, the proportion of Spaniards who deemed this 'very important' rose from 54 per cent in 2004 to 72 per cent in 2014.
39. Source: European Values Survey.
40. Source: International Social Science Program.
41. Source: International Social Science Program.
42. Source for the 'VAT gap' figures: OECD (2013b) and Poniatowski et al. (2019). I should note that one reason the tax gap did not increase after 2008 might be that the Greek government invested in tax collection facilities to reduce tax evasion after the financial crisis (I thank Professor Nicolas Dimertzis for this information).
43. The source for these data is the World Health Organization's Immunization Dashboard (https://immunizationdata.who.int/).

Conclusion

1. Source: Pew Research Center, *Public trust in government: 1958-2022* (available at: https://www.pewresearch.org/politics/2022/06/06/public-trust-in-government-1958-2022/).
2. Source: Eurobarometer 97, summer 2022.
3. I should emphasize that the focus here is on the contribution of the discipline of political science to the study of trust. I do not review the analogous contributions of other academic disciplines, although my perception is that in some of these disciplines—notably management, risk studies, and health—the study of trust has developed beyond the level achieved in political science. For example, analyses in the field of management studies have begun to explore how trust violations can be repaired (e.g. Sharma, Schoorman, and Ballinger, 2022), while health-based studies have contributed detailed explorations of how trust should be measured (Hall et al., 2002). Neither of these endeavours has been extensively replicated in the field of political science.
4. For examples of studies adopting this approach, see p. 128.

Bibliography

Aarts, Kees, Carolien van Ham, and Jacques Thomassen (2017) 'Modernization, Globalization and Satisfaction with Democracy', in Carolien van Ham et al., eds, *Myth and Reality of the Legitimacy Crisis: Explaining Trends and Cross-National Differences in Established Democracies*, New York: Oxford University Press, pp. 37–58.

Aarts, Kees and Holli A Semetko (2003) 'The Divided Electorate: Media Use and Political Involvement', *Journal of Politics*, 65:3, 759–784.

Aarts, Kees, Audun Fladmoe, and Jesper Strömbäck (2012) 'Media, Political Trust, and Political Knowledge: A Comparative Perspective', in Toril Aalberg and James Curran, eds, *How Media Inform Democracy: A Comparative Approach*, London: Routledge, pp. 98–118.

Aarts, Kees, Jacques Thomassen, and Carolien van Ham (2014) 'Globalization, Representation and Attitudes towards Democracy', in Jacques Thomassen, ed, *Elections and Democracy: Representation and Accountability*, Oxford: Oxford University Press, pp. 201–231.

Adriaansen, Maud L, Philip van Praag, and Claes H de Vreese (2012) 'Substance Matters: How News Content Can Reduce Political Cynicism', *International Journal of Public Opinion Research*, 22:4, 433–457.

Agger, Robert E, Marshall N Goldstein and Stanley A Pearl (1961) 'Political Cynicism: Measurement and Meaning', *Journal of Politics*, 23:3, 477–506.

Alford, John R (2001) 'We're All in This Together: The Decline of Trust in Government, 1958-1996', in John Hibbing and Elizabeth Theiss-Morse, eds, *What Is It about Government that Americans Dislike?* New York: Cambridge University Press.

Algan, Yann et al. (2017) 'The European Trust Crisis and the Rise of Populism', Brookings Papers on Economic Activity, Fall.

Allen, Nicholas and Sarah Birch (2015) *Ethics and Integrity in British Politics: How Citizens Judge Their Politicians' Conduct and Why It Matters*, Cambridge: Cambridge University Press.

Allen, Nicholas and Katja Sarmiento-Mirwaldt (2015) 'In It Together? The Political Consequences of Perceived Discommunions of Interest in British Politics', *Research and Politics*, 2:2, 1–10.

Allen, Trevor J (2017) 'Exit to the Right? Comparing Far Right Voters and Abstainers in Western Europe', *Electoral Studies*, 50: 103–115.

Allum, Nick (2007) 'Empirical Test of Competing Theories of Hazard-Related Trust: Case of GM Food', *Risk Analysis*, 27:4, 935–946.

Allum, Nick et al. (2010) 'Re-evaluating the Links Between Social Trust, Institutional Trust and Civic Association', in John Stilwell et al., eds, *Understanding Population Trends and Processes, Vol 2: Spatial and Social Disparities*, Netherlands: Springer, pp. 199–215.

Almond, Gabriel A and Sidney Verba (1963) *The Civic Culture: Political Attitudes and Democracy in Five Nations*, Princeton, NJ: Princeton University Press.

Andeweg, Rudy (2011) 'Approaching Perfect Policy Congruence: Measurement, Development and Relevance for Political Representation', in Martin Rosema, Bas Denters and Kees Aarts, eds, *How Democracy Works: Political Representation and Policy Congruence in Modern Societies*, Amsterdam: Pallas Publications, pp. 39–52.

Bibliography

Andeweg, Rudy (2014) 'A Growing Confidence Gap in Politics? Data versus Discourse', in Jan-Willem and Paul A M Van Lange, eds, *Power, Politics, and Paranoia: Why People Are Suspicious of Their Leaders*, Cambridge: Cambridge University Press, pp. 176–196.

André, Audrey and Sam, Depauw (2017) 'The Quality of Representation and Satisfaction with Democracy: The Consequences of Citizen-Elite Policy and Process Congruence', *Political Behavior*, 39:2, 377–397.

Ansolabehere, Stephen, Jonathan Rodden, and James M Snyder Jr (2008) 'The Strength of Issues: Using Multiple Measures to Gauge Preference Stability, Ideological Constraint, and Issue Voting', *American Political Science Review*, 102:2, 215–232.

Ares, Macarena and Enrique Hernández (2017) 'The Corrosive Effect of Corruption on Trust in Politicians: Evidence from a Natural Experiment', *Research & Politics*, 4:2, 1–8.

Armingeon, Klaus and Kai Guthmann (2014) 'Democracy in Crisis? The Declining Support for National Democracy in European Countries, 2007-2011', *European Journal of Political Research*, 53: 423–442.

Arnesen, Sveinung and Yvette Peters (2018) 'The Legitimacy of Representation: How Descriptive, Formal and Responsiveness Representation Affect the Acceptability of Political Decisions', *Comparative Political Studies*, 51:7, 868–899.

Avery, James (2009) 'Videomalaise or Virtuous Circle? The Influence of the News Media on Political Trust', *Harvard International Journal of Press/Politics*, 14:4, 410–433.

Baloyra, Enrique (1979) 'Criticism, Cynicism and Political Evaluation: Venezuelan Example', *American Political Science Review*, 73:4, 987–1002.

Bauer, Paul C (2014) *Conceptualizing and Measuring Trust and Trustworthiness*, Working Paper 61, International Political Science Association: Committee on Concepts and Methods.

Bélanger, Eric and Kees Aarts (2006) 'Explaining the Rise of the LPF: Issues, Discontent, and the 2002 Dutch Election', *Acta Politica*, 41: 4–20.

Bélanger, Eric and Richard Nadeau (2005) 'Political Trust and the Vote in Multiparty Elections: The Canadian Case', *European Journal of Political Research*, 44:1, 121–146.

Bellucci, Paolo and Vincenzo Memoli (2012) 'The Determinants of Democracy Satisfaction in Europe', in David Sanders, Pedro Magalhaes and Gabor Toka, eds, *Citizens and the European Polity: Mass Attitudes towards the European and National Polities*, Oxford: Oxford University Press, pp. 9–38.

Bennett, Stephen Earl (2001) 'Were the Halcyon Days Really Golden? An Analysis of Americans' Attitudes about the Political System, 1945-1965', in John Hibbing and Elizabeth Theiss-Morse, eds, *What Is It about Government that Americans Dislike?* New York: Cambridge University Press, pp. 47–58.

Bergman, Marcelo (2002) 'Who Pays for Social Policy? A Study on Taxes and Trust', *Journal of Social Policy*, 31:2, 289–305.

Bernstein, Jeffery L (2001) 'Linking Presidential and Congressional Approval During Unified and Divided Governments', in John R Hibbing and Elizabeth Theiss-Morse, eds, *What Is It about Government that Americans Dislike?* New York: Cambridge University Press, pp. 98–117.

Bertsou, Eri (2019a) 'Rethinking Political Distrust', *European Political Science Review*, 11:2, 213–230.

Bertsou, Eri (2019b) 'Political Distrust and Its Discontents: Exploring the Meaning, Expression and Significance of Political Distrust', *Societies*, 9:4, 72.

Besley, John C, Nicole M Lee, and Geah Pressgrove (2021) "Reassessing the Variables Used to Measure Public Perceptions of Scientists', *Science Communication*, 43:1, 3–32.

Bianco, William T (1994) *Trust: Representatives and Constituents*, Ann Arbor: University of Michigan Press.

Bickerstaff, K et al. (2008) 'Reframing Nuclear Power in the UK Energy Debate: Nuclear Power, Climate Change Mitigation and Radioactive Waste', *Public Understanding of Science*, 17:2, 145–169.

Bigley, Gregory and Jone Pearce (1998) 'Straining for Shared Meaning in Organizational Science: Problems of Trust and Distrust', *Academy of Management Review*, 23:3, 405–421.

Birch, Birch and Nicholas Allen (2012) '"There Will Be Burning and A-Looting Tonight": The Social and Political Correlates of Law-Breaking', *Political Quarterly*, 83:1, 33–43.

Bishop, George F (2005) *The Illusion of Public Opinion: Fact and Artifact in American Public Opinion Polls*, Lanham, MD: Rowman & Littlefield.

Blair, Robert A, Benjamin S Morse, and Lily L Tsai (2017) 'Public Health and Public Trust: Survey Evidence from the Ebola Virus Disease Epidemic in Liberia', *Social Science & Medicine*, 172, 89–97.

Bleich, Sara, Robert Blendon and Alyce Adams (2007) 'Trust in Scientific Experts on Obesity: Implications for Awareness and Behavior Change', *Obesity*, 15:8, 2145–2156.

Bøggild, Troels (2016) 'How Politicians' Reelection Efforts Can Reduce Public Trust, Electoral Support and Policy Approval', *Political Psychology*, 37:6, 901–919.

Bøggild, Troels (2020) 'Politicians as Party Hacks: Party Loyalty and Public Distrust in Politicians', *Journal of Politics*, 82:4, 1516–1529.

Bøggild, Troels, Lene Aaarøe, and Michael Bang Petersen (2021) 'Citizens as Complicits: Distrust in Politicians and Biased Social Dissemination of Political Information', *American Political Science Review*, 115:1, 269–285.

Booth, John A and Mitchell A Seligson (2009) *The Legitimacy Puzzle in Latin America: Political Support and Democracy in Eight Nations*, New York: Cambridge University Press.

Bradford, Ben, Jonathan Jackson, and Elizabeth A Stanko (2009) 'Contact and Confidence: Revisiting the Impact of Public Encounters with the Police', *Policing and Society*, 19:1, 20–46.

Braithwaite, Valerie (1998) 'Communal and Exchange Trust Norms: Their Value Base and Relevance to Institutional Trust', in Valerie Braithwaite and Margaret Levi, eds, *Trust and Governance*, New York: Russell Sage Foundation, pp. 46–74.

Brandenburg, Heinz and Robert Johns (2014) 'The Declining Representativeness of the British Party System, and Why It Matters', *Political Studies*, 62:4, 704–725

Brandt, Mark J (2013) 'Do the Disadvantaged Legitimize the Social System? A Large-scale Test of the Status-Legitimacy Hypothesis', *Journal of Personality and Social Psychology*, 104:5, 765–785.

Brehm, John and Wendy Rahn (1997) 'Individual-level Evidence for the Causes and Consequences of Social Capital', *American Journal of Political Science*, 41:3, 999–1023.

Brockner, Joel and Batia M Wiesenfeld (1996) 'An Integrative Framework for Explaining Reactions to Decisions: Interactive Effects of Outcomes and Procedures', *Psychological Bulletin*, 120:2, 189–208.

Bulloch, Sarah L (2013) 'Seeking Construct Validity in Interpersonal Trust Research: A Proposal on Linking Theory and Survey Measures', *Social Indicators Research*, 113:3, 1289–1310.

Burns, Calvin, Kathryn Mearns, and Peter McGeorge (2006) 'Explicit and Implicit Trust Within Safety Culture', *Risk Analysis*, 26:5, 1139–1150.

Butler, John K Jr (1991) 'Toward Understanding and Measuring Conditions of Trust: Evolution of a Conditions of Trust Inventory', *Journal of Management*, 17:3, 643–663.

Caillier, James (2010) 'Citizen Trust, Political Corruption, and Voting Behavior: Connecting the Dots', *Politics & Policy*, 38:5, 1015–1035.

Cameron, Sarah and Ian McAllister (2022) *Trends in Australian Political Opinion: Results from the Australian Election Study 1987-2022*, Canberra: The Australian National University.

Canache, Damarys, Jeffery J Mondak and Mitchell A Seligson (2001) 'Meaning and Measurement in Cross-national Research on Satisfaction with Democracy', *Public Opinion Quarterly*, 65:4, 506–528.

Capelos, Teresa et al. (2016) 'Ingredients of Institutional Reputations and Citizen Engagement with Regulators', *Regulation and Governance*, 10:4, 350–367.

Cappella, Joseph and Kathleen Hall Jamieson (1996) 'News Frames, Political Cynicism and Media Cynicism', *The ANNALS of the American Academy of Political and Social Science*, 546:1, 71–84.

Carlin, Ryan (2014) 'What's Not to Trust? Rubrics of Political Party Trustworthiness in Chile and Argentina', *Party Politics*, 20:1, 63–77.

Carnaghan, Ellen (2011) 'The Difficulty of Measuring Support for Democracy in a Changing Society: Evidence from Russia', *Democratization*, 18:3, 682–706.

Carpini, Michael Delli and Scott Keeter (1996) *What Americans Know about Politics and Why It Matters*, New Haven, CT: Yale University Press.

Catterberg, Gabriela and Alejandro Moreno (2005) 'The Individual Bases of Political Trust: Trends in New and Established Democracies', *International Journal of Public Opinion Research*, 18:1, 31–48.

Cawvey, Matthew et al. (2018) 'Biological and Psychological Influences on Interpersonal and Political Trust', in Eric Uslaner, ed, *Oxford Handbook of Social and Political Trust*, New York: Oxford University Press, pp. 119–148

Ceron, Andrea (2015) 'Internet, News and Political Trust', *Journal of Computer-Mediated Communication*, 20:5, 487–503.

Ceron, Andrea and Vincenzo Memoli (2015) 'Trust in Government and Media Slant: A Cross-Sectional Analysis of Media Effects in Twenty-Seven European Countries', *International Journal of Press/Politics*, 20:3, 339–359.

Chadee, Derek and Nakita K Ng Ying (2013) 'Predictors of Fear of Crime: General Fear versus Perceived Risk', *Journal of Experimental Social Psychology*, 43:9, 1896–1904.

Chanley, Virginia A, Thomas J Rudolph, and Wendy M Rahn (2000) 'The Origins and Consequences of Public Trust in Government: A Time Series Analysis', *Public Opinion Quarterly*, 64:3, 239–256

Chanley, Virginia A, Thomas J Rudolph and Wendy M Rahn (2001) 'Public Trust in Government in the Reagan Years and Beyond', in John Hibbing and Elizabeth Theiss-Morse, eds, *What Is It about Government that Americans Dislike?* New York: Cambridge University Press, pp. 59–78.

Charlton, Michelle, Sarah Morton and Ipsos MORI (2011) *Exploring Public Confidence in the Police and Local Councils in Tackling Crime and Anti-social Behaviour*, Research Report 50, London: Home Office

Chen, Nien-Tsu Nancy (2015) 'Predicting Vaccination Intention and Benefit and Risk Perceptions: The Incorporation of Affect, Trust, and Television Influence in a Dual-Mode Model', *Risk Analysis*, 35:7, 1268–1280.

Cheng, Helen et al. (2012) 'The Measurement and Evaluation of Social Attitudes in Two British Cohort Studies', *Social Indicators Research*, 107:2, 351–371.

Christensen, Henrik Serup (2016) 'All the Same? Examining the Link Between Three Kinds of Political Dissatisfaction and Protest', *Comparative European Politics*, 14:6, 781–801.

Christensen, Henrik Serup and Lauri Rapeli (2021) 'Immediate Rewards or Delayed Gratification? A Conjoint Survey Experiment of the Public's Policy Preferences', *Policy Sciences*, 54, 63–94.

Citrin, Jack (1974) 'Comment: The Political Relevance of Trust in Government', *American Political Science Review*, 68:3, 973–988.
Citrin, Jack et al. (1975) 'Personal and Political Sources of Political Alienation', *British Journal of Political Science*, 5:1, 1–31.
Citrin, Jack (1977) 'Political Alienation as a Social Indicator', *Social Indicators Research*, 4:4, 381–419.
Citrin, Jack and Samantha Luks (2001) 'Political Trust Revisited: Deja-Vu All Over Again?' in John Hibbing and Elizabeth Theiss-Morse, eds, *What Is It about Government that Americans Dislike?* New York: Cambridge University Press
Citrin, Jack and Christopher Muste (1999) 'Trust in Government', in John P Robinson, Phillip R Shaver, and Lawrence S Wrightsman, eds, *Measures of Political Attitudes, Volume 2*, San Diego: Academic Press, pp. 465–532.
Citrin, Jack and Donald Philip Green (1986) 'Presidential Leadership and Resurgence of Trust in Government', *British Journal of Political Science*, 16:4, 431–453.
Citrin, Jack and Laura Stoker (2018) 'Political Trust in a Cynical Age', *Annual Review of Political Science*, 21: 49–70.
Clark, April K, Michael Clark, and Daniel Monzin (2013) 'Explaining Changing Trust Trends in America', *International Research Journal of Social Sciences*, 2:1, 6–14.
Clarke, Harold D et al. (2009) *Performance Politics and the British Voter*, Cambridge: Cambridge University Press
Clarke, Harold D, Matthew Goodwin, and Paul Whiteley (2017) *Brexit: Why Britain Voted to Leave the European Union*, Cambridge: Cambridge University Press.
Clarke, Nick et al. (2018) *The Good Politician: Folk Theories, Political Interaction and the Rise of Anti-politics*, Cambridge: Cambridge University Press.
Cleary, Matthew R and Susan Stokes (2006) *Democracy and the Culture of Skepticism: The Politics of Trust in Argentina and Mexico*, New York: Russell Sage Foundation
Cohen, Roger (2016) 'The Age of Distrust', *New York Times*, 19 September (accessed online at: https://www.nytimes.com/2016/09/20/opinion/the-age-of-distrust.html)
Colquitt, Jason A, Brent A Scott and Jeffery A LePine (2007) 'Trust, Trustworthiness, and Trust Propensity: A Meta-analytic Test of their Unique Relationships with Risk Taking and Job Performance', *Journal of Applied Psychology*, 92:4, 909–927.
Cook, Timothy E and Paul Gronke (2005) 'The Skeptical American: Revisiting the Meanings of Trust in Government and Confidence in Institutions', *Journal of Politics*, 67:3, 784–803.
Cook, Karen S, Russell Hardin, and Margaret Levi (2005) *Cooperation Without Trust?* New York: Russell Sage Foundation.
Coromina, Lluis and Edurne Bartolomé Peral (2016) 'Trust in Political Institutions: Stability of Measurement Model in Europe', in Mălina Voicu, Ingvill C Mochmann, and Hermann Dülmer, eds, *Values, Economic Crisis and Democracy*, London: Routledge, pp. 50–70.
Cox, Michaelene (2003) 'When Trust Matters: Explaining Differences in Voter Turnout', *Journal of Common Market Studies*, 41:4, 757–770.
Craig, Stephen C (1980) 'The Mobilization of Political Discontent', *Political Behavior*, 2:2, 189–209.
Craig, Stephen C (1993) *The Malevolent Leaders: Popular Discontent in America*, Boulder, CO: Westview Press.
Craig, Stephen C, Richard G Niemi, and Glenn E Silver (1990) 'Political Efficacy and Trust: A Report on the NES Political Survey Items', *Political Behavior*, 12:3, 289–314.
Cramer, Katherine J (2016) *The Politics of Resentment: Rural Consciousness in Wisconsin and the Rise of Scott Walker*, Chicago, IL: University of Chicago Press.
Crepaz, Marcus et al. (2014) 'Trust Matters: The Impact of Ingroup and Outgroup Trust on Nativism and Civicness', *Social Science Quarterly*, 95:4, 938–959.

Crepaz, Michelle and Gizem Arikan (2021) 'Information Disclosure and Political Trust during the COVID-19 Crisis: Experimental Evidence from Ireland', *Journal of Elections, Public Opinion and Parties*, 31:s1, 96–108.

Crozier, Michael J, Samuel P Huntington, and Joji Watanuki (1975) *The Crisis of Democracy: Report on the Governability of Democracies to the Trilateral Commission*, New York: Oxford University Press.

Curran, Patrick J, Stephen G West, and John F Finch (1996) 'The Robustness of Test Statistics to Nonnormality and Specification Error in Confirmatory Factor Analysis', *Psychological Methods*, 1:1, 16–29.

Curtice, John (2017) 'The Vote to Leave the EU: Litmus Test or Lightning Rod?' in Elizabeth Clery, John Curtice, and Roger Harding, eds, *British Social Attitudes 34*, London: National Centre for Social Research, pp. 157–180.

Cvetkovich, George et al. (2002) 'New Information and Social Trust: Asymmetry and Perseverance of Attributions about Hazard Managers', *Risk Analysis*, 22:2, 359–367.

D'Ancona, Matthew (2017) *Post Truth: The New War on Truth and How to Fight Back*, London: Ebury Press.

Dahlberg, Stefan, Jonas Linde, and Sören Holmberg (2015) 'Democratic Discontent in Old and New Democracies: Assessing the Importance of Democratic Input and Governmental Output', *Political Studies*, 63:s1, 18–37.

Dalton, Russell J (1999) 'Political Support in Advanced Industrial Democracies', in Pippa Norris, ed, *Critical Citizens: Global Support for Democratic Governance*, New York: Cambridge University Press, pp. 57–77.

Dalton, Russell J (2004) *Democratic Challenges, Democratic Choices: The Erosion of Political Support in Advanced Industrial Democracies*, Oxford: Oxford University Press.

Dalton, Russell J (2005) 'The Social Transformation of Trust in Government', *International Review of Sociology*, 15:3, 133–154.

Dalton, Russell J (2017a) 'Political Trust in North America', in Sonja Zmerli and Tom W G, van der Meer, eds, *Handbook on Political Trust*, Cheltenham: Edward Elgar, pp. 375–394.

Dalton, Russell J (2017b) *The Participation Gap: Social Status and Political Inequality*, New York: Oxford University Press.

Dancey, Logan (2012) 'The Consequences of Political Cynicism: How Cynicism Shapes Citizens' Reactions to Political Scandals', *Political Behavior*, 34:3, 411–423.

Dassonneville, Ruth and Ian McAllister (2021) 'Explaining the Decline of Political Trust in Australia', *Australian Journal of Political Science*, 56:3, 280–297.

Dassonneville, Ruth, André Blais, and Yves Dejaeghere (2015) 'Staying with the Party, Switching or Exiting? A Comparative Analysis of Determinants of Party Switching and Abstaining', *Journal of Elections, Public Opinion & Parties*, 25:3, 387–405.

De Jonge, Chad P Kiewiet (2016) 'Should Researchers Abandon Questions about "Democracy"? Evidence from Latin America', *Public Opinion Quarterly*, 80:3, 694–716.

De Vellis, Robert F (1991) *Scale Development: Theory and Applications*, Newbury Park, CA: Sage.

De Vreese, Claes H (2005) "The Spiral of Cynicism Reconsidered', *European Journal of Communications*, 20:3, 283–301.

Dekker, Paul (2011) 'Political Trust: What Do We Measure? Should Politicians and the Public Trust Us?' Paper for *6th ECPR General Conference*, Reykjavik, 25–27 August.

Dennison, James, Eldad Davidov, and Daniel Seddig (2020) 'Explaining Voting in the UK's 2016 EU Referendum: Basic Human Values, Attitudes toward Immigration, European Identity and Trust in Politicians', *Social Science Research*, 92: 102476.

Denters, Bas, Oscar Gabriel, and Mariano Torcal (2007) 'Political Confidence in Representative Democracies: Socio-Cultural vs Political Explanations', in Jan W Van Deth, José

Ramón Montero, and Anders Westholm, eds, *Citizenship and Involvement in European Democracies: A Comparative Analysis*, Abingdon: Routledge, pp. 66–87.

Dimoka, Angelika (2010) 'What Does the Brain Tell Us about Trust and Distrust? Evidence from a Functional Neuroimaging Study', *MIS Quarterly*, 34:2, 373–396.

Dogan, Mattei (1997) 'Erosion of Confidence in Advanced Democracies', *Studies in Comparative International Development*, 32, 3–29.

Doherty, David, Conor M Dowling, and Michael G Miller (2016) 'When Is Changing Policy Positions Costly for Politicians? Experimental Evidence', *Political Behavior*, 38:2, 455–484.

Dotti Sani, Giulia M and Beatrice Magistro (2016) 'Increasingly Unequal? The Economic Crisis, Social Inequalities and Trust in the European Parliament in 20 European Countries', *European Journal of Political Research*, 55, 246–264.

Dow, Jay K (2001) 'A Comparative Spatial Analysis of Majoritarian and Proportional Elections', *Electoral Studies*, 20, 109–125.

Durr, Robert H, John B Gilmour, and Christina Wolbrecht (1997) 'Explaining Congressional Approval', *American Journal of Political Science*, 41:1, 175–207.

Dustmann, Christian et al. (2017) *Europe's Trust Deficit: Causes and Remedies*, London: Centre for Economic Policy Research.

Dyck, Joshua J, Shanna Pearson-Merkowitz, and Michael Coates (2018) 'Primary Distrust: Political Distrust and Support for the Insurgent Candidacies of Donald Trump and Bernie Sanders in the 2016 Primary', *PS: Political Science & Politics*, 51:2, 351–357.

Earle, Timothy C (2004) 'Thinking Aloud about Trust: A Protocol Analysis of Trust in Risk Management', *Risk Analysis*, 24:1, 169–183.

Earle, Timothy C (2010) 'Trust in Risk Management: A Model-based Review of Empirical Research', *Risk Analysis*, 30:4, 541–574.

Earle, Timothy C, Michael Siegrist, and Heinz Gutscher (2010) 'Trust, Risk Perception and the TCC Model of Cooperation', in Michael Siegrist, Timothy E Earle and Heinz Gutscher, eds, *Trust in Risk Management: Uncertainty and Scepticism in the Public Mind*, London: Earthscan, pp. 1–49.

Easton, David (1965) *A Systems Analysis of Political Life*, New York: Wiley.

Easton, David (1975) 'A Reassessment of the Concept of Political Support', *British Journal of Political Science*, 5:4, 435–457.

Echabe, Agustin Echebarria (2014) 'System-justifying Beliefs and Political Disaffection', *Journal of Applied Social Psychology*, 44:3, 234–240

Edelman, Richard (2017a) 'An Implosion of Trust', Edelman, 7 March (available at: https://www.edelman.com/post/an-implosion-of-trust).

Edelman (2017b) Trust in Crisis: Edelman 2017 Trust Barometer (available at: https://www.edelman.com/trust/archive).

Edlund, Jonas (1999) 'Trust in Government and Welfare Regimes: Attitudes to Redistribution and Financial Cheating in the USA and Norway', *European Journal of Political Research*, 35:3, 341–370.

Egede, Leonard E and Charles Ellis (2008) 'Development and Testing of the Multidimensional Trust in Healthcare Systems Scale', *Journal of General Internal Medicine*, 23:6, 808–815.

Eisinger, Robert M (2000) 'Questioning Cynicism', *Culture and Society*, 37:5, 55–60.

Ellinas, Antonis and Iasonas Lamprianou (2014) 'Political Trust *in Extremis*', *Comparative Politics*, 46:2, 231–250.

Emborg, Jens, Steven E Daniels, and Gregg B Walker (2020) 'A Framework for Exploring Trust and Distrust in Natural Resource Management', *Frontiers in Communication*, 5:13

Ermisch, John et al. (2009) 'Measuring People's Trust', *Journal of the Royal Statistical Society, Series A: Statistics in Society*, 172:4, 749–769.

250 Bibliography

Ervasti, Heikki, Antti Kouvo and Takis Venetoklis (2019) 'Social and Institutional Trust in Times of Crisis: Greece, 2002–2011', *Social Indicators Research*, 141, 1207–1231.

Esaiasson, Peter (2010) 'Will Citizens Take No for an Answer? On the Capacity of Procedures to Legitimize Unfavourable Bureaucratic Decisions', *European Political Science Review*, 2:3, 351–371.

Esaiasson, Peter and Mattias Ottervik (2014) 'Does Compliance Correlate with Political Support?' *Working Paper 1*, Quality of Government Institute, Gothenburg: Sweden: University of Gothenburg

Evans, Geoffrey and Anand Menon (2017) *Brexit and British Politics*, Cambridge: Polity.

Exadaktylos, Theofanis and Nikolaos Zahariadis (2014) '*Quid pro Quo*: Political Trust and Policy Implementation in Greece during the Age of Austerity', *Politics & Policy*, 42:1, 160–183.

Ezrow, Lawrence and Georgios Xezonakis (2016) 'Satisfaction with Democracy and Voter Turnout: A Temporal Perspective', *Party Politics*, 22:1, 3–14.

Fabrigar, Leandre R, Jon A Krosnick, and Bonnie L MacDougall (2005) 'Attitude Measurement: Techniques for Measuring the Unobservable', in Timothy C Brock and Melanie C Green, eds, *Persuasion: Psychological Insights and Perspectives*, Thousand Oaks, CA: Sage, pp. 17–40.

Fairbrother, Malcolm (2016) 'Trust and Public Support for Environmental Protection in Diverse National Contexts', *Sociological Science*, 3: 359–382.

Fairbrother, Malcolm (2019) 'When Will People Pay to Pollute? Environmental Taxes, Political Trust and Experimental Evidence from Britain', *British Journal of Political Science*, 49:2, 661–682.

Farnsworth, Stephen J (2003) 'Congress and Citizen Discontent: Public Evaluations of the Membership and One's Own Representative', *American Politics Research*, 31:1, 66–80.

Faulkner, Nicholas, Aaron Martin, and Kyle Peyton (2015) 'Priming Political Trust: Evidence from an Experiment', *Australian Journal of Political Science*, 50:1, 164–173.

Feldman, Stanley (1983) 'The Measurement and Meaning of Trust in Government', *Political Methodology*, 9:3, 341–354.

Feldman, Yuval (2013) 'Five Models of Regulatory Compliance Motivation: Empirical Findings and Normative Implications', in David Levi-Faur, *Handbook on the Politics of Regulation*, Cheltenham: Edward Elgar, pp. 335–346.

Finifter, Ada (1970) 'Dimensions of Political Alienation', *American Political Science Review*, 64:2, 389–410.

Finney, Sara J and Christine DiStefano (2006) 'Non-normal and Categorical Data in Structural Equation Modeling', in Gregory R Hancock and Ralph O Muller, eds, *Structural Equation Modeling: A Second Course*, Charlotte, NC: Information Age Publishing, pp. 269–314.

Firebaugh, Glenn (1997) *Analyzing Repeated Surveys*, QASS 115, Thousand Oaks, CA: Sage.

Fisher, Justin, Jennifer van Heerde and Andrew Tucker (2010) 'Does One Trust Judgement Fit All? Linking Theory and Empirics', *British Journal of Politics and International Relations*, 12:2, 161–188.

Fiske, Susan T (1980) 'Attention and Weight in Person Perception: The Impact of Negative and Extreme Behavior', *Journal of Personality and Social Psychology*, 38:6, 889–906.

Fiske, Susan T (1986) 'Schema-based versus Piecemeal Politics: A Patchwork Quilt, but Not a Blanket of Evidence', in Richard R Lau and David O Sears, eds, *Political Cognition: The 19th Annual Carnegie Symposium on Cognition*, Hillsdale, NJ: Erlbaum, pp. 41–53.

Fiske, Susan T and Federica Durante (2014) 'Never Trust a Politician? Collective Distrust, Relational Accountability, and Voter Response', in Jan-Willem van Prooijen and Paul A M van Lange, eds, *Power, Politics, and Paranoia: Why People Are Suspicious of their Leaders*, Cambridge: Cambridge University Press, pp. 91–105.

Fiske, Susan T and Stephen L Neuberg (1990) 'A Continuum Model of Impression Formation, from Category-based to Individuating Processes: Influence of Information and Motivation on Attention and Interpretation', in Mark P Zanna, ed, *Advances in Experimental Social Psychology*, New York: Academic Press, pp. 1–74.

Fitzgerald, Jennifer and Jennifer Wolak (2016) 'The Roots of Trust in Local Government in Western Europe', *International Political Science Review*, 37:1, 130–146

Ford, Robert and Matthew Goodwin (2014) *Revolt on the Right: Explaining Support for the Radical Right in Britain*, Abingdon: Routledge

Fowler, Floyd J Jr (2009) *Survey Research Methods*, Thousand Oaks, CA: Sage Publications.

Frazier, M Lance, Paul D Johnson and Stav Fainshmidt (2013) 'Development and Validation of a Propensity to Trust Scale', *Journal of Trust Research*, 3:2, 76–97.

Freimuth, Vicki S et al. (2014) 'Trust during the Early Stages of the 2009 H1N1 Pandemic', *Journal of Health Communication*, 19:3, 321–339.

Frewer, L J et al. (1996) 'What Determines Trust in Information about Food-related Risks? Underlying Psychological Constructs', *Risk Analysis*, 16:4, 473–486.

Fukuyama, Francis (1989) 'The End of History', *The National Interest*, 16: 3–18.

Fuchs, Christoph and Adamantios Diamantopoulos (2009) 'Using Single-item Measures for Construct Measurement in Management Research: Conceptual Issues and Application Guidelines', *Business Administration Review*, 69:2, 195–210.

Funk, Carolyn L (1996) 'The Impact of Scandal on Candidate Evaluations: An Experimental Test of the Role of Candidate Traits', *Political Behavior*, 18:1, 1–24.

Funk, Carolyn L (2001) 'Process Performance: Public Reaction to Legislative Policy Debate', in John Hibbing and Elizabeth Theiss-Morse, eds, *What Is It about Government that Americans Dislike?* New York: Cambridge University Press.

Gabriel, Oscar W (1995) 'Political Efficacy and Trust', in Jan Van Deth and Elinor Scarbrough, eds, *The Impact of Values*, Oxford: Oxford University Press, pp. 357–389.

Gabriel, Oscar W and Eva-Maria Trüdinger (2011) 'Embellishing Welfare State Reforms? Political Trust and Support for Welfare State Reforms in Germany', *German Politics*, 20:2, 273–292.

Gainous, Jason, Stephen C Craig, and Michael D Martinez (2008) 'Social Welfare Attitudes and Ambivalence about the Role of Government', *Politics and Policy*, 36:6, 972–1004.

Gallup (2018) *Indicators of News Media Trust: A Gallup/Knight Foundation Survey*, Washington, DC: Gallup.

Gallup, George H (1976) *The Gallup International Public Opinion Polls – Great Britain: 1937-1975*, New York: Random House.

Gambetta, Diego (1988) 'Can We Trust Trust?' in Diego Gambetta, ed, *Trust: Making and Breaking Cooperative Relations*, Oxford: Basil Blackwell, pp. 213–237.

Gamson, William A (1968) *Power and Discontent*, Homewood, IL: Dorsey Press.

Gangl, Amy (2003) 'Procedural Justice Theory and Evaluations of the Lawmaking Process', *Political Behavior*, 25:2, 119–149.

Gershtenson, Joseph and Dennis Plane (2011) 'An Alternative Measure of Political Trust: Reconciling Theory and Practice', in John H Aldrich and Kathleen M McGraw, eds, *Improving Public Opinion Surveys: Interdisciplinary Innovation and the American National Election Studies*, Princeton, NJ: Princeton University Press, pp. 117–136.

Gesser-Edelsburg, Anat, Yaffa Shir-Raz, and Manfred S Green (2016) 'Why Do Parents Who Usually Vaccinate their Children Hesitate or Refuse? General Good vs. Individual Risk', *Journal of Risk Research*, 19:4, 405–424.

Gibson, James L (2011) 'A Note of Caution about the Meaning of "The Supreme Court Can Usually be trusted...", *Law & Courts: Newsletter of the Law & Courts Section of The American Political Science Association*, 21:3, 10–15.

Gibson, James L and Gregory A Caldeira (1996) 'The Legal Cultures of Europe', *Law & Society Review*, 30:1, 55–85.

Gibson, James L, Gregory A Caldeira and Lester Kenyatta Spence (2003) 'Measuring Attitudes toward the United States Supreme Court', *American Journal of Political Science*, 47:2, 354–367.

Gibson, James L, Gregory A Caldeira and Lester Kenyatta Spence (2005) 'Why Do People Accept Public Policies They Oppose? Testing Legitimacy Theory with a Survey-Based Experiment', *Political Research Quarterly*, 58:2, 187–201.

Gilles, Ingrid et al. (2011) 'Trust in Medical Organizations Predicts Pandemic (H1N1) 2009 Vaccination Behavior and Perceived Efficacy of Protection Measures in the Swiss Public', *European Journal of Epidemiology*, 26:3, 203–210.

Goubin, Silke and Stafan Kumlin (2022) 'Political Trust and Policy Demand in Changing Welfare States: Building Normative Support and Easing Reform Acceptance?' *European Sociological Review*, 38:4, 590–604.

Graham, Jenny et al. (2002) *Guiding Principles: Public Attitudes towards Conduct in Public Life*, London: National Centre for Social Research

Grimes, Marcia (2006) 'Organizing Consent: Role of Procedural Fairness in Political Trust and Compliance', *European Journal of Political Research*, 45:2, 285–315.

Grimmelikhuijsen, Stephan and Eva Knies (2017) 'Validating a Scale for Citizen Trust in Government Organizations', *International Review of Administrative Sciences*, 83:3, 583–601.

Grönlund, Kimmo and Maija Setälä (2012) 'In Honest Officials We Trust: Institutional Confidence in Europe', *American Review of Public Administration*, 42:5, 523–542.

Gross, Kimberley, Paul R Brewer, and Sean Aday (2009) 'Confidence in Government and Emotional Responses to Terrorism After September 11, 2001', *American Politics Research*, 37:1, 107–128.

Guglielmi, S et al. (2020) 'Public Acceptability of Containment Measures during the COVID-19 Pandemic in Italy: How Institutional Confidence and Specific Political Support Matter', *International Journal of Sociology and Social Policy*, 40: 9–10, 1069–1085.

Gunther, Richard, José Ramón Montero and Mariano Torcal (2007) 'Democracy and Intermediation: Some Attitudinal and Behavioural Dimensions', in Richard Gunther, Jose Ramon Montero and Hans-Jürgen Puhle, eds, *Democracy, Intermediation, and Voting on Four Continents*, Oxford: Oxford University Press, pp. 29–74.

Gunther, Richard P and José Ramón Montero (2006) 'The Multidimensionality of Political Support for New Democracies: Conceptual Redefinition and Empirical Refinement', in Mariano Torcal and José Ramón Montero, eds, *Political Disaffection in Contemporary Democracies: Social Capital, Institutions and Politics*, London: Routledge, pp. 46–78.

Habibov, Nazim (2014) 'Individual and Country-level Institutional Trust and Public Attitude to Welfare Expenditures in 24 Transitional Countries', *The Journal of Sociology & Social Welfare*, 41:4, 23–48.

Hall, Mark et al. (2002) 'Trust in the Medical Profession: Conceptual and Measurement Issues', *Health Services Research*, 37:5, 1419–1439.

Hamm, Joseph et al. (2011) 'Exploring Separable Components of Institutional Confidence', *Behavioral Sciences and the Law* 29:1, 95–115.

Hamm, Joseph et al. (2013a) 'Deconstructing Public Confidence in State Courts', *Journal of Trust Research*, 3:1, 11–31

Hamm, Joseph A et al. (2013b) 'Trust and Intention to Comply with a Water Allocation Decision: The Moderating Role of Knowledge and Consistency', *Ecology and Society*, 18:4, 49.
Hamm, Joseph A, Corwin Smidt, and Roger C Mayer (2019) 'Understanding the Psychological Nature and Mechanisms of Political Trust', *PLoS One*, 14:5, e0215835.
Harbridge, Laurel, Neil Malhotra, and Brian F Harrison (2014) 'Public Preferences for Bipartisanship in the Policymaking Process', *Legislative Studies Quarterly*, 39:3, 327–355.
Hardin, Russell (2002) *Trust and Trustworthiness*, New York: Russell Sage Foundation.
Hardin, Russell (2006) *Trust*, Cambridge: Polity.
Hardin, Russell (2013) 'Government without Trust', *Journal of Trust Research*, 3:1, 32–52.
Harrebye, Silas and Anders Ejrnæs (2015) 'European Patterns of Participation: How Dissatisfaction Motivates Extra-parliamentary Activities Given the Right Institutional Conditions', *Comparative European Politics*, 13:2, 151–174.
Hart, Vivien (1978) *Distrust and Democracy: Political Distrust in Britain and America*, Cambridge: Cambridge University Press.
Heath, Anthony F et al. (2013) *The Political Integration of Ethnic Minorities in Britain*, Oxford: Oxford University Press.
Heath, Oliver (2008) 'Triggers for Protest: Modelling Responses to the Political Context in Britain, 2000-02', *European Journal of Political Research*, 47:4, 489–509.
Herian, Mitchel N et al. (2012) 'Public Participation, Procedural Fairness and Evaluations of Local Governance: The Moderating Role of Uncertainty', *Journal of Public Administration Research and Theory*, 22:4, 815–840.
Hernández, Enrique (2016) 'Europeans' View of Democracy: The Core Elements of Democracy', in Monica Ferrín and Hanspeter Kriesi, eds, *How Europeans View and Evaluate Democracy*, Oxford: Oxford University Press, pp. 43–63.
Hernández-Lagos, Pablo and Dylan Minor (2020) 'Political Identity and Trust', *Quarterly Journal of Political Science*, 15:3, 337–367.
Hetherington, Marc J (2005) *Why Trust Matters: Declining Political Trust and the Demise of American Liberalism*, Princeton, NJ: Princeton University Press.
Hetherington, Marc J and Thomas J Rudolph (2008) 'Priming, Performance, and the Dynamics of Political Trust', *Journal of Politics*, 70:2, 498–512.
Hetherington, Marc J and Thomas J Rudolph (2015) *Why Washington Won't Work: Polarization, Political Trust and the Governing Crisis*, Chicago, IL: Chicago University Press.
Hetherington, Mark J and Jason A Husser (2012) 'How Trust Matters: The Changing Political Relevance of Political Trust', *American Journal of Political Science*, 56:2, 312–325.
Hibbing, John R and Elizabeth Theiss-Morse (1995) *Congress as Public Enemy Public Attitudes toward American Political Institutions*, Cambridge: Cambridge University Press.
Hibbing, John R and Elizabeth Theiss-Morse (2001) 'How Trustworthy Politicians Decrease Mass Political Participation', Paper for the Annual Meeting of the Midwest Political Science Association, San Francisco.
Hibbing, John R and Elizabeth Theiss-Morse (2002) *Stealth Democracy: Americans' Beliefs about How Government Should Work*, New York: Cambridge University Press.
Hill, David B (1981) 'Attitude Generalization and the Measurement of Trust in American Leadership', *Political Behavior*, 3:3, 257–270.
Hillen, Marij, Hanneke C J M de Haes, and Ellen M A Smets (2011) 'Cancer Patients' Trust in their Physician: A Review', *Psycho-Oncology*, 20:3, 227–241.
Hirschman, Albert O (1970) *Exit, Voice, and Loyalty: Responses to Decline in Firms, Organizations, and States*, Cambridge, MA: Harvard University Press.

Hobolt, Sara Binzer (2009) *Europe in Question: Referendums on European Integration*, Oxford: Oxford University Press.

Holmberg, Sören (2014) 'Feeling Policy Represented', in Jacques Thomassen, ed, *Elections and Democracy: Representation and Accountability*, Oxford: Oxford University Press, pp. 132–152.

Hooghe, Marc (2011) 'Why There is Basically Only One Form of Political Trust', *British Journal of Politics and International Relations*, 13:2, 269–275.

Hooghe, Marc and Ruth Dassonneville (2018a) 'A Spiral of Distrust: A Panel Study on the Relation Between Political Distrust and Protest Voting in Belgium', *Government & Opposition*, 53:1, 104–130.

Hooghe, Marc and Ruth Dassonneville (2018b) 'Explaining the Trump Vote: The Effect of Racist Resentment and Anti-immigrant Sentiments', *PS: Political Science & Politics*, 51:3, 528–534.

Hooghe, Marc and Sofie Marien (2013) 'A Comparative Analysis of the Relationship Between Political Trust and Forms of Political Participation in Europe', *European Societies*, 15:1, 131–152.

Hooghe, Marc and Martin Okolikj (2020) 'The Long-term Effects of the Economic Crisis on Political Trust in Europe: Is There a Negativity Bias in the Relation Between Economic Performance and Political Support?' *Comparative European Politics*, 18:6, 879–898.

Hooghe, Marc and Sonja Zmerli, eds (2011) *Political Trust: Why Context Matters*, Colchester, Essex: ECPR Press

Hooghe, Marc, Sofie Marien, and Teun Pauwels (2011) 'Where Do Distrusting Voters Turn If There Is No Viable Exit or Voice Option? The Impact of Political Trust on Electoral Behaviour in the Belgian Regional Elections of June 2009', *Government & Opposition*, 46:2, 245–273.

Hooghe, Marc, Sofie Marien, and Thomas de Vroome (2012) 'The Cognitive Basis of Trust: The Relation Between Education, Cognitive Ability, and Generalized and Political Trust', *Intelligence*, 40:6, 604–613

Hough, Mike, Jonathan Jackson, and Ben Bradford (2013) 'Legitimacy, Trust, and Compliance: An Empirical Test of Procedural Justice Theory using the European Social Survey', in Justice Tankebe and Alison Liebling, eds, *Legitimacy and Criminal Justice: An International Exploration*, Oxford: Oxford University Press, pp. 326–352.

Howe, Paul (2017) 'Eroding Norms and Democratic Deconsolidation', *Journal of Democracy*, 28:4, 15–29.

Hvidman, Ulrich (2019) 'Citizens' Evaluations of the Public Sector: Evidence from Two Large-Scale Experiments', *Journal of Public Administration and Theory*, 29:2, 255–267.

Intawan, Chanita and Stephen P Nicholson (2018) 'My Trust in Government Is Implicit: Automatic Trust in Government and System Support', *Journal of Politics*, 80:2, 601–614.

Ipsos (2019) *Trust: The Truth?* London: Ipsos Mori.

Ipsos (2022) *Veracity Index: Trust in Professions Survey*, London: Ipsos.

Jackson, Jonathan et al. (2011) 'Developing European Indicators of Trust in Justice', *European Journal of Criminology*, 8:4, 267–285.

Jackson, Jonathan et al. (2012) 'Why Do People Comply with the Law? Legitimacy and the Influence of Legal Institutions', *British Journal of Criminology*, 52:6, 1051–1071

Jackson, Jonathan and Jacinta M Gau (2016) 'Carving Up Concepts? Differentiating between Trust and Legitimacy in Public Attitudes towards Legal Authority', in Ellie Shockley et al., eds, *Interdisciplinary Perspectives on Trust: Towards Theoretical and Methodological Integration*, Switzerland: Springer International Publishing, pp. 49–69

Jacobs, Alan M and J Scott Matthews (2012) 'Why Do Citizens Discount the Future? Public Opinion and the Timing of Policy Consequences', *British Journal of Political Science*, 42:4, 903–935.

Jacobs, Alan M and J Scott Matthews (2017) 'Policy Attitudes in Institutional Context: Rules, Uncertainty, and the Mass Politics of Public Investment', *American Journal of Political Science*, 61:1, 194–207.

Jacobs, Kristof, Agnes Akkerman, and Andrej Zaslove (2018) 'The Voice of Populist People? Referendum Preferences, Practices and Populist Attitudes', *Acta Politica*, 53:4, 517–541.

James, Oliver (2011) 'Performance Measures and Democracy: Information Effects on Citizens in Field and Lab Experiments', *Journal of Public Administration Research and Theory*, 21:3, 399–418.

James, Oliver and Alice Moseley (2014) 'Does Performance Information about Public Services Affect Citizens' Perceptions, Satisfaction, and Voice Behaviour? Field Experiments with Absolute and Relative Performance Information', *Public Administration*, 92:2, 493–511.

James, Oliver and Gregg G Van Ryzin (2017) 'Incredibly Good Performance: An Experimental Study of Source and Level Effects on the Credibility of Government', *American Review of Public Administration*, 47:1, 23–35.

Jefferys, Kevin (2007) *Politics and the People: A History of British Democracy Since 1918*, London: Atlantic Books.

Jennings, Will et al. (2017) 'The Decline in Diffuse Support for National Politics: The Long View of Political Discontent in Britain', *Public Opinion Quarterly*, 81:3, 748–758.

Jennings, Will et al. (2021) 'How Trust, Mistrust and Distrust Shape the Governance of the COVID-19 Crisis', *Journal of European Public Policy*, 28:8, 1174–1196.

Johnson, Branden B (1999) 'Exploring Dimensionality in the Origins of Hazard-related Trust', *Journal of Risk Research*, 2:4, 325–354.

Johnson, Branden B (2010) 'Getting Out of the Swamp: Towards Understanding Sources of Local Officials' Trust in Wetlands Management', in Michael Siegrist, Timothy C Earle, and Heinz Gutscher, eds, *Trust in Risk Management: Uncertainty and Scepticism in the Public Mind*, London: Continuum, pp. 211–240.

Johnson, Branden B (2020) 'Probing the Role of Institutional Stereotypes in Americans' Evaluations of Hazard-managing Institutions', *Journal of Risk Research*, 23:3, 313–329.

Johnson, Branden B and Mathew P White (2010) 'The Importance of Multiple Performance Criteria for Understanding Trust in Risk Managers', *Risk Analysis*, 30:7, 1099–1115.

Jones, David R (2015) 'Declining Trust in Congress: Effects of Polarization and Consequences for Democracy', *The Forum*, 13:3, 375–394.

Jones, David R and Monika L McDermott (2010) *Americans, Congress and Democratic Responsiveness: Public Evaluations of Congress and Electoral Consequences*, Ann Arbor: University of Michigan Press.

Kampen, Jarl K, Steven Van De Walle, and Geert Bouckaert (2006) 'Assessing the Relation Between Public Service Delivery and Trust in Government', *Public Performance and Management Review*, 29:4, 387–404.

Kavanagh, Jennifer et al. (2020) *The Drivers of Institutional Trust and Distrust*, Santa Monica, CA: RAND Corporation.

Kawalerowicz, Juta and Michael Biggs (2015) 'Anarchy in the UK: Economic Deprivation, Social Disorganization, and Political Grievances in the London Riot of 2011', *Social Forces*, 94:2, 673–698.

Kay, Aaron C and John T Jost (2003) 'Complementary Justice: Effects of 'Poor but Happy' and 'Poor but Honest' Stereotype Exemplars on System Justification and Implicit Activation of the Justice Motive', *Journal of Personality and Social Psychology*, 85:5, 823–837.

Keele, Luke (2005) 'The Authorities Really Do Matter: Party Control and Trust in Government', *Journal of Politics*, 67:3, 873–886.
Keele, Luke (2007) 'Social Capital and the Dynamics of Trust in Government', *American Journal of Political Science*, 51:2, 241–254.
Kelleher, Christine A and Jennifer Wolak (2007) 'Explaining Public Confidence in the Branches of State Government', *Political Research Quarterly*, 60:4, 707–721.
Keller, Carmen et al. (2011) 'The General Confidence Scale: Coping with Environmental Uncertainty and Threat', *Journal of Applied Social Psychology*, 41:9, 2200–2229.
Kelley, Stanley Jr and Thad W Mirer (1974) 'The Simple Act of Voting', *American Political Science Review*, 68:2, 572–591.
Kemmers, Roy et al. (2015) State of Disgrace: Popular Political Discontents about the Dutch State in the 2000s', *Parliamentary Affairs*, 68:3, 476–493.
Kestilä-Kekkonen, Elina and Peter Söderlund (2015) 'Political Trust, Individual-level Characteristics and Institutional Performance: Evidence from Finland, 2004–13', *Scandinavian Political Studies*, 39:2, 138–160.
Kinder, Donald R (1986)) 'Presidential Character Revisited', in Richard R Lau and David O Sears, eds, *Political Cognition: The 19th Annual Carnegie Symposium on Cognition*, Hillsdale, NJ: Erlbaum, pp. 233–255.
Kinder, Donald R (1998) 'Opinion and Action in the Realm of Politics', in Daniel T Gilbert, Susan T Fiske, and Lindzey Gardner, eds, *The Handbook of Social Psychology*, Boston, MA: Oxford University Press, pp. 778–867.
Kleinnijenhuis, Jan, Anita M J van Hoof, and Dirk Oegema (2006) 'Negative News and the Sleeper Effect of Distrust', *The International Journal of Press/Politics*, 11:2, 86–104.
Klingemann, Hans-Dieter (1999) 'Mapping Political Support in the 1990s: A Global Analysis', in Norris, Pippa, ed, *Critical Citizens: Global Support for Democratic Government*, New York: Oxford University Press, pp. 31–56.
Klingemann, Hans-Dieter (2014) 'Dissatisfied Democrats: Democratic Maturation in Old and New Democracies', in Russell J Dalton and Christian Welzel, eds, *The Civic Culture Transformed: From Allegiant to Assertive Citizens*, New York: Cambridge University Press, pp. 116–157.
Klingemann, Hans-Dieter and Dieter Fuchs (1995) *Citizens and the State*, Oxford: Oxford University Press.
Konisky, David M, Jeffrey Milyo and Lilliard E Richardson Jr (2008) 'Environmental Policy Attitudes: Issues, Geographical Scale, and Political Trust', *Social Science Quarterly*, 89:5, 1066–1085.
Kooistra, E B and Benjamin van Rooij (2020) 'Pandemic Compliance: A Systematic Review of Influences on Social Distancing Behaviour during the First Wave of the COVID-19 Outbreak', Amsterdam Law School Research Paper No. 2022-29.
Kramer, Roderick M (1999) 'Trust and Distrust in Organizations: Emerging Perspectives, Enduring Questions', *Annual Review of Psychology*, 50, 569–598.
Kriesi, Hanspeter and Julia Schulte-Cloos (2020) 'Support for Radical Parties in Western Europe: The Role of Long- and Short-term Dynamics', *Electoral Studies*, 65, 102138.
Kuklinski, James et al. (1991) 'The Cognitive and Affective Bases of Political Tolerance Judgments', *American Journal of Political Science*, 35:1, 1–27.
Kumlin, Staffan (2011) 'Dissatisfied Democrats, Policy Feedback and European Welfare States, 1976–2001', in Sonja Zmerli and Marc Hooghe, eds, *Political Trust: Why Context Matters*, Colchester, Essex: ECPR Press, pp. 163–186.
Kunda, Ziva (1990) 'The Case for Motivated Reasoning', *Psychological Bulletin*, 108:3, 480–498.

Lang, John T and William K Hallman (2005) 'Who Does the Public Trust? The Case of GM Food in the United States', *Risk Analysis*, 25:5, 1241–1252.

Larsen, Heidi J et al. (2018) 'Measuring Trust in Vaccination: A Systematic Review', *Human Vaccines and Immunotherapeutics*, 14:7, 1599–1609.

Lasswell, Harold D (1936) *Politics: Who Gets What, When, How*, New York: Whittlesey House.

Lau, Richard R (1982) 'Negativity in Political Perception', *Political Behavior*, 4:4, 353–377.

Laustsen, Lasse and Alexander Bor (2017) 'The Relative Weight of Character Traits in Political Candidate Evaluations: Warmth is More Important than Competence, Leadership and Integrity', *Electoral Studies*, 49, 96–107.

LaVeist, Thomas A, Lydia A Isaac, and Karen Patricia Williams (2009) 'Mistrust of Health Care Organizations is Associated with Underutilization of Health Services', *Health Services Research*, 44:6, 2093–2105.

Lee, Lucy and Penny Young (2013) 'A Disengaged Britain? Political Interest and Participation over 30 Years', in Alison Park et al., eds, *British Social Attitudes: The 30th Report*, London: NatCen Social Research, pp. 62–86.

Lenard, Patti Tamara (2008) 'Trust Your Compatriots, but Count Your Change: The Roles of Trust, Mistrust and Distrust in Democracy', *Political Studies*, 56:2, 312–332.

Lerman, Amy E (2019) *Good Enough for Government Work: The Public Reputation Crisis in America (And What We Can Do To Fix It)*, Chicago, IL: University of Chicago Press.

Lerman, Amy E and Daniel Acland (2020) 'United in States of Dissatisfaction: Confirmation Bias across the Partisan Divide', *American Politics Research*, 48:2, 227–237

Levi, Margaret (1998) 'A State of Trust', in Valerie Braithwaite and Margaret Levi, eds, *Trust and Governance*, New York: Russell Sage Foundation, pp. 77–101.

Levi, Margaret (2022) 'The Power of Beliefs', *Annual Review of Political Science*, 25, 1–19.

Levi, Margaret and Laura Stoker (2000) 'Political Trust and Trustworthiness', *Annual Review of Political Science*, 3, 475–507.

Lewicki, Roy J, Daniel J McAllister, and Robert J Bies (1998) 'Trust and Distrust: New Relationships and Realities', *Academy of Management Review*, 23:3, 438–458.

Lewis, J David and Andrew Weigert (1985) 'Trust as a Social Reality', *Social Forces*, 63:4, 976–985.

Lewis, Paul et al. (2011) 'Rioters Say Anger with Police Fuelled Summer Unrest', *The Guardian*, 5 December (available at: http://www.theguardian.com/uk/2011/dec/05/anger-police-fuelled-riots-study).

Li, Peter Ping (2015) 'Trust as a Leap of Hope for Transaction Value: A Two-way Street Above and Beyond Trust Propensity and Expected Trustworthiness', in Brian H Bornstein and Alan J Tomkins, eds, *Motivating Cooperation and Compliance with Authority: The Role of Institutional Trust*, Springer, pp. 37–53.

Lind, E Allan and Tom Tyler (1988) *The Social Psychology of Procedural Justice*, New York: Plenum Press.

Liu, James H et al. (2018) 'The Global Trust Inventory as a "Proxy Measure" for Social Capital: Measurement and Impact in 11 Democratic Societies', *Journal of Cross-Cultural Psychology*, 49:5, 789–810.

Lodge, Milton and Charles S Taber (2013) *The Rationalizing Voter*, New York: Cambridge University Press.

Loewenberg, Gerhard (1971) 'The Influence of Parliamentary Behavior on Regime Stability: Some Conceptual Clarifications', *Comparative Politics*, 3:2, 177–200.

Long, J Scott and Jeremy Freese (2006) *Regression Models for Categorical Dependent Variables Using Stata*, College Station, TX: Stata Press.

Loosveldt, Geert and Koen Beullens (2017) 'Interviewer Effects on Non-differentiation and Straightlining in the European Social Survey', *Journal of Official Statistics*, 33:2, 409–426.
Lu, Jie and Bruce Dickson (2020) 'Revisiting the Eastonian Framework on Political Support: Assessing Different Measures of Regime Support in Mainland China', *Comparative Politics*, 52:4, 671–701.
Lubbers, Marcel, Mérove Gijsberts, and Peer Scheepers (2002) 'Extreme Right Wing Voting in Western Europe', *European Journal of Political Research*, 41:3, 345–378.
Lubell, Mark (2007) 'Familiarity Breeds Trust: Collective Action in a Policy Domain', *Journal of Politics*, 69:1, 237–250.
Luhmann, Niklas (1979) *Trust and Power*, London: Wiley.
Luhmann, Niklas (1988) 'Familiarity, Confidence, Trust: Problems and Alternatives', in Diego Gambetta, ed, *Trust: Making and Breaking Cooperative Relations*, Oxford: Basil Blackwell, pp. 94–107.
Lundmark, Sebastian, Henrik Oscarsson, and Marcus Weissenbilder (2020) 'Confidence in an Election Authority and Satisfaction with Democracy: Evidence from a Quasi-natural Experiment of a Failed Election in Sweden', *Electoral Studies*, 67, 102216.
Lupia, Arthur and Mathew D McCubbins (1998) *The Democratic Dilemma: Can Citizens Learn What They Need to Know?* New York: Cambridge University Press.
Macdonald, David (2020) 'Trust in Government and the American Public's Responsiveness to Rising Inequality', *Political Research Quarterly*, 73:3, 790–804.
MacInnis, Bo and Jon A Krosnick (2016) 'Trust in Scientists' Statements about the Environment and American Public Opinion on Global Warming', in Jon A Krosnick, I-Chant A Chiang, and Tobias H Stark, eds, *Political Psychology: New Explorations*, New York: Psychology Press, pp. 483–522.
Macke, Anne Statham (1979) 'Trends in Aggregate-level Political Alienation', *The Sociological Quarterly*, 20:1, 77–87.
Magalhães, Pedro C (2014) 'Government Effectiveness and Support for Democracy', *European Journal of Political Research*, 53:1, 77–97.
Magalhães, Pedro C (2016) 'Economic Evaluations, Procedural Fairness and Satisfaction with Democracy', *Political Research Quarterly*, 69:3, 522–534.
Mair, Peter (2013) *Ruling the Void: The Hollowing of Western Democracy*, London: Verso.
Malka, Ariel, Jon A Krosnick, and Gary Langer (2009) 'The Association of Knowledge with Concern about Global Warming: Trusted Information Sources Shape Public Thinking', *Risk Analysis*, 29:5, 633–647.
Manin, Bernard (1997) *The Principles of Representative Government*, Cambridge: Cambridge University Press.
Marcinkowski, Frank and Christopher Starke (2018) 'Trust in Government: What's News Media Got to Do with It?' *Studies in Communication Sciences*, 18:1, 87–102.
Marien, Sophie (2011) 'Measuring Political Trust across Time and Space', in Marc Hooghe and Sonja Zmerli, eds, *Political Trust: Why Context Matters*, Colchester, Essex: ECPR Press, pp. 13–46.
Marien, Sophie and Marc Hooghe (2011) 'Does Political Trust Matter? An Empirical Investigation into the Relation Between Political Trust and Support for Law Compliance', *European Journal of Political Research*, 50:2, 267–291.
Martin, Aaron et al. (2020) 'Political Probity Increases Trust in Government: Evidence from Randomized Survey Experiments', *PLoS ONE*, 15:2, e0225818.
Martini, Sergio and Mario Quaranta (2020) *Citizens and Democracy in Europe: Contexts, Changes and Political Support*, Cham: Palgrave Macmillan.

Marvel, John D (2015) 'Public Opinion and Public Sector Performance: Are Individuals' Beliefs about Performance Evidence-Based or the Product of Anti-public Sector Bias?' *International Public Management Journal*, 18:2, 209–227

Marvel, John D (2016) 'Unconscious Bias in Citizens' Evaluations of Public Sector Performance', *Journal of Public Administration Research and Theory*, 26:1, 143–158.

Mason, William M, James S House and Steven S Martin (1985) 'On the Dimensions of Political Alienation in America', *Sociological Methodology*, 15:111–151.

Mauk, Marlene (2020) *Citizen Support for Democratic and Autocratic Regimes*, Oxford: Oxford University Press.

Mayer, Roger C, James H Davis and David F Schoorman (1995) 'An Integrative Model of Organizational Trust', *Academy of Management Review*, 20:3, 709–734.

Mayne, Quinton and Armen Hakhverdian (2017) 'Education, Socialization and Political Trust', in Sonia Zmerli and Tom WG van der Meer, eds, *Handbook on Political Trust*, Cheltenham: Edward Elgar, pp. 176–196.

McAllister, Daniel J (1995) 'Affect- and Cognition-based Trust as Foundations for Interpersonal Cooperation in Organizations', *Academy of Management Journal*, 38:1, 24–59.

McAllister, Ian (1999) 'The Economic Performance of Government', in Pippa Norris, ed, *Critical Citizens: Global Support for Democratic Governance*, New York: Cambridge University Press, pp. 188–203.

McClosky, Herbert and John Zaller (1984) *The American Ethos: Public Attitudes towards Capitalism and Democracy*, Cambridge, MA: Harvard University Press.

McEvily, Bill and Marco Tortoriello (2011) 'Measuring Trust in Organisational Research: Review and Recommendations', *Journal of Trust Research*, 1:1, 23–63.

McGraw, Kathleen M and Brandon Bartels (2005) 'Ambivalence toward American Political Institutions', in Stephen C Craig and Michael D Martinez, eds, *Ambivalence and the Structure of Political Opinion*, New York: Palgrave Macmillan, pp. 105–126.

McKnight, D Harrison and Norman Chervany (1996) 'The Meanings of Trust', Minnesota Research Center Working Paper No. 4, University of Minnesota.

Meredith, Lisa et al. (2007) 'Trust Influences Response to Public Health Messages during a Bioterrorist Event', *Journal of Health Communication*, 12:3, 217–232.

Metlay, Daniel (1999) 'Institutional Trust and Confidence: A Journey into a Conceptual Quagmire', in George Cvetkovich and Ragnar E Loftstedt, eds, *Social Trust and the Management of Risk*, London: Earthscan, pp. 100–116.

Miller, Alan S and Tomoko Mitaruma (2003) 'Are Surveys on Trust Trustworthy?' *Social Psychology Quarterly*, 66:1, 62–70.

Miller, Arthur H and Stephen A Borelli (1991) 'Confidence in Government during the 1980s', *American Politics Quarterly*, 19:2, 147–173.

Miller, Arthur H (1974) 'Political Issues and Trust in Government: 1964-1970', *American Political Science Review*, 68:3, 951–972.

Miller, Arthur H et al. (1979) '"Type-Set Politics: Impact of Newspapers on Public Confidence', *American Political Science Review*, 73:1, 67–84

Mishler, William and Richard Rose (1997) 'Trust, Distrust and Skepticism: Popular Evaluations of Civil and Political Institutions in Post-communist Societies', *Journal of Politics*, 59:2, 418–451.

Mishler, William and Richard Rose (2001) 'What are the Origins of Political Trust? Testing Institutional and Cultural Theories in Post-communist Societies', *Comparative Political Studies*, 34:1, 30–62.

Möllering, Guido (2001) 'The Nature of Trust: From Georg Simmel to a Theory of Expectation, Interpretation and Suspension', *Sociology*, 35:2, 403–420.

Mondak, Jeffery J et al. (2007) 'Does Familiarity Breed Contempt? The Impact of Information on Mass Attitudes towards Congress', *American Journal of Political Science*, 51:1, 34–48.

Mondak, Jeffrey J, Matthew Hayes, and Damarys Canache (2017) 'Biological and Psychological Influences on Political Trust', in Sonia Zmerli and Tom WG van der Meer, eds, *Handbook on Political Trust*, Cheltenham: Edward Elgar, pp. 143–159.

Mondak, Jeffrey J and Karen D Halperin (2008) 'A Framework for the Study of Personality and Political Behaviour', *British Journal of Political Science*, 38:2, 335–362.

Morgeson, Forrest V III and Claudia Petrescu (2011) 'Do They All Perform Alike? An Examination of Perceived Performance, Citizen Satisfaction and Trust with US Federal Agencies', *International Review of Administrative Science*, 77:3, 451–479.

MORI (2003) *Trust in Public Institutions – New Findings: National Quantitative Survey*, London: MORI Social Research Institute.

Morrell, Michael E (2003) 'Survey and Experimental Evidence for a Reliable and Valid Measure of Internal Political Efficacy', *Public Opinion Quarterly*, 67:4, 589–602.

Mounk, Yascha (2018) *The People vs. Democracy: Why Our Freedom is in Danger and How to Save It*, Cambridge, MA: Harvard University Press.

Moy, Patricia and Dietram Scheufele (2000) 'Media Effects on Political and Social Trust', *Journalism and Mass Communication Quarterly*, 77:4, 744–759.

Mueller, Jan-Werner (2016) *What Is Populism?* Philadelphia, PA: University of Pennsylvania Press.

Muller, Edward N and Thomas O Jukam (1977) 'On the Meaning of Political Support', *American Political Science Review*, 71:4, 1561–1595.

Muller, Edward N and Carol J Williams (1980) 'Dynamics of Political Support-Alienation', *Comparative Political Studies*, 13:1, 33–59.

Murphy, Kristina (2004) 'The Role of Trust in Nurturing Compliance: A Study of Accused Tax Avoiders', *Law and Human Behavior*, 28:2, 187–209.

Murphy, R and A Guter-Sandu (2018) 'Resources Allocated to Tackling the Tax Gap: A Comparative EU study', Working Paper, London: City University of London.

Murtin, Fabrice, Lara Fleischer, and Vincent Siegerink (2018) *Trust and Its Determinants: Evidence from the Trustlab Experiment*, OECD Statistics Working Paper 89, Paris: OECD.

Mutz, Diana C and Byron Reeves (2005) 'The New Videomalaise: Effects of Televised Incivility on Political Trust', *American Political Science Review*, 99:1, 1–15.

Myhill, Andy and Ben Bradford (2012) 'Can Police Enhance Public Confidence by Improving Quality of Service? Results from Two Surveys in England and Wales', *Policing & Society*, 22:4, 397–425.

Nakayachi, Kazuya (2015) 'Examining Public Trust in Risk-managing Organizations after a Major Disaster', *Risk Analysis*, 35:1, 57–67.

Naurin, Elin (2011) *Election Promises, Party Behaviour and Voter Perceptions*, Basingstoke: Palgrave.

Neumann, Robert (2016) 'Understanding Trustworthiness: Using Response Latencies from CATI Surveys to Learn about the 'Crucial' Variable in Trust Research', *Quality & Quantity*, 50:1, 43–64.

Newton, Kenneth (1999a) 'Social and Political Trust in Established Democracies', in Pippa Norris, ed, *Critical Citizens: Global Support for Democratic Governance*, New York: Cambridge University Press, pp. 169–187.

Newton, Kenneth (1999b) 'Mass Media Effects: Mobilization or Media Malaise?' *British Journal of Political Science*, 29:4, 577–599.

Newton, Kenneth (2006) 'Political Support: Social Capital, Civil Society and Political and Economic Performance', *Political Studies*, 54:4, 846–864.

Newton, Kenneth (2019) *Surprising News: How the Media Affect—and Do Not Affect—Politics*, Boulder, CO: Lynne Riener.

Noordzij, Kjell, Willem de Koster, and Jeroen van der Waal (2021a) "They Don't Know What It's Like to Be at the Bottom": Exploring the Role of Perceived Cultural Distance in Less-educated Citizens' Discontent with Politicians', *British Journal of Sociology*, 72:3, 566–579.

Noordzij, Kjell, Willem de Koster, and Jeroen van der Waal (2021b) 'The Micro–Macro Interactive Approach to Political Trust: Quality of Representation and Substantive Representation across Europe', *European Journal of Political Research*, 60:4, 954–974.

Norris, Pippa, ed (1999) *Critical Citizens: Global Support for Democratic Government*, New York: Oxford University Press.

Norris, Pippa (2011) *Democratic Deficit: Critical Citizens Revisited*, New York: Cambridge University Press.

Norris, Pippa (2022) *In Praise of Skepticism: Trust but Verify*, New York: Oxford University Press.

Norris, Pippa and Ronald Inglehart (2019) *Cultural Backlash: Trump, Brexit, and Authoritarian Populism*, New York: Cambridge University Press.

O'Brien, Thomas C, Ryan Palmer, and Dolores Albarracin (2021) 'Misplaced Trust: When Trust in Science Fosters Belief in Pseudoscience and the Benefits of Critical Evaluation', *Journal of Experimental Social Psychology*, 96, 104184.

O'Neill, Onora (2002) *A Question of Trust: The BBC Reith Lectures 2002*, Cambridge: Cambridge University Press.

OECD (2013a) *Strategic Orientations of the Secretary General: 2013 and Beyond*, Paris: OECD Publishing.

OECD (2013b) *Study to Quantify and Analyse the VAT Gap in the EU-27 Member States: Final Report*, TAXUD/2012/DE/316, The Hague: Netherlands Bureau for Economic Policy Analysis.

OECD (2021) *Enhancing Public Trust in COVID-19 Vaccination: The Role of Governments*, Paris: OECD Publishing.

OECD (2022) *Building Trust to Reinforce Democracy: Main Findings from the 2021 OECD Survey on Drivers of Trust in Public Institutions*, Paris: OECD Publishing.

Offe, Claus (1999) 'How Can We Trust Our Fellow Citizens?' in Mark E Warren, ed, *Democracy and Trust*, New York: Cambridge University Press, pp. 42–87.

Oldendick, Robert W and Stephen E Bennett (2019) 'The Polls – Federal Government Power', *Public Opinion Quarterly*, 83:1, 135–158.

Oliver, Richard L (2014) *Satisfaction: A Behavioral Perspective on the Consumer*, Abingdon: Routledge.

Oliveira, Thiago et al. (2021) 'Are Trustworthiness and Legitimacy 'Hard to Win, Easy to Lose'? A Longitudinal Test of the Asymmetry Thesis of Police-Citizen Contact', *Journal of Quantitative Criminology*, 37: 1003–1045.

Olsen, Asmus Leth (2015) 'Citizen (Dis)satisfaction: An Experimental Equivalence Framing Study', *Public Administration Review*, 75:3, 469–478.

Omodie, M M and J McLennan (2000) 'Conceptualising the Measuring Global Interpersonal Mistrust-Trust', *Journal of Social Psychology*, 140:3, 279–294.

Osuna, Jose, Max Kiefel, and Kira Gartzou Katsouyanni (2021) 'Place Matters: Analyzing the Roots of Political Distrust and Brexit Narratives at a Local Level', *Governance*, 34:4, 1019–1038.

Ouattara, Ebe and Tom van der Meer (2023) 'Distrusting Democrats: A Panel Study into the Effects of Structurally Low and Declining Political Trust on Citizens' Support for Democratic Reform', *European Journal of Political Research*, 62:4, 1101–1021.

Owen, Diana and Jack Dennis (2001) 'Trust in Federal Government: The Phenomenon and Its Antecedents', in John Hibbing and Elizabeth Theiss-Morse, eds, *What Is It about Government that Americans Dislike?* New York: Cambridge University Press, pp. 209–226

Ozawa, Sachiko and Pooja Sripad (2013) 'How Do You Measure Trust in the Health System? A Systematic Review of the Literature', *Social Science and Medicine*, 91, 10–14.

Paige, Jeffery M (1971) 'Political Orientation and Riot Participation', *American Sociological Review*, 36:5, 810–820.

Parker, Suzanne L, Glenn R Parker, and Terri L Towner (2015) 'Rethinking the Meaning and Measurement of Political Trust', in Christina Eder, Ingvill C Mochmann, and Markus Quandt, eds, *Political Trust and Disenchantment with Politics: International Perspectives*, Leiden: Brill, pp. 59–82.

Parry, Geraint (1976) 'Trust, Distrust and Consensus', *British Journal of Political Science*, 6:2, 129–142.

Pasek, Josh (2018) 'It's Not My Consensus: Motivated Reasoning and the Sources of Scientific Illiteracy', *Public Understanding of Science*, 27:7, 787–806.

Patterson, Orlando (1999) 'Liberty Against the Democratic State: On the Historical and Contemporary Sources of American Distrust', in Mark E Warren, ed, *Democracy and Trust*, New York: Cambridge University Press, pp. 151–207.

Patterson, Samuel C and Gregory A Caldeira (1990) 'Standing Up for Congress: Variations in Public Esteem since the 1960s', *Legislative Studies Quarterly*, 15:1, 25–47.

Pattie, Charles and Ron Johnston (1998) 'Voter Turnout at the British General Election of 1992: Rational Choice, Social Standing or Political Efficacy?' *European Journal of Political Research*, 33:2, 263–283.

Pattie, Charles and Ron Johnston (2001) 'Losing the Voters' Trust: Evaluations of the Political System and Voting in the 1997 British General Election', *British Journal of Politics and International Relations*, 3:2, 191–222.

Pattyn, Sven et al. (2012) 'Stripping the Political Cynic: A Psychological Exploration of the Concept of Political Cynicism', *European Journal of Personality*, 26, 566–579.

Peffley, Mark and Robert Rohrschneider (2014) 'The Multiple Bases of Democratic Support: Procedural Representation and Governmental Outputs', in Jacques Thomassen, ed, *Elections and Democracy: Representation and Accountability*, Oxford: Oxford University Press, pp. 181–200.

Peterson, David A M et al. (2020) 'Macrointerest', *British Journal of Political Science*, 52:1, 200–220.

Petrescu, Maria (2013) 'Marketing Research using Single-Item Indicators in Structural Equation Models', *Journal of Marketing Analytics*, 1:2, 99–117.

Pew Center (1998) *Deconstructing Distrust: How Americans View Government*, Washington, DC: Pew Research Center.

Pew Center (2015) *'Beyond Distrust: How Americans View Their Government'*, Washington DC: Pew Research Center.

Pew Center (2019a) *'Public Trust in Government, 1958-2019'*, Washington, DC: Pew Research Center.

Pew Center (2019b) *'Trust and Distrust in America'*, Washington, DC: Pew Center.

Pew Center (2022) *'Americans' Trust in Scientists, Other Groups Declines'*, Washington, DC: Pew Center.

Peyton, Kyle (2020) 'Does Trust in Government Increase Support for Redistribution? Evidence from Randomized Survey Experiments', *American Political Science Review*, 114:2, 596–602.

Pharr, Susan J and Robert D Putnam, eds (2000) *Disaffected Democracies: What's Troubling the Trilateral Countries?* Princeton, NJ: Princeton University Press.

Poniatowski, Grzegorz et al. (2019) *Study and Reports on the VAT Gap in the EU-28 Member States: 2019 Final Report*, CASE Reports, No. 500, Warsaw: Center for Social and Economic Research (CASE)

Poortinga, Wouter and Nick F Pidgeon (2003) 'Exploring the Dimensionality of Trust in Risk Regulation', *Risk Analysis*, 23:5, 961–972.

Poortinga, Wouter and Nick F Pidgeon (2004) 'Trust, the Asymmetry Principle and the Role of Prior Beliefs', *Risk Analysis*, 24:6, 1475–1486.

Poortinga, Wouter and Nick F Pidgeon (2006) 'Prior Attitudes, Salient Value Similarity, and Dimensionality: Toward an Integrative Model of Trust in Risk Regulation', *Journal of Applied Social Psychology*, 36:7, 1674–1700.

Proszowska, Dominika, Giedo Jansen, and Bas Denters (2022) 'On Their Own Turf? The Level Specificity of Political Trust in Multilevel Political Systems', *Acta Politica*, 57, 510–528.

PytlikZillig, Lisa M et al. (2016) 'The Dimensionality of Trust-Relevant Constructs in Four Institutional Domains: Results from Confirmatory Factor Analyses', *Journal of Trust Research*, 6:2, 111–150.

PytlikZillig, Lisa M et al. (2017) 'A Longitudinal and Experimental Study of the Impact of Knowledge on the Bases of Institutional Trust', *PLoS ONE*, 12:4, e0175387.

PytlikZillig, Lisa M and Christopher D Kimbrough (2016) 'Consensus on Conceptualizations and Definitions of Trust: Are We There Yet?' in Ellie Shockley et al., eds, *Interdisciplinary Perspectives on Trust: Towards Theoretical and Methodological Integration*, Switzerland: Springer International Publishing, pp. 17–47.

Quaranta, Mario (2018) 'How Citizens Evaluate Democracy: An Assessment using the European Social Survey', *European Political Science Review*, 10:2, 191–217.

Quilter-Pinner, Harry et al. (2021) *Trust Issues: Dealing with Distrust in Politics*, London: Institute for Public Policy Research.

Quinn, Sandra Crouse et al. (2009) 'Public Willingness to Take a Vaccine or Drug under Emergency Use Authorisation during the 2009 H1N1 Pandemic', *Biosecurity and Bioterrorism*, 7:3, 275–290.

Quintelier, Ellen and Jan W. van Deth (2014) 'Supporting Democracy: Political Participation and Political Attitudes. Exploring Causality using Panel Data', *Political Studies*, 62:s1, 153–171.

Quintelier, Ellen and Marc Hooghe (2012) 'Political Attitudes and Political Participation: A Panel Study on Socialization and Self-Selection Effects among Late Adolescents', *International Political Science Review*, 33:1, 63–81.

Rahn, Wendy M (2000) 'Affect as Information: The Role of Public Mood in Political Reasoning', in Arthur Lupia, Mathew D McCubbins, and Samuel L Popkin, eds, *Elements of Reason: Cognition, Choice and the Bounds of Rationality*, New York: Cambridge University Press, pp. 130–150.

Ramirez, Mark D (2008) 'Procedural Perceptions and Support for the U.S. Supreme Court', *Political Psychology*, 29:5, 675–698.

Ramirez, Mark D (2009) 'The Dynamics of Partisan Conflict on Congressional Approval', *American Journal of Political Science*, 53:3, 680–693.

Riccucci, Norma M, Gregg G Van Ryzin, and Cecilia F Lavena (2014) Representative Bureaucracy in Policing: Does It Increase Perceived Legitimacy?' *Journal of Public Administration Research and Theory*, 24:3, 537–551.

Richardson, Grant (2008) 'The Relationship Between Culture and Tax Evasion across Countries: Additional Evidence and Extensions', *Journal of International Accounting, Auditing and Taxation*, 17, 67–78.

Richardson, Lilliard E Jr, David Houston, and Chris Sissie Hadjiharalambous (2001) 'Public Confidence in the Leaders of American Governmental Institutions', in John Hibbing and

Elizabeth Theiss-Morse, eds, *What Is It about Government that Americans Dislike?* New York: Cambridge University Press.

Robbins, Blaine G (2016) 'What is Trust? A Multidisciplinary Review, Critique and Synthesis', *Sociology Compass*, 10:10, 972–986.

Robbins, Blaine and Edgar Kiser (2020) 'State Coercion, Moral Attitudes, and Tax Compliance: Evidence from a National Factorial Survey Experiment of Income Tax Evasion', *Social Science Research*, 91, 102448.

Rooduijn, Matthijs, Wouter van der Brug and Sarah L de Lange (2016) 'Expressing or Fuelling Discontent? The Relationship between Populist Voting and Political Discontent', *Electoral Studies*, 43, 32–40.

Rose, Abigail et al. (2014) 'Development and Testing of the Health Care System Distrust Scale', *Journal of General Internal Medicine*, 19:1, 57–63.

Rose, Jonathan (2014) *The Public Understanding of Political Integrity: The Case for Probity Perceptions*, Basingstoke: Palgrave Macmillan.

Rose, Richard and Bernhard Wessels (2019) 'Money, Sex and Broken Promises: Politicians' Bad Behaviour Reduces Trust', *Parliamentary Affairs*, 72:3, 481–500.

Rothstein, Bo (2000) 'The Universal Welfare States as a Social Dilemma', in Mark van Vugt et al., eds, *Cooperation in Modern Society: Promoting the Welfare of Communities, States and Organizations*, London: Routledge, pp. 210–228.

Rothstein, Bo and Dietlind Stolle (2008) 'The State and Social Capital: An Institutional Theory of Generalized Trust', *Comparative Politics*, 40:4, 441–459.

Rotter, Julian B (1967) 'A New Scale for the Measurement of Interpersonal Trust', *Journal of Personality*, 35:4, 561–565.

Rousseau, Denise M et al. (1998) 'Not So Different After All: A Cross-Discipline View of Trust', *Academy of Management Review*, 23:3, 393–404.

Rudolph, Thomas (2021) 'Populist Anger, Donald Trump, and the 2016 Election', *Journal of Elections, Public Opinion and Parties*, 31:1, 33–58.

Rudolph, Thomas J and Jillian Evans (2005) 'Political Trust, Ideology, and Public Support for Government Spending', *American Journal of Political Science*, 49:3, 660–671.

Rutto, Filippo, Silvia Russo and Christina Mosso (2014) 'Development and Validation of a Democratic System Justification Scale', *Social Indicators Research*, 118, 644–655.

Safran, Dana Gelb et al. (1998) 'Linking Primary Care Performance to Outcomes of Care', *Journal of Family Practice*, 47:3, 213–220.

Sasaki, Masamichi, ed (2019) *Trust in Contemporary Society*, Leiden: Brill.

Saunders, Mark and Adrian Thornhill (2004) 'Trust and Mistrust in Organisations: An Exploration using an Organisational Justice Framework', *European Journal of Work and Organisational Psychology*, 13:4, 493–515.

Saunders, Mark NK, Graham Dietz, and Adrian Thornhill (2014) 'Trust and Distrust: Polar Opposites, or Independent but Co-existing?' *Human Relations*, 67:6, 639–665.

Schaffer, Frederick Charles (2010) Thin Descriptions: The Limits of Survey Research on the Meaning of Democracy', Political Concepts Working Paper 45, International Political Science Association Committee on Concepts and Methods.

Scharpf, Fritz (1999) *Governing in Europe: Effective and Democratic?* Oxford: Oxford University Press.

Schnaudt, Christian (2019) *Political Confidence and Democracy in Europe: Antecedents and Consequences of Citizens' Confidence in Representative and Regulative Institutions and Authorities*, Springer International Publishing.

Scholz, John T and Mark Lubell (1998) 'Trust and Taxpaying: Testing the Heuristic Approach to Collective Action', *American Journal of Political Science*, 42:2, 398–417.

Schoon, Ingrid and Helen Cheng (2011) 'Determinants of Political Trust: A Lifetime Learning Model', *Developmental Psychology*, 47:3, 619–631.

Schoorman, F David, Roger C Mayer, and James H Davis (2007) 'An Integrative Model of Organizational Trust: Past, Present, Future', *Academy of Management Review*, 32:2, 344–354.

Schuck, Andreas R T (2017) 'Media Malaise and Political Cynicism', in Patrick Rossler, ed, *International Encyclopedia of Media Effects*, Chichester: John Wiley and Sons, pp. 1045–1064.

Searle, Rosalind H, Ann-Marie I Nienaber, and Sim B Sitkin, eds (2017) *The Routledge Companion to Trust*, New York: Routledge.

Sears, David O et al. (1978) 'Political System Support and Public Response to the Energy Crisis', *American Journal of Political Science*, 22:1, 56–82.

Segatti, Paolo (2006) 'Italy: Forty Years of Political Disaffection', in Mariano Torcal and José Ramón Montero, eds, *Political Disaffection in Contemporary Democracies: Social Capital, Institutions and Politics*, London: Routledge, pp. 244–276.

Seligson, Mitchell A (1983) 'On the Measurement of Diffuse Support: Some Evidence from Mexico', *Social Indicators Research*, 12:1, 1–24.

Selnes, Fred (1998) 'Antecedents and Consequences of Trust and Satisfaction in Buyer-Seller Relationships', *European Journal of Marketing*, 32:3–4, 305–322.

Seyd, Ben, John Curtice, and Jonathan Rose (2018) 'How Might Reform of the Political System Appeal to Discontented Citizens?' *British Journal of Politics and International Relations*, 20:2, 263–284.

Seyd, Ben and Feifei Bu (2022) 'Perceived Risk Crowds Out Trust? Trust and Public Compliance with Coronavirus Restrictions Over the Course of the Pandemic', *European Political Science Review*, 14:2, 155–170.

Sharma, Kinshuk, F David Schoorman, and Gary A Ballinger (2022) 'How Can It Be Made Right Again? A Review of Trust Repair Research', *Journal of Management*, 49:1, 363–399.

Sheldon, Ruth et al. (2009) *Exploring Attitudes to GM Food*, Social Science Research Unit report 2, London: Food Standards Agency.

Shepherd, Steven and Aaron C Kay (2012) 'On the Perpetuation of Ignorance: System Dependence, System Justification, and the Motivated Avoidance of Sociopolitical Information', *Journal of Personality and Social Psychology*, 102:2, 264–280.

Shepherd, Steven and Aaron C Kay (2014) 'When Government Confidence Undermines Public Involvement in Modern Disasters', *Social Cognition*, 32:3, 206–216.

Shockley, Ellie et al., eds (2016) *Interdisciplinary Perspectives on Trust: Towards Theoretical and Methodological Integration*, Switzerland: Springer International Publishing

Siegrist, Michael, Timothy C Earle, and Heinz Gutscher (2003) 'Test of a Trust and Confidence Model in the Applied Context of Electromagnetic Field (EMF) Risks', *Risk Analysis*, 23:4, 705–716.

Siegrist, Michael (2019) 'Trust and Risk Perception: A Critical Review of the Literature', *Risk Analysis*, 413, 480–490.

Siegrist, Michael and Alexandra Zingg (2014) 'The Role of Public Trust During Pandemics: Implications for Crisis Communication', *European Psychologist*, 19:1, 23–32.

Sigelman, Lee and Carol K Sigelman (1986) 'Shattered Expectations: Public Responses to "Out of Character" Presidential Actions', *Political Behavior*, 8:3, 262–286.

Sitkin, Sim and Nancy Roth (1993) 'Explaining the Limited Effectiveness of Legalistic Remedies for Trust/Distrust', *Organization Science*, 4:3, 367–392.

Skogan, Wesley G (2006) 'Asymmetry in the Impact of Encounters with Police', *Policing & Society*, 16:2, 99–126.

Slemrod, Joel (2002) 'Trust in Public Finances', NBER Working Paper 9187, Cambridge, MA: National Bureau of Economic Research.

Slovic, Paul (1999) 'Perceived Risk, Trust and Democracy', in George Cvetkovich and Ragnar E Loftstedt, eds (1999) *Social Trust and the Management of Risk*, London: Earthscan, pp. 42–52.

Smith, Jordan W et al. (2013) 'Community/Agency Trust: A Measurement Instrument', *Society and Natural Resources*, 26:4, 472–477.

Soroka, Stuart N (2014) *Negativity in Democratic Politics: Causes and Consequences*, New York: Cambridge University Press.

Spector, Paul E (1992) *Summated Rating Scale Construction: An Introduction*, Quantitative Applications in the Social Sciences 82, Newbury Park, CA: Sage.

Steinmo, Sven H, ed (2018) *The Leap of Faith: The Fiscal Foundations of Successful Government in Europe and America*, Oxford: Oxford University Press.

Stoker, Gerry, Colin Hay, and Matthew Barr (2016) 'Fast Thinking: Implications for Democratic Politics', *European Journal of Political Research*, 55:1, 3–21.

Stoker, Gerry (2017) *Politics Matters: Making Democracy Work*, Basingstoke: Palgrave.

Stokes, Donald (1962) 'Popular Evaluations of Government: An Empirical Assessment', in Harlen Cleveland and Harold Lasswell, eds, *Ethics and Bigness: Scientific, Academic, Religious, Political, and Military*, New York: Harper, pp. 61–72.

Strömbäck, Jesper, Monika Djerf-Pierre and Adam Shehata (2016) 'A Question of Time? A Longitudinal Analysis of the Relationship between News Media Consumption and Political Trust', *The International Journal of Press/Politics*, 21:1, 88–110.

Sturgis, Patrick and Patten Smith (2010) 'Assessing the Validity of Generalized Trust Questions: What Kind of Trust Are We Measuring?' *International Journal of Public Opinion Research*, 22:1, 74–92.

Tankebe, Justice (2013) 'Viewing Things Differently: The Dimensions of Public Perceptions of Police Legitimacy', *Criminology*, 51:1, 103–135.

Teodoro, Manuel P, Samantha Zuhlke and David Switzer (2022) *The Profits of Distrust: Citizen-Consumers, Drinking Water, and the Crisis of Confidence in American Government*, Cambridge: Cambridge University Press.

Teperoglou, Eftichia and Emmanouil Tsatsanis (2014) 'Dealignment, De-legitimation and the Implosion of the Two-Party System in Greece: The Earthquake Election of 6 May 2012', *Journal of Elections, Public Opinion and Parties*, 24:2, 222–242.

Terwel, Bart W et al. (2009) 'Competence-based and Integrity-based Trust as Predictors of Acceptance of Carbon Dioxide Capture and Storage (CCS)', *Risk Analysis*, 29:8, 1129–1140.

Theiss-Morse, Elizabeth, Dona-Gene Barton, and Michael W Wagner (2015) 'Political Trust in Polarized Times', in Brian H Bornstein and Alan J Tomkins, eds, *Motivating Cooperation and Compliance with Authority: The Role of Institutional Trust*, Springer, pp. 167–190.

Thomassen, Jacques (2013) 'Representation from Above and a Revolt from Below', in Stefan Dahlberg, Henrik Oscarsson, and Lena Wängnerudet, eds, *Stepping Stones: Research on Political Representation, Voting Behavior and Quality of Government*, Gothenburg: University of Gothenburg, pp. 15–38.

Thomassen, Jacques (2015) 'What's Gone Wrong with Democracy, or with Theories Explaining Why it Has?' in Thomas Puguntke et al., eds, *Citizenship and Democracy in an Era of Crisis: Essays in Honour of Jan W. Van Deth*, Abingdon: Routledge, pp. 34–52.

Thornton, Emily M et al. (2019) 'Prosocial Perceptions of Taxation Predict Support for Taxes', *PLoS One*, 14:11, e0225730.

Torcal, Mariano, Jordi Muñoz and Eduard Bonet (2012) 'Trust in the European Parliament: From Affective Heuristics to Rational Cueing', in David Sanders, Pedro Magalhaes, and

Gabor Toka, eds, *Citizens and the European Polity: Mass Attitudes towards the European and National Polities*, Oxford University Press, pp. 140–168.
Torcal, Mariano (2014) 'The Decline of Political Trust in Spain and Portugal: Economic Performance or Political Responsiveness', *American Behavioral Scientist*, 58:12, 1542–1567.
Torcal, Mariano (2017) 'Political Trust in Western and Southern Europe', in Sonia Zmerli and Tom WG van der Meer, eds, *Handbook on Political Trust*, Cheltenham: Edward Elgar, pp. 418–439.
Tourangeau, Roger, Lance J Rips, and Kenneth Rasinski (1989) 'Carryover Effects in Attitude Surveys', *Public Opinion Quarterly*, 53:4, 495–524.
Tourangeau, Roger, Lance J Rips, and Kenneth Rasinski (2000) *The Psychology of Survey Response*, Cambridge: Cambridge University Press.
Trachtenberg, Felicia, Elizabeth Dugan, and Mark A Hall (2005) 'How Patients' Trust Relates to Their Involvement in Medical Care', *Journal of Family Practice*, 54: 4, 344–352.
Twenge, Jean M, W Keith Campbell, and Nathan T Carter (2014) 'Declines in Trust in Others and Confidence in Institutions among American Adults and Late Adolescents, 1972–2012', *Psychological Science*, 25:10, 1914–1923.
Twyman, Matt, Nigel Harvey, and Clare Harries (2008) 'Trust in Motives, Trust in Competence: Separate Factors Determining the Effectiveness of Risk Communication', *Judgment and Decision Making*, 3:1, 111–120.
Tyler, Tom R (1988) 'What is Procedural Justice? Criteria used by Citizens to Assess the Fairness of Legal Procedures', *Law & Society Review*, 22:1, 103–135.
Tyler, Tom R (2006) 'Psychological Perspectives on Legitimacy and Legitimation', *Annual Review of Psychology*, 57:1, 375–400.
Tyler, Tom R and Steven L Blader (2000) *Cooperation in Groups: Procedural Justice, Social Identity and Behavioral Engagement*, Philadelphia, PA: Psychology Press.
Tyler, Tom R and Andrew Caine (1981) 'The Influence of Outcomes and Procedures on Satisfaction with Formal Leaders', *Journal of Personality and Social Psychology*, 41:4, 642–655.
Tyler, Tom R and Peter Degoey (1996) 'Trust in Organizational Authorities: The Influence of Motive Attributions on Willingness to Accept Decisions', in Roderick M Kramer and Tom R Tyler, eds, *Trust in Organizations: Frontiers of Theory and Research*, Thousand Oaks, CA: Sage, pp. 331–356.
Tyler, Tom R, Kenneth A Rasinski and Eugene Griffin (1986) 'Alternative Images of the Citizen: Implications for Public Policy', *American Psychologist*, 41:9, 970–978.
Ulbig, Stacy G (2002) 'Policies, Procedures and People: Sources of Support for Government?' *Social Science Quarterly*, 83:3, 789–809.
Ullmann-Margalit, Edna (2004) 'Trust, Distrust and in Between', in Russell Hardin, ed, *Distrust*, New York: Russell Sage Foundation, pp. 60–82.
Uslaner, Eric M (2001) 'Is Washington Really the Problem?' in John Hibbing and Elizabeth Theiss-Morse, eds, *What is it About Government that Americans Dislike?* New York: Cambridge University Press, pp. 118–133.
Uslaner, Eric M (2002) *The Moral Foundations of Trust*, New York: Cambridge University Press.
Uslaner, Eric M (2016) 'Who Do You Trust?' in Ellie M Shockley et al., eds, *Interdisciplinary Perspectives on Trust: Towards Theoretical and Methodological Integration*, Springer, pp. 71–83.
Uslaner, Eric M, ed (2018) *The Oxford Handbook of Social and Political Trust*, Oxford: Oxford University Press.
Van Assche, Jasper et al. (2019) 'Broadening the Individual Differences Lens on Party Support and Voting Behavior: Cynicism and Prejudice as Relevant Attitudes Referring to Modernday Political Alignments', *European Journal of Social Psychology*, 49:1, 190–199.

Van Craen, Maarten and Wesley G Skogan (2015) 'Trust in the Belgian Police: The Importance of Responsiveness', *European Journal of Criminology*, 12:2, 129–150.

Van Damme, Anjuli (2015) 'The Impact of Police Contact on Trust and Police Legitimacy in Belgium', *Policing and Society*, 272, 205–228.

Van de Walle, Steven, Steven Van Roosbroek, and Geert Bouckaert (2008) 'Trust in the Public Sector: Is There any Evidence for a Long-term Decline? *International Review of Administrative Sciences*, 74:1, 47–64.

Van de Walle, Steven and Frédérique Six (2014) 'Trust and Distrust as Distinct Concepts: Why Studying Distrust in Institutions is Important', *Journal of Comparative Policy Analysis*, 16:2, 158–174.

Van den Bekerom, Petra, Joris van der Voet, and Johan Christensen (2021) 'Are Citizens More Negative about Failing Service Delivery by Public than Private Organizations? Evidence from a Large-scale Survey Experiment', *Journal of Public Administration Research and Theory*, 31:1, 128–149.

Van der Brug, Wouter and Philip van Praag (2007) 'Erosion of Political Trust in the Netherlands: Structural or Temporary? A Research Note', *Acta Politica*, 42, 433–458.

Van der Meer, Tom (2010) 'In What We Trust? A Multi-level Study into Trust in Parliament as an Evaluation of State Characteristics', *International Review of Administrative Sciences*, 76:3, 517–536.

Van der Meer, Tom and Armen Hakhverdian (2017) 'Political Trust as the Evaluation of Process and Performance: A Cross-National Study of 42 European Countries', *Political Studies*, 65:1, 81–102.

Van der Meer, T.W.G. and E. Ouattara (2019) 'Putting 'Political' Back in Political Trust: An IRT Test of the Unidimensionality and Cross-national Equivalence of Political Trust Measures', *Quality & Quantity*, 53:6, 2983–3002.

Van Deth, Jan W (2017) 'Compliance, Trust and Norms of Citizenship', in Sonia Zmerli and Tom WG van der Meer, eds, *Handbook on Political Trust*, Cheltenham: Edward Elgar, pp. 212–227.

Van Elsas, Erika (2015) 'Political Trust as a Rational Attitude: A Comparison of the Nature of Political Trust across Different Levels of Education', *Political Studies*, 63:5, 1158–1178.

Van Elsas, Erika et al. (2020) 'How Political Malpractice Affects Trust in EU Institutions', *West European Politics*, 43:4, 944–968.

Van Erkel, Patrick and Tom WG van der Meer (2016) 'Macroeconomic Performance, Political Trust and the Great Recession: A Multilevel Analysis of the Effects of Within-country Fluctuations in Macroeconomic Performance on Political Trust in 15 EU Countries, 1999-2011', *European Journal of Political Research*, 55:1, 177–197.

Van Ham, Carolien and Jacques Thomassen (2017) 'The Myth of Legitimacy Decline: An Empirical Evaluation of Trends in Political Support in Established Democracies', in Van Ham, Carolien et al., eds (2017) *Myth and Reality of the Legitimacy Crisis: Explaining Trends and Cross-national Differences in Established Democracies*, New York: Oxford University Press.

Van Ham, Carolien et al., eds (2017) *Myth and Reality of the Legitimacy Crisis: Explaining Trends and Cross-National Differences in Established Democracies*, New York: Oxford University Press.

Van Ryzin, Gregg G (2011) 'Outcomes, Process and Trust of Civil Servants', *Journal of Public Administration Research and Theory*, 21:4, 745–760.

Van Schuur, Wijbrandt (2003) 'Mokken Scale Analysis: Between the Guttman Scale and Parametric Item Response Theory', *Political Analysis*, 11:2, 139–163.

Van Schuur, Wijbrandt (2011) *Ordinal Item Response Theory: Mokken Scale Analysis*, Thousand Oaks: Sage.

Van Wessel, Margit (2010) 'Political Disaffection: What We Can Learn from Asking the People', *Parliamentary Affairs*, 63:3, 504–523.
Van Wessel, Margit (2017) 'Citizens as Sense-Makers: Towards a Deeper Appreciation of Citizens' Understanding of Democratic Politics', *Political Studies*, 65:1S, 127–145.
Wallis, Ed (2012) 'Another Planet', *Fabian Review*, 124:3, 8–10.
Walls, John et al. (2004) 'Critical Trust: Understanding Lay Perceptions of Health and Safety Risk Regulation', *Health, Risk and Society*, 6:2, 133–150.
Warren, Mark E (1999) 'Democratic Theory and Trust', in Mark E Warren, ed, *Democracy and Trust*, New York: Cambridge University Press, pp. 310–345.
Warren, Mark E (2017) 'What Kinds of Trust Does a Democracy Need? Trust from the Perspective of Democratic Theory', in Sonja Zmerli and Tom W.G, van der Meer, eds, *Handbook on Political Trust*, Cheltenham: Edward Elgar, pp. 33–52.
Warren, Mark E and John Gastil (2015) 'Can Deliberative Minipublics Address the Cognitive Challenges of Democratic Citizenship?' *Journal of Politics*, 77:2, 562–574.
Weatherford, M Stephen (1987) 'How Does Government Performance Influence Political Support?' *Political Behavior*, 9:1, 5–28.
Weatherford, M Stephen (1991) 'Mapping the Ties that Bind: Legitimacy, Representation and Alienation', *The Western Political Quarterly*, 44:2, 251–276.
Weatherford, M Stephen (1992) 'Measuring Political Legitimacy', *American Political Science Review*, 86:1, 149–166.
Weil, Frederick D (1989) 'The Sources and Structure of Political Legitimation in Western Democracies', *American Sociological Review*, 54:5, 682–706.
Weinschenk, Aaron C and Christopher T Dawes (2019) 'Moral Foundations, System Justification, and Support for Trump in the 2016 Presidential Election', *The Forum*, 17:2, 195–208.
Werner, Annika (2016) 'Party Responsiveness and Voter Confidence in Australia', *Australian Journal of Political Science*, 51:3, 436–457.
Wessels, Bernhard (2009) 'Trust in Political Institutions', in Jacques Thomassen, ed, *Legitimacy of the EU After Enlargement*, Oxford: Oxford University Press, pp. 165–183.
White, Mathew P et al. (2003) 'Trust in Risky Messages: The Role of Prior Attitudes', *Risk Analysis*, 23:4, 717–726.
White, Mathew P and J Richard Eiser (2005) 'Information Specificity and Hazard Risk Potential as Moderators of Trust Asymmetry', *Risk Analysis*, 25:5, 1187–1198
White, Mathew P and J Richard Eiser (2006) 'Marginal Trust in Risk Managers: Building and Losing Trust Following Decisions under Uncertainty', *Risk Analysis*, 26:5, 1187–1203.
Whiteley, Paul et al. (2013) *Affluence, Austerity and Electoral Change in Britain*, Cambridge University Press.
Whiteley, Paul et al. (2016) 'Why Do Voters Lose Trust in Governments? Public Perceptions of Government Honesty and Trustworthiness in Britain 2000-2013', *British Journal of Politics and International Relations*, 18:1, 234–254.
Whiteley, Paul et al. (2023) *Brexit Britain: The Consequences of the Vote to Leave the European Union*, Cambridge: Cambridge University Press.
Widmer, Eric and Ivan de Carlo (2010) 'Why Do the Swiss Trust Their Government Less and Other People More Than They Used To? The Impact of Cohorts and Periods on Political Confidence and Interpersonal Trust in Switzerland', in Simon Hug and Hanspeter Kriesi, eds, *Value Change in Switzerland*, Lexington Books, pp. 171–190.
Wilson, Rick K and Catherine C Eckel (2011) 'Trust and Social Exchange', in James N Druckman et al., eds, *Cambridge Handbook of Experimental Political Science*, New York: Cambridge University Press, pp. 243–257.

Wilson, Rick K and Catherine C Eckel (2017) 'Political Trust in Experimental Designs', in Sonja Zmerli and Tom W G van der Meer, eds, *Handbook on Political Trust*, Cheltenham: Edward Elgar, pp. 125–139.

Winston, J S et al. (2002) 'Automatic and Intentional Brain Responses during Evaluation of Trustworthiness of Faces', *Nature Neuroscience*, 5:3, 277–283

Wolak, Jennifer and Christine Kelleher Palus (2010) 'The Dynamics of Public Confidence in U.S. State and Local Government', *State Politics and Policy Quarterly*, 10:4, 421–445.

Wong, Catherine Mei Ling and Olivia Jensen (2020) 'The Paradox of Trust: Perceived Risk and Public Compliance during the COVID-19 Pandemic in Singapore', *Journal of Risk Research*, 23:7–8, 1021–1030.

Wright, Tony (2013) 'What is it About Politicians?' *Political Quarterly*, 84:4, 448–453.

Wroe, Andrew, Nicholas Allen, and Sarah Birch (2013) 'The Role of Political Trust in Conditioning Perceptions of Corruption', *European Political Science Review*, 5:2, 175–195.

Wu, Cary and Rima Wilkes (2018) 'Finding Critical Trusters: A Response Pattern Model of Political Trust', *International Journal of Comparative Sociology*, 59:2, 110–138.

Wuthnow, Robert (2018) *The Left Behind: Decline and Rage in Small-town America*, Princeton, NJ: Princeton University Press.

Wuttke, Alexander, Konstantin Gavras and Harald Schoen (2022) 'Have Europeans Grown Tired of Democracy? New Evidence from Eighteen Consolidated Democracies, 1981–2018', *British Journal of Political Science*, 52, 416–428.

Yamagishi, Toshio and Midori Yamagishi (1994) 'Trust and Commitment in the United States and Japan', *Motivation and Emotion*, 8:2, 129–166.

Yaqub, Ohid et al. (2014) 'Attitudes to Vaccination: A Critical Review', *Social Science & Medicine*, 112, 1–11.

YouGov (2022) 'How Much Confidence Brits Have in Police to Deal with Crime' (available at: https://yougov.co.uk/topics/legal/trackers/how-much-confidence-brits-have-in-police-to-deal-with-crime).

Zaller, John (1992) *The Nature and Origins of Mass Opinion*, New York: Cambridge University Press

Zeineddine, Fouad Bou and Felicia Pratto (2014) 'Political Distrust: The Seed and Fruit of Popular Empowerment', in Jan-Willem van Prooijen and Paul A M van Lange (eds) *Power, Politics, and Paranoia: Why People are Suspicious of their Leaders*, Cambridge: Cambridge University Press, pp. 106–129.

Ziller, Conrad and Thomas Schübel (2015) '"The Pure People" versus "the Corrupt Elite"? Political Corruption, Political Trust and the Success of Radical Right Parties in Europe', *Journal of Elections, Public Opinion and Parties*, 25:3, 368–386.

Zmerli, Sonja et al. (2007) 'Trust in People, Confidence in Political Institutions and Satisfaction with Democracy', in Jan van Deth, José Ramón Montero, and Anders Westholm, eds, *Citizenship and Involvement in European Democracies*, Routledge, pp. 35–65.

Zmerli, Sonja (2012) 'Social Structure and Political Trust in Europe: Mapping Contextual Preconditions of a Relational Concept', in Silke I Keil and Oscar W Gabriel, eds, *Society and Democracy in Europe*, London: Routledge, pp. 111–138.

Zmerli, Sonja and Tom W G van der Meer, eds (2017) *Handbook on Political Trust*, Cheltenham: Edward Elgar.

Zmerli, Sonja and Ken Newton (2017) 'Objects of Political and Social Trust: Scales and Hierarchies', in Sonja Zmerli and Tom W G van der Meer, eds, *Handbook on Political Trust*, Cheltenham: Edward Elgar, pp. 104–124.

Index

For the benefit of digital users, indexed terms that span two pages (e.g., 52–53) may, on occasion, appear on only one of those pages.

Alienation, 7, 50, 54–56, 62, 74

Blair, Tony, 129–130, 132, 139–140
Brexit referendum (2016), 16, 33–34, 159, 189

Consequences of low trust, 147
  Acceptance of official information, 16–17, 169
  Compliance with official rules, 171
  Compliance with the law, 16–17, 174–179, 190
  Demands for reform of the political system, 157
  Democratic norms, 157–158, 182–183
  Electoral turnout, 16–17, 167
  In Greece, 182–185, 190–191
  In Spain, 182–183, 190–191
  Payment of tax, 63, 149–150, 173, 174–175, 182, 183–184
  Political protest, 3–4, 16, 63, 150, 189
  Support for anti-system parties, 154
  Support for government activism, 159, 190
  Vaccination, 171, 184–185
Coronavirus pandemic, 3, 9, 16–17, 171–172, 180, 190, 195–196, 198–199
Cynicism, 7, 26, 50, 54–57, 60, 62–66, 70, 74, 170

Dissatisfaction, 7, 50, 55–56, 60, 63–66, 70, 170
Distrust, 12, 21–22, 24–27, 47, 54–55, 60, 63–66, 80, 83–84, 92–93, 149, 170, 194
  see also Measuring trust: Distinguishing trust and distrust

Financial crash (2007–2008), 16–17, 30, 95–96, 141–142, 182–185, 190–192

Iraq war (2003) 91, 98, 141

Legitimacy, 7, 50, 54–57, 70, 74, 80–81

Measuring trust, 71, 201
  Ambivalence, 24–25, 78, 80, 193–194
  Distinguishing trust and distrust, 25–27, 83–84, 194, 201
  Effects of social desirability biases, 80
  Implicit trust, 80, 194
  Limitations of existing measures, 71, 73, 76–78, 201
  Validity of single-item survey measures, 73, 83–84
Media, *see* Trust, media and
MPs' expenses scandal (2009), 30, 91, 98, 168, 192

'Negativity bias', 13, 36

Office for National Statistics (ONS), 79
O'Neill, Onora, 28, 33, 81–82

Political support, 7, 14, 48–50

Scepticism, 47, 60, 63–66, 147, 170
Social (interpersonal) trust, 36, 77–78, 127, 136, 150, 174–175

Trump, President, 3–4, 52–53, 59–60, 155–157, 189
Trust
  Age and, 102–104, 114
  Ambivalence, 24–25, 78, 80, 193–194
  Among demographic groups, 15, 88, 99, 114, 187
    see also Age and; Education and; Generations and
  As belief or action, 22, 81
  Benevolence and, 123, 129–135

Trust (*Continued*)
  Biased information processing and, 198–199
  Changes in levels of, 33, 90
  Cognition and affect, influence on, 38
  Competence and, 120, 129, 130–135
  'Crisis' of, 4–5, 87–88, 97, 188, 191
  Definitions of, 22
  Dimensionality of, 60, 73
  Distinctiveness of, 56
  Domains of, 31, 192–193
  Economic evaluations and, 141, 197–198
  Economic status and, 101–102, 188
  Education and, 100, 114, 188
  Expectations and, 106–108, 114–115
  Explanations of, 15
  Explanations of, at one point in time, 118
  Explanations of, over time, 98, 141
  Fairness and, 119–120, 126, 130–134, 139–142
  Generations and, 15, 99, 102–104, 187
  Government performance and, 105–106, 129, 131–134, 137–140
  In the health service, 82
  Information and, 67–68, 136, 193
  Integrity and, 124, 134–135
  In the justice system, 95–96
  Levels in Britain and other countries, 94, 187
  Measurement of, *see* Measuring trust
  Media and, 111, 114–115
  Nature of, 6–7, 12–13, 191
    see also Trust: definitions of
  Negative and positive information, effect on, 42
  Outcomes of, 8–9, 61
    see also Consequences of low trust
  Personality, effect on, 36
  Policy representation and, 108, 114–115, 123–124, 129–132, 137–138
  Political engagement, and, 112, 114–115
  In public office-holders, Britain, 87
  As specific *v* generalized judgement, 28
  Stability of, 33, 192–193
  Status of, 7, 13–14, 48
Trustworthiness, 23–24, 31–33, 35–36, 40, 67–68, 120, 130–131

Variations in factors associated with trust
  At different time-points, 141, 192
  Between different individuals, 136, 192
  Between different institutions, 138, 192